BETTY BOOTHROYD

The Autobiography

'Somehow Betty Boothroyd came to transcend politics. She was a persona who had become a British institution before she chose to retire ... Unsurprisingly, her *Autobiography* is of profound human interest and should command greater sales than ministerial – or prime ministerial – memoirs ... The concluding chapters constitute a powerful defence of Parliamentary democracy, transcending any tinge of *amour-propre* or self-importance on the part of the House of Commons ... Betty Boothroyd has completed a beautifully written text in record time. But then, she always was brisk! I believe her when she tells us: "I have written at this pace because I believe Parliament is worth defending, and that this book will help persuade others to do so."' *The Times*

'This is what Betty Boothroyd is like: by turns, frank, fun and generous and much of this shines through her autobiography ... This is an uncomplicated book by a straightforward lady ... When Betty was in the Chair, she added to the liveliness and character of Parliament. And so, having lived her life through the medium of two great political institutions, she arguably became one herself.' William Hague in the *Sunday Telegraph*

'Nobody ever queued for a seat in the Strangers Gallery in the hope of catching a glimpse of the Speaker. At least, nobody did until 1997. Then Betty Boothroyd was elected – and, after 20 anonymous years buried on the back benches ... a star was born ... She possessed personal qualities that guaranteed she would bring a glitter to the job – a job which, with previous incumbents, had been nothing but dull.' Roy Hattersley in the *Daily Mail*

'Almost half the book is devoted to her crowning achievement in serving as Common's Speaker and with the underlying message that the independence and sovereignty of Parliament is under threat ... Above all, the memoirs reveal her love for the Speaker's job she gave up just 12 months ago and her abiding passion for Parliament.' *Yorkshire Post*

'Boothroyd had palpable star quality and, consequently, when she was at the helm, she made parliament seem to count for something' Gyles Brandreth in the *Sunday Telegraph*

'The Elizabeth I of our era' Oona King

'Unlike Margaret Thatcher, she manages to be strong without compromising her femininity. And unlike the Iron Lady, she comes across as very much a woman's woman ... Her positive impact on Westminster cannot be overstated' *Sunday Times*

'Betty Boothroyd was the first Speaker to become a political superstar – one of the most popular women in Britain and known around the world ... The first woman Speaker in eight centuries of parliamentary history [to make] the Commons sexy' *Mail on Sunday*

'A warm, nourishing platter, which should equal the appetites of the former Speaker's many admirers' *Independent on Sunday*

'Betty Boothroyd is an admirable woman and her book is an important document for our times. It should be required reading for anyone interested in the survival of parliamentary democracy.' *Evening Standard*

BETTY
BOOTHROYD

The Autobiography

ARROW

Published by Arrow Books in 2002

1 3 5 7 9 10 8 6 4 2

First published by Century in 2001

Arrow Books
The Random House Group Limited
20 Vauxhall Bridge Road, London, SW1V 2SA

Random House Australia (Pty) Limited
20 Alfred Street, Milsons Point, Sydney
New South Wales 2061, Australia

Random House New Zealand Limited
18 Poland Road, Glenfield
Auckland 10, New Zealand

Random House (Pty) Limited
Endulini, 5a Jubilee Road
Parktown 2193, South Africa

The Random House Group Limited Reg. No.954009

www.randomhouse.co.uk

A CIP catalogue record for this book is available from the British Library

Acknowledgement is due for permission to quote from *The Autobiography*
of John Major (HarperCollins), *Breaking the Code: Westminster Diaries*
by Gyles Brandreth (Weidenfeld and Nicolson), *A Positively Final
Appearance* by Alec Guinness (Penguin Books) and *The Tiller Girls*
by Doremy Vernon (Robson Books).

Papers used by Random House are natural, recyclable products made from
wood grown in sustainable forests. The manufacturing processes conform
to the environmental regulations of the country of origin

Typeset in Times New Roman by MATS, Southend-on-Sea, Essex
Printed and bound in the United Kingdom by
Bookmarque Ltd, Croydon, Surrey

ISBN 0 09 942704 4

For my parents,
Mary and Archie Boothroyd

Contents

Illustrations

———

An MP at last (*Three Star Press Agency*)
James Callaghan (*Hulton Getty*)
John Stonehouse (*Hulton Getty*)
Bob Mellish (*Hulton Getty*)
Militant's last stand at a Wembley rally (*Hulton Getty*)
Three cheers for Labour! (*Express and Star, Wolverhampton*)
Admiring British pork (*Birmingham Evening Mail*)
The European Parliament, 1976
The Thatcher victory of 1979 (*Hulton Getty*)
Michael Foot (*Hulton Getty*)
Eric Heffer and Tony Benn (*Hulton Getty*)
'The Gang of Four' (*Hulton Getty*)
Neil Kinnock (*Hulton Getty*)
After I was elected Speaker, 1992 (*Popperfoto*)

Colour

Robed in Speaker's House (*Maz Mashru*)
In the Chair with Sir Nicolas Bevan alongside
In my Pugin study in Speaker's House (*Charles Green*)
On the Royal bed in Speaker's House (*Michael Jones*)
Speakers' Reunion (*PA Photos*)
The staff of Speaker's House
A State occasion
Dinner with the Queen
With Margaret Thatcher
Steamrolling the Opposition
'Madam Speaker' rose (*Express Newspapers*)

Unless otherwise attributed, all the photographs are from Betty Boothroyd's collection

Acknowledgements

―――

UNLIKE MINISTERS OF the Crown, whose activities are minuted in volumes of official documents, Speakers of the House of Commons operate in an environment that requires them to make verbal, often unrecorded decisions on which the smooth running of Parliament depends. My gratitude for the help I have received in writing these memoirs is therefore immense. Many friends and colleagues have delved into their own records and shared their reminiscences. Some prefer not to be named because of the positions they hold. All of them have my profound thanks.

Michael Jones, Associate Editor (Politics) of the *Sunday Times* and a friend for twenty-five years, has been enthusiastic and unstinting in his efforts from the start. Without his energy and professionalism, the book could not have proceeded. In all the months of hard labour, we never exchanged a cross word!

I prevailed on many friends to raid their memory banks and am especially grateful to Terry Lancaster,

Lord Weatherill, Charlie Turnock, Lord Whitty, Donald Gray, Margaret Watson of the *Dewsbury Reporter*, Jane Kennedy, Peter Butler, Gwyneth Dunwoody, Oliver Walston, Jennifer Beever, Joan Booth, Roseanne O'Reilly, Yvonne Carson, Chris Moncrieff, Chuck Mallet and John Muirhead.

The Libraries of the House of Commons and House of Lords have provided their usual first-class service. Valuable material on my life and those most closely associated with me has been provided by institutions across the world whose co-operation I acknowledge – the Open University, Sheffield University, the Bodleian Library, Oxford, the W.E.B. DuBois Library of the University of Massachusetts, the University of the Witwatersrand, the British Library of Political and Economic Science, the Templeman Library of the University of Kent, the National Museum of Labour History, the Wiener Library, West Yorkshire Archive Service, the Usher Gallery, Lincoln and the Special Collections of Bedfordshire and Lincolnshire County Libraries.

My publishers at Random House have been unfailingly supportive and I could not have wished for two more reassuring pilots for my maiden voyage in unfamiliar waters than Kate Parkin and Tony Whittome. Their skill, encouragement and patience have helped overcome every obstacle and technical glitch. Sheila Dawes was untiringly conscientious in reading and commenting on the text, John Jones put my papers in temporary order, Sarah Kinson and Trushar Barot rallied to the cause as the deadline neared and Toby Zeegen's IT skills prevented disaster at a critical time.

Barely a year has passed since I retired from the Speakership. I have written at this pace because I believe Parliament is worth defending and that this book will help persuade others to do so.

Betty Boothroyd, September 2001

Preface

———

Politics is as much about character
as it is about the blueprint of policies.
Barbara Castle

A PROFESSOR AT CAMBRIDGE UNIVERSITY recently said that one does not have to be a Freudian to know that what happens to you before the age of twenty-five matters more than anything that happens afterwards. He might have had me in mind. By twenty-five, my dreams of taking the West End by storm as a dancer had crashed, and my father's ambition to see me settled in a safe office job had been tried and abandoned. But by then I had won a national speaking award, had stood for election to the local council, had begun to travel and had become a full-time worker for the Labour Party. Nothing would ever again part me from politics, or close my eyes to the wider world.

My great good luck was to be born into a working-class Yorkshire family that endowed me with a strong constitution, insisted on a disciplined approach to life and gave me the confidence to fulfil my ambitions. Looking back, I have to admit that my lack of a rounded academic education affected me at times. I was also taken aback by the prejudice that my northern roots aroused in a few narrow-minded people when I first tried to earn a living in London. I could not understand it – and it hurt. It was not the last time I was to come up against people who thought I had set my sights too high.

I was determined, however, to make my own contribution. When I was four years old, J. B. Priestley visited West Bromwich in search of material for his book *English Journey*. What he found there inspired him to one of his finest passages which sums up everything I entered politics to change. It was a wet, foggy Sunday in 1933 and he lunched with a man who owned a sheet metal warehouse in a place Priestley called Rusty Lane. He said he had never seen 'such a picture of grimy desolation' and was appalled at the conditions the local children grew up in. Boys threw stones at the warehouse while he and his hosts, four Black Country businessmen, ate and drank inside. Outside, they found three frightened little girls with round eyes and wet smudgy faces who said the boys had run off.

'They need not have run away for me', wrote Priestley, who was not easily shocked by poverty and despair. 'Nobody can blame them if they grow up to smash everything that can be smashed' until something was done to rid Britain of its Rusty Lanes.

Priestley would find a vastly changed Black Country if he were to visit it today. Much, however, remains to be done and those who pick up the banner of progressive politics bear as heavy a responsibility as my generation did. Huge and unacceptable discrepancies remain in the quality of life of places like West Bromwich and the leafy suburbs and towns and villages of Middle England. My father would rub his eyes now at the material prosperity most people enjoy, but he would be shocked by the social problems that have yet to be solved. That is why political action and the democratic process remain as vital today as they were when I was a little girl with round eyes and a wet smudgy face.

Having political ambitions was hard enough for a young woman in the days when men dominated public life; I was doubly suspect because I was unmarried. In that respect the Labour Party was little different from the Conservatives. But I grew up in a family whose convictions were set in granite, and I would not be beaten. The strength of my parents, who faced adversity with courage and dignity, flowed in my veins. They bore their hardships lightly and never wavered in their high standards. Their love and example were my bedrock.

CHAPTER ONE

Roots

What is this the sound and rumour? What is this that all
   men hear?
Like the wind in hollow valleys when the storm is drawing
   near,
Like the rolling on of ocean in the eventide of fear?
'Tis the people marching on.

William Morris

SHORTLY BEFORE 1 a.m. on a cold starry night on 18 February 1949, a crowd of 3,000 cheering people heard the Mayor of Batley declare the results of the town's parliamentary by-election. Many had waited for two hours and Mum and I were among them. She had toiled in the mill all day and I had come from the office where I worked as a secretary. My brief ambition to be a professional dancer on the West End stage was long over. I was on the point of becoming totally committed to politics.

Batley was a short bus ride away from our home in the West Riding of Yorkshire and we had campaigned for Labour's man, Dr A. D. D. Broughton.

I did not know what his initials stood for until I caught up with him in the House of Commons a few years later. But that did not matter. They gave his supporters the homespun slogan: 'ADD Broughton to Labour's majority at Westminster!' which was what the good folk of Batley and Morley duly did, with a thumping turnout of 82 per cent.

There were no spin-doctors to advise us how to win votes but we managed well enough without them. We had enthusiasm and energy and faith in what Mr Attlee's Government was doing to make life better for working people, and that is what we were in my family.

When Dr Broughton's victory was announced, Mum and I joined other party supporters in singing the first and last verses of the Red Flag, after which we walked home because the buses had stopped. I was nineteen and this was the perfect ending to an experience that would influence everything that followed. I had loved every minute of the election – the comradeship, the hustle and bustle in the party committee rooms where we were told which streets to canvass, and the fascination of meeting the people who opened their doors to us. Above all, there was the fun of meeting other youngsters in the Labour League of Youth, which became my passport to a lifetime in politics and public service.

No conversion to a cause was required to make me what I became. What followed confirmed everything I had known since childhood. The Labour Party defined our inborn convictions and outward hopes. It was social as much as political. I graduated as a

campaigner during years of accompanying my
mother to weekly meetings of the Labour women's
section in Ben Riley Hall, Dewsbury, where everyone
enjoyed each other's company over tea and biscuits
as they embroidered pillowcases and tray-covers to
raise funds for the party at Christmas bazaars.

Nothing could have been more natural than my
becoming an active party member. My route was
only unusual because my teenage ambition was to
entertain people and help them forget their worries,
not to transform their lives through political action.

In March, Mum and I canvassed to save another
Labour seat in nearby Sowerby, after the resignation
of John Belcher, a junior Minister in the Attlee
Government who was questioned about allegations
of corruption by the Lynskey Tribunal. Labour held
on but the Tory vote surged and went on rising in the
Leeds West by-election in July, where we worked to
get Charlie Pannell elected. Attlee called a general
election in the following February and scraped back
at the head of an exhausted and soon to be divided
party.

But that did not deter me. I had found my real
vocation. I wanted to work for the Labour Party and
one day, maybe, become an MP myself.

We lived at 24 Marriott Street, Dewsbury, a back-to-
back stone house in the heavy textile area of
Yorkshire. I was born there on 8 October 1929, three
years after the General Strike and three weeks before
the Wall Street Crash. My parents were Archibald
and Mary Boothroyd. He was forty-three and she

was twenty-seven, and I was their only child. My arrival, seven months after their wedding, delighted them both, but especially Dad, who had thought he would never be a father.

He wanted to call me Hannah, but Mum thought otherwise and I was duly named Betty. She may have objected to Hannah because it was the name of Dad's first wife, who had died two years previously, as well as his mother's name. At any rate, I am glad Mum had her way. Betty suited me fine.

I suppose we were what people call a house-proud family, even though we had few amenities. Mum and I took it in turns to wash our front steps and the flagstones on either side. I was very good at it, and neighbours gave me tuppence pocket money for doing theirs on Friday nights and Saturday mornings. We rubbed the edges of the black steps with a white pebble we got from the beach at Bridlington. That showed each step clearly when we were going in and out. Then we ruddled – or reddened – the flagstones nearest the wall on each side of the steps to make the front of the house look nice. We bought the ruddling stone from a tinkerman who came round on a horse and cart, selling pots and pans and the like. Everybody in our street did it. It was an old Yorkshire custom. We also scrubbed the front windowsill, where we grew nasturtiums in a window-box, sharing the seeds with our neighbours. Our life revolved around a regular routine: good preparation for the disciplines of my later years.

Everything in our house was done methodically. Dad lit the boiler on Mondays to provide hot water

to wash our clothes, and again on Fridays for
bathtime in a zinc tub in front of the open fire. The
black-leaded fireplace sparkled from our polishing.
Dad scattered wet tea leaves on the carpets to draw
out the dust, which he then swept up with a bristle
hand-brush, on his hands and knees. Monday nights
were washnights, Tuesday nights were spent ironing,
Wednesday nights were for cleaning the bedrooms,
Thursday nights for cleaning the rest of the house.
On Friday nights Mum did the weekend baking.
Some of the best Yorkshire puddings ever tasted
came out of the side oven of the fireplace.

Mum served her puddings separately with onion
gravy, at Sunday dinner. During the hard-up 1930s
this was a commonplace means of reducing our
appetite for meat and saving money. Vegetables were
boiled on a gas ring and other dishes on the fire,
where a kettle of hot water was always on hand.

We lived in a part of Dewsbury called Eastborough, a close-knit community in which people
shared their problems and looked out for each other.
Our front door opened directly on to the terraced
street and our house was joined to those on either
side and at the rear – hence the term back-to-back.
Such houses had no gardens or even a yard. The
density of population, some 700–1,000 people
packed into rows of small houses that have long since
been demolished, is now a folk memory in the North
of England. But it was not all bad. There was no
crime, and children could play safely and wander at
will.

We were better off than many. Dad had earned

good money when he was younger and bought some high-quality furniture when he was first married. He and Hannah Boothroyd lived a few doors away from where I was later born. The houses were all rented and people moved from one to another, as we did, with little formality.

Dad was a proud, independent man, who put family life first and my welfare before anything else. My arrival gave his life new meaning at a time when he most needed it. For him, as for millions of others, the Great Depression between the wars led to long stretches of unemployment. But he was neither bitter nor dejected, and stressed the importance of maintaining high personal standards. He and Mum were a remarkable partnership of loving, practical and hard-working people who poured all their ambitions into me. And being an only child meant that I was at the undisputed centre of their lives. No matter how fierce the gales outside, I was always watched over.

Mum found work easier to get than Dad did, for the simple reason that women's wages were much lower than men's, a fact she drilled into me. So while she worked in the woollen mills, he spent his time on the dole busying himself with household chores behind drawn curtains so that the neighbours could not see him. He and Mum met in a local mill where he was a weftman and she was a weaver. As weftman, he had a lot of responsibility: he was the warehouse stockman who checked that the count, size and colour of the yarn were correct before it was supplied to a particular loom. Mum married late for those times, probably because of family responsibilities.

My first real memory is of Dad standing by the fireplace when I was small and of feeling totally loved. He was my earliest playmate and I was never lonely or bored. I had no need of expensive playthings, for he taught me rhymes as soon as I could talk and made rough toys for me with bits of wood and leather. He was wonderfully inventive and full of fun. He put wheels on a box and pushed me around the house as if I were a lady in a chauffeur-driven car. When it snowed, he made me a sledge. Hard winters were doubly appreciated because he found work shovelling snow for the Town Corporation.

But Eastborough was undeniably grim. Washing hung on lines across the street and there were passages every six houses or so, called ginnels, through which children ran from street to street. However, we had enough to eat and our neighbours took me into their homes as if I was one of their own. There was a huge sense of community in my home town – and much the same spirit exists there still. That strong feeling of belonging is something I've always found in the North of England and even now, if asked, I say that my home is in the West Riding of Yorkshire. It's often hard to explain to outsiders exactly where such feelings come from, but I believe that local papers play a big part in capturing the essence of their communities, and the *Dewsbury Reporter* has always had a key role in our town's life. Weekly markets, too, are a feature of country-town communities, especially in the North, and I for one miss the bustle and excitement we used to feel every market day. Supermarkets just aren't the same!

We've been lucky in Dewsbury, too, that the rows of old terraced houses in which I was brought up haven't been replaced by tower blocks. New, clean, low-rise public housing has allowed our town to retain a sense of neighbourliness and a pride in itself that I don't see in the high-rise developments of the big cities.

The boundaries of my childhood were marked by Caulms Wood, a hilly area at the end of our street, a school and two churches on the road to the town centre. I was christened in one of them, St Philip's Church of England, and went to Brownies at the other, the Baptist chapel. I have been ecumenically minded ever since.

Our house had a good-sized living room, carpeted with a linoleum surround, and a kitchen area in one corner, served by a cold-water tap. Food was stored on stone slabs in the cellar, where we kept the bread fresh in a large stone jar. We had two bedrooms. My parents had a mirrored wardrobe in theirs, where we hung all our clothes. My room contained a bamboo table and a whatnot in the corner.

Three popular prints hung on the walls. There was *The Laughing Cavalier*, Cromwell's Roundheads asking the Royalist boy when he last saw his father, and *The Boyhood of Raleigh*, in which young Walter points out to sea as he talks excitedly to two old worthies. Dewsbury was a long way from the open seas, but this picture appealed to my romantic instincts. The seaside meant a lot to working people in the old

West Riding of Yorkshire, situated halfway between
the Irish Sea (across the Pennines) and the North Sea
(across the Yorkshire Dales).

Visiting the town centre on Saturday afternoons
was a great treat too. Mum dressed me up and a ten-
minute walk brought us to the covered market place,
where thousands of shoppers poured in from the
surrounding towns. Dewsbury's confident Victorian
character had a huge influence on my adolescent
years. We could do little about the Depression that
was blighting the whole of industrial Britain, but we
could make our own fun – and we did so with
panache.

Dewsbury was blessed with its own theatre, the
Empire Palace, built in 1901 and offering escapism,
drama, glamour and popular entertainment in large
doses. It was one of the best-loved theatres in the
provinces and I found its appeal irresistible. Charlie
Chaplin and Stan Laurel played on the same bill
there before leaving to make their names in
Hollywood. Top stars could attract audiences of
1,600 sitting, with another 1,300 standing. The crush
was so great that the balcony's metal girder buckled
once under the strain.

George Formby, Vera Lynn, the young Anthony
Newley and the Irish tenor Josef Locke all appeared
at the Empire. Eric Morecambe and Ernie Wise
starred there in pantomime before they won the
nation's hearts on television. Ernie was born nearby,
at Ardsley, and bought his wife's engagement ring in
Dewsbury. I was thrilled when he and his wife
Doreen attended the ceremony to make me a

Freeman of the City of London in 1993 and we recalled the Empire with great affection. Sadly, it closed in 1955, a victim of television. But to us it was a special place, where working people could exchange the rigours of their daily lives for the opulence of upholstered seating, velvet curtains and an eight-hundredweight chandelier.

My family's antecedents are something of a blur and I never knew my grandparents. Dad's father, Walter Boothroyd, was described on my parents' marriage certificate as a chemical worker; Mum's father, Harry Butterfield, as a blanket finisher. Her own mother died soon after giving birth to Mum, who was brought up by Grandad Butterfield. He lived with us for a while before moving in with Aunty Sarah, another of his daughters, who had a bigger house. Poor people who could no longer look after themselves were often forced to live in the municipal workhouse, where married couples were separated. None of my family suffered that, thank God. We would not have allowed it to happen. But we did not escape the low life-expectancy that cut a swathe through many working-class families in the first decades of the twentieth century.

One aspect of our family's history did register with me. Mum and Dad had different religions; she was a Catholic and he, in so far as he was anything, was a Protestant. The Butterfields were presumably Catholics, because Grandad Butterfield sent Mum and her sister Sarah to St Paulinus RC School in Dewsbury. It was not a happy experience for Mum. She was left-handed when the conventional theory was that children ought to be right-handed, and this made her a disciplinary target for the nuns, who decided to cure what they regarded as an impediment. They rapped her knuckles whenever they saw her writing with her left hand and finally forced her into submission. It was a cruel but common punishment for left-handers and meant that her handwriting was barely legible for the rest of her life.

As a right-hander, I didn't have this particular problem, but in general Mum was determined that I would be spared such a rigid regime. Her wedding at St Ignatius Catholic Church in Ossett was her final act as a Catholic. Dad must have promised that any child would be raised a Catholic – and I was already on the way. But he reneged and I was not, even though the nuns regularly tried to take me to church and to the local Catholic school. This led to doorstep rows, during which Dad refused to back down. He ignored the nuns' protests and sent them angrily away.

Mum hated rows and hid during these confrontations, but she must have been a willing party to the breach. None of this was explained to me at the time and I did not enquire about it. She was content for me to go with my playmates to the Church of England, where I sang in the choir. I enjoyed it, but was never confirmed.

When I became Speaker, I cherished my links with St Margaret's, Parliament's parish church. But I have never been a regular church-goer. I am happy to pray with anybody and to meet people of any denomination – be they a cardinal, rabbi, Muslim elder or Salvation Army captain.

Dad's parents died before I was one year old, leaving memories of a spirited couple who enjoyed ballroom dancing, an unusual pastime for working-class people in the Victorian era. They may have passed on their dancing genes to me. I like to think so.

Dad had two brothers, Sam and Charles, and a sister Gladys. Sam was a popular but unqualified veterinarian and ran his own dog kennels. Charles lived in a better part of town and was secretary of the local Co-operative Society and a Labour councillor. Vera, his only child, was much older than me. We thought she would never marry because she clung to her mother, who doted on her. Mum tried to teach her to weave, but she was hopeless at it. In the end she surprised us all by running off to Hull, where we lost track of her.

Dad's sister Gladys settled a few miles away in Thornhill and had two children, Margaret and Raymond. I spent a week with them during the summer holidays, playing in their garden, which had red-hot poker flowers and lay next to a field. Margaret and Raymond both married and had families, and I called on them from time to time when I was in Dewsbury and always invited them to Speaker's House for the annual State Opening party. But I never really knew their children and, for one reason or another, my Boothroyd family connections shrank as the years went by.

As with so many families, relationships were sometimes tangled. Dad's mother-in-law from his first marriage, whom I called 'Granny' Bould, lived

opposite us in Marriott Street. For whatever reason,
the Boulds did not speak to my mother when she
married Dad; they simply ignored her. That stopped
when Granny Bould, with the wisdom of age, ended
the rift one Christmas by telling Mum to 'bring that
bairn [me] into this house'. Her home was open to me
ever after and I was bridesmaid at her granddaughter's wedding and remain close to her great-
granddaughter, Jackie, my godchild, who still lives in
Dewsbury.

Mum and Dad thought the sun shone out of me,
but on the whole they were reserved people. Even
when I became an MP, long after Dad's death, Mum
kept her emotions in check. 'Win, lose or draw,
you're still my daughter,' she told me when my nerve
broke at one election and I feared defeat. I won, but
her reaction was typical. The maternal link was all
that really mattered to her and when I forged ahead
in my parliamentary career she remained the warm,
loving and kind person she always was – a remarkable woman whom I didn't fully appreciate until
much later.

She worked in textiles all her life, running two
looms at the same time, which was hard graft. She
was exploited because she was a woman, and ever
since I have hated discrimination, on whatever
grounds. Dad's presence at home must have had a
subconscious effect on me, because I sensed something was wrong. A family friend thought that his
strong trade-union views made it difficult for him to
find a job in Dewsbury, but I never heard him say he
was victimised.

It was true that he and Mum were both staunch members of the Textile Workers' Union and the Labour Party. Dad was also a committee member of the local Working Men's Club during the 1926 General Strike, when no child was turned away without a bowl of soup. He was certainly more outspoken than Mum about the rights and wrongs of the world. She seldom expressed her opinions outside the home; inside was a different matter.

When I began my lifetime's habit of smoking, thinking it was the height of sophistication, Dad warned me: 'Don't let your mother catch you. Blow it up the chimney so she won't smell it.' He bought Navy Cut and taught me how to smoke. He also told me never to mix the grape and the grain when I drank. It was good advice, but there was none of either in our house. Elderberry wine was our Christmas tipple. I collected the berries in the autumn and Dad made the wine, which we served with Christmas cake and cheese to visitors. One year he used too much yeast and the corks jumped out of the bottles, turning the ceiling a definite elderberry colour.

Mum worked in the mills without complaint from 7 a.m. to 5.30 p.m. on weekdays and till noon on Saturdays. It was easier for her when she had a job in the town, because she could walk to the mill in twenty minutes, but when she started at Stubley Mill in Batley she had to get there by bus and risked arriving late – a grievous offence. Turning up just five minutes late was punished by a ninety-minute wait outside the gate and being docked a quarter of a day's pay. The textile union was too weak to prevent such monstrous treatment.

The whole trade-union movement had taken a beating during the General Strike and the textile employers cut wages in the year I was born. These were the conditions that made my parents unwavering members of the Labour Party in its formative decades. My own loyalty to Labour was umbilical. Like my parents, I yearned for change and a better future for people who were forced to live such narrow lives.

It is hardly credible today that my parents, and others of their generation, were certified fit for manual labour as children. My mother's work certificate was issued under the Factory and Workshop Act of 1901 on 28 December 1914. That was just thirteen days after her thirteenth birthday during the first winter of the 1914–18 war. Dad's work certificate was dated 10 June 1899 under the terms of the 1891 Act. He was thirteen years and five months old. The law allowed children to enter full-time manual employment at eleven under the 1891 Act and at twelve under the 1901 Act, so at least my parents were spared the drudgery of the mills for a while. Working-class parents, with large families to feed and no welfare state to turn to, had little choice.

Mum's long working life took its inevitable toll. She never smoked a cigarette in her life, but developed emphysema, from which she eventually died. Her condition was almost certainly contracted from the fine hairs thrown out by the looms that she worked. It should have been declared an industrial disease.

Despite our closeness, it was difficult for me to appreciate the nineteenth-century influences that moulded Dad's outlook. He grew up in the late Victorian and Edwardian eras, when a father's word was law and children were expected to do as they were told. He was disciplined and expected others to be. He took his paternal duties very seriously – sometimes, I thought, too much so. I suppose it came from being middle-aged when I was born and my being an only child, the sole one in our neighbourhood. Dad could not understand why I refused to accept that parents had absolute authority over their children. As I grew up, I baffled him.

I challenged him in terms he must have found almost scandalous. 'I'm not your property. I didn't ask to be born into this world,' I would say. 'I'm a person in my own right.'

But he was adamant. 'You belong to us and you do as you're told.'

He must have found my independent spirit hard to bear, all the more so since he felt acutely his own position as the unemployed head of the family. Men of his generation believed they were the natural breadwinners and that a woman's first duty was to the home, whether or not she worked outside.

He looked for work, but there were few opportunities for unemployed manual workers of his age until the war came in 1939. He scanned the Situations Vacant in the *Dewsbury Reporter*, which we shared with our neighbours, but worked infrequently for much of the 1930s. Most days he walked to the local library to read the newspapers, while I was looked after by neighbours or went to school. It must have been a galling way to pass the time for an active, mentally alert man.

When I was seven or eight I tried to get him work with one of the local rag dealers, who played an important part in the textiles chain. Dewsbury's mills owed their origin to the invention of the rag-grinding machine in 1813. This made it possible to reprocess woollen cloth into recycled fibres called 'shoddy', from which blankets, coats and uniforms were made. Our nearest shoddy dealer had a warehouse a few streets away and knew us well. He used to chase us off when we children got in and played among his bales. As we ran away, I shouted at him on several occasions, 'Can you give my dad a job?'

He must have thought about it, because he called on Dad for a chat. In the end Dad did become a rag ware-houseman, but he must have hated it. He had a natural taste for fine clothes and taught me to value them too. He trained me to be as disciplined as he was in the way he brushed his clothes before hanging them up and packed his shoes with newspaper to make the leather last longer. Economies were made on the size of clothes, not the cost. They were always bought one size too large, so that the sleeves of any new coat covered my fingers. Whitsun was a traditional time for buying clothes in the textile towns and usually brought a new summer dress, a light coat or a gabar-dine raincoat my way. 'Spend a little more than you can afford and you will not regret it,' Dad would say. A lifetime's practice has proven him right.

A presumptuous journalist once asked how a Dewsbury girl like me managed to develop any dress sense at all. The exchange went like this:

Question: You are known for your glamorous and colourful wardrobe, but from where does a lass from a drab environment like Dewsbury acquire this fashion sense?
Answer: Don't you think this question just a little patronising? Why shouldn't somebody from Dewsbury have good taste? If I have got good taste, I know where I inherited it – from my father.

Dad also appreciated good furniture. We cherished the pieces he brought from his first marriage: a glass-panelled sideboard with brass handles, a horsehair settee with mahogany back and matching horsehair chair, and a rocking chair. We covered the polished legs of the living-room table with old woollen socks on weekdays to prevent them being kicked or scratched. Our prize possession was a glorious rosewood gramophone on four legs, a wind-up His Master's Voice model, with a speaker just like the one in the famous trademark. We seldom used it, but when we did, it was to listen to Gilbert and Sullivan, George Formby and Gracie Fields.

Neighbours borrowed our four dining chairs for weddings and funerals. The Yorkshire expression – 'she's got all her chairs at home' – probably originated from situations like that. I used to think it meant that Mum managed to get her chairs back, but it probably meant she was a smart lady and nobody could 'put one over' her. She also let people use her fine china teaset for special occasions, looking anxiously for any chips when it was returned.

Mum and Dad hated the thought of my having to struggle as they did and wanted me to get an office job. Father dreamed of me working in the Town Hall rates department – somewhere safe and warm – but they never passed their anxieties on to me. They were very down-to-earth and never promised anything they could not fulfil. 'Wait and see' was their stock answer.

Blackpool was the town's favourite destination when the mills closed for the annual holidays. Mum packed our clothes in Dad's leather Gladstone bag and we crossed the Pennines by coach, stopping to eat our packed snacks and drink our flasks of tea. We set out at 7 a.m. and reached Blackpool in the late afternoon, meeting up with our neighbours, who had gone on ahead. I used to think that, apart from being by the sea, it was just like being at home.

We made our own fun as children. One way to reach Caulms Wood beyond the recreation ground was to cut through a piggery at the top of Camroyd Street. It was owned by a man whom we called 'Piggy' Littlewood. If there was a Mrs Piggy, we did not see her; he was enough of an adversary. The challenge was to crawl under the window of his house and cross the piggery without startling the pigs and alerting him. A drystone wall marked the boundary between his property and the wood. Once across it we were safe. If he caught us on his side, we believed we were at his mercy. After a time the wall fell down, but the rules of the game were unchanged.

Piggy's litter usually detected our presence and snorted their alarms, setting him after us shouting obscenities and waving his cane. We thought this was high sport, but he regarded me as the chief culprit, even though Rita Coulter, the Waring boys and Irene and Mary Boyes joined me in these escapades. He had several talks to my father, but they were on friendly terms and usually had a laugh about it.

Mum was more relaxed than Dad about my wanting to be in the thick of anything that was happening. But she was very methodical. She managed the household accounts and made sure we were never in arrears with the rent. Dad spent little on himself and was content to leave financial matters to her. She slipped him something for his Sunday visit to the Working Men's Club and paid the regular bills with money put away in various boxes. There was one for the rent, another for the rates, another for the electric meter and yet another for the insurance man who called on Fridays. We often talked by the light of the fireside at the end of the day. Mother was always conscious of electricity costs and later compared the number of lights left burning in my home to Blackpool's famous illuminations.

Breakfast was usually bread and Bovril, and I also ate meals at neighbours' houses. I made them honorary relatives, which is what they were. 'Grandma' Teale lived a few doors away, and Mum would wrap me in a blanket when I was a baby and pop me in Grandma Teale's bed on her way to work. 'Aunty' Sally, one of Grandma Teale's daughters, bathed me in soap bubbles in the sink. When I went to school, the Teales fed me at midday and four o'clock. They never asked for payment; it was just a natural part of a close-knit, working-class life. All the Teale grown-ups became 'uncles' and 'aunties', giving me a ready-made extended family of the kind that was dealt a hammer blow in parts of England when the bulldozers moved in to clear the old terraced streets. Better housing was undoubtedly needed, but it did not come without a loss of community, especially in the high-rise estates that replaced the Coronation Streets in some of the old urban areas.

Mavis, one of my 'cousins', and I had scarlet fever together. We were sent to an isolation hospital, where our families inspected us through the windows. Treatment was rudimentary but effective. Before we were discharged the nurses pumped a disinfectant mixture into our noses through a rubber pipe to clear any lingering infection. John Teale, another 'uncle', fought in Burma during the war. I knitted him socks and we all longed for his return. When he came back in his army uniform after VJ Day, we wept with joy for ages. He brought me a pair of white oriental buckskin shoes with high wedges.

I went to Eastborough School from the age of four and enjoyed it. We played with sand, slept during the afternoon rest period and learned arithmetic with the help of large numbered cards pinned on the wall. They still flash before me when I do mental arithmetic. In 1938 we were given gas masks and taught how to wear them, in case of enemy attack. The uneasy peace prevailed for another year and it was not until school closed for the whole of September and October in 1939 that we realised what was happening in the world.

We returned to school part-time on 6 November to find workmen building air-raid shelters under the school arches. These were great places to play hide-and-seek in pitch black during the midday break, but we were found out and got into terrible trouble. Miss Ganter, the headmistress of the senior Girls' School, sat at a raised desk on a small platform so that she could see right through the half-glass partitions that divided the classrooms. Every child passed her desk on entering the school and latecomers had to explain themselves, a chastening experience that made me conscious for the rest of my life of the need to be five minutes early, rather than a minute late. It was a discipline that served me well in preparing for the daily Speaker's Procession that leaves Speaker's House at 2.26-and-a-half minutes and arrives in the Commons chamber for prayers at 2.30 prompt. Miss Ganter would have been pleased that I was never late.

Another formidable teacher was Miss Fox. Her way of teaching the proper use of the apostrophe was to take an erring pupil to the school signboard and show them the apostrophe after the 's' in Girls' School. 'That's because the school belongs to all the girls and not just one. You must remember by that example.' She and other teachers gave me a good

basic education and a round, classical style of
handwriting. The school was well regarded by the
inspectors and rightly so.

Our teachers always wore suits or dresses and
looked what they were – pillars of society. Visiting
schools and colleges in later years, I found it hard to
tell the difference between teachers and students:
they wore the same casual clothes and looked alike.

Eastborough School was ambitious for its pupils,
who included Betty Lockwood, later Baroness
Lockwood, chairman of the Equal Opportunities
Commission, and – in the Boys' School – Sir Marcus
Fox, chairman of the 1922 Committee of
Conservative MPs during Margaret Thatcher's
premiership. Eddie Waring, the sports commentator,
was another old boy.

Local employment picked up during the war and
the mills worked flat out making blankets and
essential supplies for the services. Dad found regular
work again and also became an air-raid warden.
Sirens sounded on the first night and I was placed
under the kitchen table with Malcolm and Gordon
Waring, two boys who lived opposite us. Our fathers
got stirrup pumps and sandbags ready, in case of fire,
but there was no bombing that night, and Dewsbury
was largely spared the destruction that other towns
suffered.

We followed the news on the wireless, but I
already knew about the Nazis before the fighting
began. A wonderful teacher called Miss Smith had
travelled a lot and told us something of what was
going on in Hitler's Germany. I must have been

about seven and remember her dramatising her account by asking us about our family's politics, a daunting question for children of that age. When she asked us to raise our hands to show whether we were Labour or Conservative, most children wavered, although I had no doubts.

I knew we were Labour and my hand shot up. 'Because you're Labour and you're dark and you look like a gypsy, the Nazis would make you wash the pavements with your very best clothes,' she told me. It was an appalling prospect. She spared us the details of Hitler's racial laws, but her warning of what I could expect if the Nazis came to Britain struck home.

We were lucky in Dewsbury during the war – and our family was luckier than many, for we didn't lose any of our loved ones. Because of Miss Smith's powerful lesson on the very real dangers that I and my family would have faced, had the Nazis invaded Britain, I followed the war more closely than most of my friends. While Dad was out doing his air-raid warden duties, saving the nation with his stirrup pump and bucket of sand, I was planning an escape route. I knew every nook and cranny of the caves in Caulms Wood and made sure that all my friends knew just where to hide, should the German tanks come rolling through.

We took cover in the sandbagged shelter under the school arches whenever the sirens went and the ack-ack guns began firing at the top of Caulms Wood. We passed the time playing games, singing songs and sleeping on bunk beds until the All Clear came.

Mum, always intensely practical, took our insurance policies with her in a tin box, in case we needed to claim for life, limb or damaged property. My air-raid garb was a zipped-up siren suit made of dark-red blanketing with a hood, lined in purple silk. A photograph of me outside our house with my first bicycle shows how happy my childhood was and how empty of traffic the streets were. I rode errands on it to the Co-operative shop, where they weighed the butter, lard and sugar on scales and packed it in brown paper.

I did not mind the war at all. My immediate family was largely unaffected and the community spirit brought everybody together. The school's Christmas parties were especially enjoyable, and I raved so much about the sandwiches they served that Mum asked what was in them. It was only the same potted meat we bought from Alfie Wilson, the butcher in Battye Street; it just tasted different at parties.

Towards the end of the war we moved to a better house nearby in East Parade which had a small front garden and a back yard, where my friends and I played. Mum and Dad were both working at this time, and I lit the fire and laid the table for tea before they came home. This led to a rare clash at school when Mr Hardy, one of my teachers, told me to stay behind because of some petty misdemeanour. I flatly refused and walked out, saying that I would accept any other punishment but would not let my parents, who worked damned hard, come home to a cold house. He must have been a wise old bird, because he never mentioned it again.

Other relatives were less well placed than we were. Mother's elder sister, Sarah, received £200 compensation to bring up five children under the age of fourteen when her husband Cyril was killed in a coal-mining accident. He was crushed when the pit roof collapsed shortly before the pits were nationalised in 1946. We walked across the fields to see her on Sunday afternoons at her home in Gawthorpe, near Ossett, taking a tin of salmon or ham or some fruit. My cousins greatly outnumbered me at these gatherings and I cannot say I enjoyed them.

We became much closer as we grew up, though, and I owe them a great deal. Two of my cousins, Margaret and Joan, were wonderfully supportive when Mum was not well. When I became an MP they visited her regularly, telephoned daily and took her to hospital for various tests. I knew she was in good and loving hands.

I failed the eleven-plus examination, which divided children into academic and non-academic streams, but neither my parents nor I were upset about this. I had never been particularly bookish and they had set their hopes on my winning a scholarship to Dewsbury College of Commerce and Art at the age of thirteen. When I did, they were over the moon. My being qualified for a job meant everything to them, for at thirteen they had been child labourers slaving for a pittance.

Failing the eleven-plus destroyed the self-confidence of many children, wasting valuable talents and blighting their prospects. Mercifully, I was spared that experience and have always mixed easily with people, regardless of their educational background. The Labour Party has always attracted old boys and girls from fee-paying schools. I worked for two of them without any sense of inferiority.

My parents wanted me to be literate and numerate, to learn shorthand and typewriting and to become a fully qualified secretary, working in an office. That was their ambition for me – and it was a good one. It made everything else possible. I could have had all the political drive in the world, but I doubt if I would have made it to Parliament as a female manual worker. At the very least, I would have needed trade-union sponsorship in the days when the unions were totally male-dominated. It would have been hopeless.

I studied English and a smattering of accountancy, bookkeeping, mathematics and French. I did well at essay writing and even better at sports, especially athletics and swimming, becoming captain of my house, Spartan House. Dad never allowed me to slacken. I suffered lots of sports injuries and was laid up for weeks when I broke an ankle, but he kept me hard at it by collecting and returning my homework each day.

The college shared his disciplined attitude. When I refused to eat a fatty mutton dish for lunch one day, I was made to sit in front of it all afternoon by a teacher who berated me about the wartime suffering of the French people. They had no food at all, she said; so eventually I succumbed by swallowing the congealed meat without complaint.

I had a brush with authority during my teens when I arrived very late at Leeds railway station in the

Christmas season to find the ticket office besieged and the last Dewsbury train about to leave. I told the ticket collector I would pay at the other end, but he refused to allow me through. Determined not to miss the train, I made a dash for it, chased by the collector and a policeman, who wanted to know what all the noise was about.

Their legs were longer than mine and they caught me. However, I told the policeman that if he did not let me go, I would be his responsibility that night; he thought twice and then asked the collector if he would accept a penny for a platform ticket as part-payment for the fare. The collector, who did not want me on his hands any more than the policeman did, nodded and the policeman duly paid the penny and I went home. Had the collector been more reasonable, I would have paid the penny myself. As I pointed out, I was no fare dodger.

Some members of the family saw my future in singing and encouraged me to take lessons. I was reckoned to have a big voice that would hold people's attention – a comment that was to recur over the years. Aunty Fanny, an elderly lady on Dad's side, who was convinced that I had a great future as a singer, paid for me to have lessons with a Mr Auty and bought me a second-hand piano. I gave it a go, singing scales to Mr Auty's tuning fork, but I was no good at it and sloped off, playing truant – something I never did at dancing school. Dad also thought I was another Clara Butt and was deeply disappointed when Mr Auty and I parted company.

My first job after leaving school was working at

Bickers, Dewsbury's top department store, where they sold everything. As a child, I used to gawp at their windows. I had dreamed of being a window dresser in one of Dewsbury's top stores – either Bickers or perhaps J & B's or Hodgsons – where I would be surrounded by smells of perfume and lovely clothes. J & B's whalebone corsets and enormous bras represented the height of middle-class luxury. I would have given anything to rearrange its display of pins and needles and haberdashery.

Dewsbury's town centre had shops of all kinds, as well as department stores: food shops, milliners, drapers, tailors, hairdressers, dress shops and market stalls that stayed open late on Saturday nights. The town centre was a clean, well-lit, bustling place, with plenty of activity and entertainment.

Bickers took me on at a wage of one pound a week and gave me a ten-shilling (fifty-pence) rise as soon as I arrived, so my enthusiasm must have impressed them. I sat at the centre of my own small financial empire and enjoyed it for a while. My job was to handle the money that customers gave to the sales staff, stamp their receipts and return them with the right change. The sales assistants put the money and bill in a cylinder and sent it to me along a system of pulleys that made a whooshing noise. All I had to do was be quick and accurate – but it was not enough. I wanted something more challenging that required initiative and absorbed more of my youthful energy.

The war had given great scope to my love of dance and entertaining people. I had appeared at the Empire as principal boy in amateur pantomime – our

annual show at the Dewsbury Empire was the
highlight of my year. I was the right shape – and I
suppose I had the legs – for principal boy and I
danced and sang my way through my wartime
teenage years in *Cinderella*, *Aladdin* and *Babes in the
Wood*. Compared with modern pantos it was all
innocent stuff. There were no topical references, no
celebrity appearances, no blue jokes. We took
everything very seriously and the whole community
turned out and cheered us to the rafters. There's
nothing quite like playing to an audience full of
people you know, all willing you on to do well. Even
with the war on, we were determined to look our
best. I remember going into Leeds with Alice
Whitworth, who made our gorgeous costumes, and
scouring the place for sequins – not easy to come by
in those drab times. No matter how the audience
cheered and no matter on what clouds we exited
stage left, it was down to earth with a bump, and
school, on Monday.

Later I joined a teenage jazz band called the Swing
Stars, which entertained servicemen in camps and
airfields across Yorkshire. We appeared under the
auspices of ENSA (Entertainments National Service
Association), the morale-boosting organisation
jocularly known as Every Night Something Awful. I
sang and tap-danced, and what I lacked in polish I
made up for in exuberance and cosmetics. Service
audiences, a long way from home and with time on
their hands, gave us a warm welcome. Photographs
of me show a smiling, stage-struck brunette enjoying
herself hugely.

We travelled cross-country in a coach with other artists who gave their services free – operetta singers, a comedian and a conjuror. Dad did not object, even though we returned very late, because I was in the company of grown-ups and it was all in a good cause. Our excursions were organised by Jack Booth, who always wore a dinner jacket and black tie, which impressed Dad.

Everything about dancing appealed to me and people said I had a natural talent for it. Marcus Fox, who went to my dancing school with his twin sister Marcia, was kind enough to recall when I became Speaker that 'Betty was a lovely mover'. By the time I reached my teens, other parents were saying they would send their children to me, if ever I opened a dancing school. I had no such ambitions but Mum indulged me and I went to advanced classes at a Leeds dancing academy, where I was put through some tough routines.

I was better at some aspects than others: very good at tap and movement, quite good at splits and high kicks but no good at ballet, much as I liked it. Mum saved the dividends from the local Co-op to help pay for my lessons. Our Co-op number was 12249, which we knew by heart.

When the opportunity arose, Dad fought hard to stop me becoming a full-time dancer. It went against everything he wanted for me – security, safety and a settled way of life. He hated even the thought of my being out late with friends in Dewsbury, and once lost his temper in a ferocious burst of anger when I returned home well after midnight.

I was fifteen or sixteen at the time. Mr and Mrs Whitely, neighbours of ours, ran the cloakroom at the Dewsbury Town Hall dance and Dad always timed my return by theirs. When they told him they had not seen me that night, he feared the worst. He thought I must have been abducted. By midnight he was beside himself, pacing the streets and getting increasingly wound up.

There was a simple explanation. Dewsbury Town Hall was packed out and unknown to him or Mum, I had gone dancing with friends in Ossett, five miles away. We had to walk back afterwards because the bus service had stopped. However, Dad refused to listen when I turned up and laid into me with the belt on which he used to hone his razor. I still had my coat on and was merely shaken. So was Mum. But I understood Dad's anger. He had been through hours of worry and could not control himself.

It blew over, but he never reconciled himself to my wish to become a professional dancer, especially in London. Why should a respectable working-class girl leave her home and a good job for a risky future on the stage in, of all places, London? Helping the war effort was one thing. Leaving home for the perils of show business was a totally different matter.

Inevitably, I longed for greater freedom and snatched the chance when it came. It was an adventure that was blown out of all proportion by the press in later years. Some of the girls at the Leeds academy went on to become professionals, and my teachers thought I might follow them. They wrote to the John Tiller School in London, which invited me

for a local audition and interview. The Tiller Girls
were famous for their precision dancing and
everything about them appealed to me. I was
auditioned at the Alhambra Theatre in Bradford and
told I might have potential. The school followed this
up by inviting me to London, instructing me to bring
two pairs of black satin shorts, a couple of blouses
and a black bow.

I was told to write for accommodation to the
Theatre Girls' Club in Greek Street, Soho, where
they would let me have a bed. After another
interview and audition, the Tiller organisation sent
Mum a contract to sign on my behalf, because I was
still a junior. I thought I was on my way to stardom
– but I was wrong. I was seventeen and it was the
bitterly cold winter of 1946–7. I had never been away
from home on my own and London was an alien
world. I was too excited to be nervous, and eager to
please, but there were huge rows at home before I
left, and Dad agreed only when Mum persuaded him
that I needed to get this out of my system.

The misery of living in London did that soon
enough, but I was unhappy there for other reasons
too. A lady called Bobbie played her part. Her job
was to take us for workouts in a former chapel
around the corner from Greek Street, where the
dance mistress put us through tough routines that
made our limbs ache. I did not mind either the
training or the dance mistress. 'Come on – jump kick,
jump kick, carry on smiling all the while, show your
teeth, come on – kick those legs.'

I worked hard, but I did not fit in. Bobbie, like all

bullies, exploited her position of authority. She pounced when she heard me tell a girl that I would see her 'back at t'club'. She screamed with mocking laughter at my Yorkshire accent. 'There's no back to this club. Can't you speak properly?' I smarted at her sarcasm and remember it still.

We were paid about three pounds a week in rehearsal, which was half the Tiller Girls' performing rate. The club took half of that and Mum sent me ten shillings when she could afford it, which meant that I could get home for occasional weekends. I had great respect for the Tiller School, but the club was a different matter. I had 'provincial' written all over me and did not know a soul; it was a hostile environment a long way from home. The cold was made worse by heating, lighting and food shortages. The girls slept in shared cubicles, where it was so cold once that we jumped into bed together. That caused a tremendous kerfuffle.

Doremy Vernon, in her book *The Tiller Girls*, describes how fusty the club had become. It was a place where 'time had stood still' and security mattered more than anything else:

> The front door had numerous locks and bolts to be undone each time it was opened. Immediately a Girl had come inside, it would be noisily locked up again. To add to the jail-like atmosphere, there was the sight of Miss Bell, in charge since the 20s, walking about with an enormous bunch of keys round her waist. However, it was excellent value at only 30 shillings a week.

I do not remember Miss Bell, but I do recall everything that belonged to the club being locked up and having to keep our clothes packed under our beds because we had no wardrobes. As Doremy Vernon remarks, most girls thought the place 'too dreary for any lengthy stay' – and I was one of them.

After training, we went into rehearsal and I was sent for a try-out at the London Palladium, one of the first four London theatres to be allowed to reopen after the war. The show was Val Parnell's *High Time!*, described as 'an opulent and boisterous production without the Crazy Gang but in the same tradition'. It ran for 571 performances from April 1946 to February 1947 and the curtain came down nightly at 10.45 p.m., a sign of the gradual return to normal life after six years of war. Public transport had been virtually non-existent after 9.30 p.m. during the blackout and although there were late-night bus and underground services again, theatre managements hesitated before returning to later 'curtain down' times.

Parnell was the first producer to bring back a second house at 8.30 p.m. and his gamble paid off. The winter was so fierce that many London theatres were empty, but *High Time!* and other variety shows did well. Parnell also broke new ground by hiring a dance band called the Skyrockets, instead of the usual pit orchestra, where players came and went. The Skyrockets were one of the best dance bands in the country and stayed at the Palladium until commercial television took it over in 1955. By the time I appeared, towards the end of the show's run, Parnell was the undisputed king of variety.

On the face of it, my progression from hoofing it with the Swing Stars to high-kicking to the Skyrockets was meteoric. I danced at the Palladium for six pounds a week, doing three routines for each performance. But my run lasted for just a few weeks and I never saw the whole show. It was built around a constantly changing cast, and mine was a fleeting appearance that has caused more subsequent comment than it deserved.

The experience proved my mother right. I accepted the stage discipline, but was unsuited to Tiller life. Being behind the footlights was a constant struggle. We wore stage make-up called 'leg white', but were expected to wash it off before returning to the club. The problem was finding a vacant basin in the dressing rooms. My solution was to slip on a pair of trousers and clean up later. We took turns to scour the stage for sequins that fell off our dresses. The knack was to pick them up on a wet fingertip, put them into a box and return them to the wardrobe mistress to be used again.

I foolishly thought that show business was going to be terribly exciting and glamorous. But it was just like politics – damned hard work. How we survived is a mystery. We supplemented our meagre diet with milkshakes and toasted buns at the Moo-cow Milkbars in Tottenham Court Road or Leicester Square during rehearsal breaks, or on the way between the club and the old chapel. The weight we put on from eating stodgy food was quickly lost in dancing. Austerity Britain lived up to its name and I hated it.

My parents were so concerned about me that they asked a family friend, Harry Barker, a Royal Navy seaman based at Portsmouth, to look me up if he was ever in London. I had been bridesmaid at his wedding to Grandma Bould's granddaughter, so there could have been nothing more natural than his checking up on me. But that was not how the club reacted, especially when he arrived without giving notice, either to them or to me.

His visit caused consternation. Nobody believed he was a close family friend. My parents were not on the telephone, so they could not verify what he said. I was placed under immediate suspicion, refused permission to leave with him and told that he could not enter the club lounge. The only place we could talk was in the foyer, under the scrutiny of a sceptical receptionist. It was deeply embarrassing and upsetting for me. Harry was bemused by the whole episode, but I was appalled. The club had made it clear that they neither liked nor trusted me and I was deeply unhappy.

I longed for the comforts of home, but I was still under contract and had to go where the Tiller School sent me. After the Palladium, they thought I would benefit from pantomime experience and sent me to Luton, the professional equivalent of exile in Siberia. In January 1947 it had the weather to match. I was gloomier than ever. My assignment was a one-week run of *Goldilocks and the Three Bears* at the Grand Theatre, Luton. The local press liked it, especially the 'first-rate acrobatic dancing', and my parents braved the snow to come and see it. But my dancing nemesis was near. A foot infection from a nail gave me the excuse I needed to return home. I did not like Luton any more than I liked London. I returned to Dewsbury chastened but wiser.

So I never made it to the Tiller line at London's Victoria Palace or their second line at Blackpool's Winter Gardens. I had to wait nearly thirty years before I appeared on that platform as a member of the Labour's Party's non-singing, non-dancing National Executive. My Tiller days ended in disappointment, but my admiration for professional dancers remains.

It had been a big setback, but the truth is that I was too young to cope with being away from home at that period of my life. I had always been fairly successful at anything I attempted, but had relied more on my parents' support than I cared to admit. It took me quite a time to recover, and although my parents carried on as if nothing had happened, others had expected me to succeed and I was embarrassed to have failed them. The Tiller episode was a tough lesson in survival, the first of many.

Some time after my return, Dad fell ill. He was bedridden but uncomplaining. Dr Hamilton called regularly but could do little for Dad's heart condition. His bedside greeting was 'How are you today, Archie? You're my best patient.' Dad regarded him as a good 'horse doctor' and did not want anybody else. He got up for a short time in the afternoons and Mrs Whitely came in to make him a

cup of tea and something to eat while Mum and I
were at work. There was no meals-on-wheels service
from the council. Neighbours looked after each
other more than they do today.

My father died in March 1948, aged sixty-two. I
was eighteen and Mum had prepared me for it. He
had suffered from heart disease for a long time and,
although his death did not shock me, it made me
realise the sacrifices they both had made for me. Now
there were just the two of us. There was nothing for
it but to buckle down. I had a humdrum job as a
secretary in the nationalised British Road Services
office in Batley, dealing with long-distance lorry
drivers and ran hither and thither. I still danced but
this time it was for my own enjoyment and worthy
causes. Years later I received a letter from J.
Kendrick, a retired BRS driver and concert secretary
of the Heckmondwike Working Men's Club, then in
his eighties.

> I was standing inside the door of the concert room
> watching a beautiful creature dancing on the stage
> in a RAFA charity concert. I sensed someone
> standing beside me and heard him say: 'What a
> beautiful leg.' It was George Burns, another BRS
> driver. I said: 'Never mind the leg, look at who it
> is.' He went pop-eyed and said: 'My God, it's our
> Betty.'

He was used to seeing me at work looking prim and
proper. He could not believe his eyes.

*

Doremy Vernon says that it was rare for Tiller Girls to venture into a totally different world when they left the organisation. In her book, published in 1988, she wrote:

> When they did, their choices were fascinating, whether it was Betty Boothroyd becoming an MP for 14 years, a woman from the 50s joining the prison service or one from the 60s becoming a Moonie.

One thing is sure. Although my Tiller days cured me of my show-business ambitions, the daily routine of synchronised high kicks and co-ordinated teamwork taught me much about the need for rigorous preparation. Politicians, like Tiller Girls, are public performers – they forget it at their peril.

CHAPTER TWO

Spreading My Wings

—

*For anyone who cares about the state of the world
and thinks he may improve it, there can be no escape
from politics.*

Denis Healey

MY FATHER HAD done most of the talking at home, but he was more interested in local than national affairs. Mum had a wider perspective than he sometimes realised. He believed strongly that Dewsbury people should support Dewsbury shops and that a pound spent outside the town in Leeds, Bradford or Huddersfield was money lost to the local economy.

Mum did not argue about it. As money became a little more plentiful with full employment, she shopped where she wanted, swearing me to secrecy. 'Mind, not a word to your dad,' she told me when she paid ten pounds for my bridesmaid's dress in Leeds for Elsie Ferguson's wedding.

It was she, not Dad, who took me to party

meetings and rallies from an early age. When I think of how hard she worked all her life, her energy and determination were quite remarkable. In later years she thought nothing of travelling all over the country supporting me. In her quiet but persistent way, she widened my horizons beyond the closed community in which she had always lived. She made it possible for me to think politically, and to understand the importance of argument and debate and of communicating one's beliefs to other people.

For her, politics was about helping people to build a better life by working together for common ends. Being Labour meant sharing what you had and caring for others, especially the less fortunate. Dad felt that keenly too, but I never heard them talk about the philosophy of it. There was no socialism – or any other -ism – in their conversation. They were down-to-earth people with no time for theorising.

She was the more outgoing of the two and enjoyed the social side of local politics, especially in the women's section of the Labour Party, which had a flourishing life of its own before political correctness became the rage.

She loved nothing better than taking me to hear the party's leaders when they visited Yorkshire. A rally in Leeds meant a succulent feast: 'butties' comprising lashings of ham overhanging the sides of soft bread, washed down by a glass of milk from a stall in the market place. Sometimes the local party would hire a coach and Mum would take jam sandwiches, in the hope that she could swap one for Spam.

Labour's star was in the ascendant after the 1945 general election, which was the first in ten years. Winston Churchill's defeat gave me my first sense of the power of the people. In the idea that a nation could get rid of its great war leader and vote for change, I found the stirrings of my own political instincts and interests and became more actively involved in the Labour Party.

Clement Attlee, the new Prime Minister, was a great hero of ours. His modesty and straightforward approach to problems inspired confidence. We knew he was doing the best he could and admired his integrity and conscientiousness. Violet, his wife, also made a great impression on me as she sat knitting on the platform, flashing her painted fingernails. I painted mine as soon as I could and started smoking as well. I thought this was a sign of sophistication, and I have long been a lost cause to the non-smoking lobby.

Aneurin Bevan was as different from Attlee in background and temperament as it was possible for two men in the same party to be, but that was Labour's strength. At least, it was until Bevan resigned from Attlee's Cabinet in 1951 over the imposition of the first prescription charges in the NHS and we began fighting among ourselves. Nobody who heard Bevan speak to a large audience could fail to be impressed by his wit and passion. He almost knocked us off our feet with the strength of his convictions. I became an admirer as soon as I heard him. I knew him and Jennie Lee, his formidable wife, when I became an MPs' secretary, and they always sent telegrams of support at my early election attempts. Despite its difficulties, the National Health Service remains Bevan's lasting achievement. Sadly, my father did not live long enough to see the welfare state come into existence, or to benefit from the NHS. We take it for granted today and some find fault with it, but it took decades of struggle to create and those who remember the harsh conditions that working people endured before the war know how hard – and necessary – the struggle was.

Labour's Yorkshire roots go back well before the party was officially founded in 1908. A Labour man stood in Halifax in 1868 and a delegate from the Yorkshire textile workers sat on the platform at the historic conference in London that decided to send the first Labour MPs to Westminster in 1900. Dewsbury ran a Labour candidate in the 1906 general election. He failed, but the seeds of change were planted and industrial Yorkshire soon became a Labour stronghold.

The League of Youth gave me my first experience of front-line politics – and I relished it. I was the party's assistant agent for Dewsbury in the 1950 general election and became a Yorkshire representative on the league's national committee, which took me to London for meetings at the party's headquarters in Transport House in Smith Square.

We worked happily alongside party veterans, who did all they could to encourage us. The social side of Labour's programme was a major attraction for teenagers in the pre-television era when money was

scarce. We organised galas and hikes, campaigned in
local elections and joined 4,500 other Labour
supporters in 1949 at a rally in a Filey holiday camp
on the Yorkshire coast. Apathy was unheard-of in
post-war politics. The Filey rally gave us the chance
to voice our opinions at open-air meetings, attend
study courses and lectures and make our own fun. I
entered a beauty contest and won a prize. The
Yorkshire Evening News published my picture
accepting an award from Alice Bacon, MP for Leeds
North-East. Such contests are not part of the scene
these days, but we had no such inhibitions. The
country was still picking itself up after the war.
During the week of the rally shortages were so acute
that restrictions were placed on the transport of
potatoes from Lincolnshire to Yorkshire.

Old copies of the duplicated magazine that we
produced for Yorkshire members show how
enthusiastic we were. Called *Venture*, it was an
amateur threepenny newsletter run off on rough
yellow paper. Colin Beever, a gifted organiser who
went on to Ruskin College, edited its mixture of
gossip, light-hearted observation and youthful
punditry and I wrote bits and pieces. One column,
signed Aunty BeBe, discussed the importance of
women's handbags and their 'vital trivialities' and
what happened when they were spilled while saying
goodbye to a boyfriend on a railway station:

It's all very well for men to mock us but we don't
have pockets or, if we do, we don't put anything in
them . . . There were photographs I didn't really

want, but couldn't throw away either. Notebooks with people's addresses I never really knew and a shopping list for the League's New Year social. Combs, mirrors, hairpins, a needle stuck through a reel of cotton, a copy of the Absent Voters Register, and four pencil stumps used in past elections.

There was a key ring containing six keys I knew nothing about, an empty perfume bottle, the back off my old clothing coupon book and half a dozen assorted buttons.

The contents of a woman's handbag are a clue to her personality, and if she's a hoarder – and aren't we all – much of her life's history. Fashion columns always tell us to be chic and soignée, we should never carry anything but the bare essentials: make-up, comb, scented wisps of hand-kerchief, and, when we go out with men, plenty of money. But bare, indeed, would be the woman whose bag was as bare as that . . . our bags are part of us, not just impersonal accessories . . .

I won the League's national speaking award in 1952 in a competition sponsored by the *Daily Herald*, Labour's paper (and the forerunner of the *Sun*) in Leeds. Denis Healey took time off from his parliamentary campaign in Leeds South-East to judge it. With a first-class Oxford degree and a valiant war record to his name, Denis had already made his mark on the party by addressing its 1945 conference in his major's uniform and becoming International Secretary at Transport House headquarters. He recalled in his memoirs that he had chosen 'a bonny lass from Dewsbury who danced as a Tiller girl in the chorus of the local pantomimes'. We were to become close comrades in the fight to save the Labour Party during the 1970s and 1980s, although nobody could have guessed it then.

By 1952 I was keen to address meetings and eager for advice on how to improve. Sarah Barker, the party's Yorkshire organiser, gave me some tips that I have never forgotten. 'Capture your audience with your first sentence,' she said. 'Don't go in for long preambles. They put people off.'

My dancing debacle was well behind me and I was making my voice heard on weightier subjects than the bric-a-brac in women's handbags. I stood for a hopeless seat in Dewsbury's town council elections in May 1952 and lost by a narrow margin. My opponent was a chartered accountant, a Conservative running as an Independent. Our manifesto warned: 'Don't be misled by the Independent label. A vote for them is a vote of confidence in the Tory Government.' They gave it nevertheless and the Tories went on to win another two general elections.

I stood on a platform that promised to build houses to let, resist cuts in education and extend health services, especially for the elderly. Uncle Charles, the secretary of the local Co-op, had no problem in holding his seat in St John's East but I did better than anybody had hoped, coming within 200 votes of victory. My ambitions soared. The political bug would now infect me for life. My friends were pleased for me, but I kept my feet on the ground after

observations such as the one in *Venture* printed after
another camp at Filey: 'Was Betty Boothroyd a very
well-behaved girl, or didn't she get found out?'
enquired its gossip column.

Aunty BeBe's own article in the same issue was
brazenly subtitled 'The Page that appeals to men'. It
seemed that I had discovered the opposite sex – and
they me. But my political ambitions were also noted.
The number of young party members rose in
Dewsbury under my chairmanship of the local
League of Youth. I had learned how to organise and
express myself. Invitations to other parts of the
country followed and I supported Labour candidates
wherever I could.

So nobody was surprised when in 1952 I quit my
job with British Road Services in Batley to work full-
time for the party. For me it was the natural thing to
do. This time Dad would have been pleased with my
return to London.

It was traumatic leaving my mother again, without
any close relation nearby, but we understood each
other and she knew I had to go. A job in the party's
research department at Transport House was too
good an opportunity to miss. I was in daily contact
with party officials and MPs. I had found my
vocation at last.

'The folk down here are grand to work with, but
keep me informed of how and what you're doing in
Yorkshire,' I wrote to *Venture*. The message was
clear. I wanted to remain in touch with them, but this
time I was in London to stay. Ironically, David
Ginsburg, the party's research secretary who ran my

department, moved in the other direction by
becoming Labour MP for Dewsbury from 1959 until
1981, when he joined the Social Democratic Party.
He was a great change from his predecessor Will
Paling, the old miner MP who had studied at evening
classes and had won a scholarship to a Labour
college. Ginsburg went to public school and Balliol
College, Oxford. He finally lost the seat in 1983,
letting the Tories in for a few years.

I found the whole business of his election galling.
How I would have loved to represent my home town!
When Will Paling retired, I sought nominations for
the seat and won the backing of the town's bus
drivers and conductors in the Transport and General
Workers' Union (the TGWU). They sent the form
proposing me to the union's regional office in Leeds
and I waited for news. But nothing happened. An old
friend smelled a rat and we went to Leeds to see if he
was right. He was; the union had arbitrarily rejected
the wishes of its members and had nominated
Ginsburg, a TGWU member. The bus workers were
naive for thinking that the Yorkshire officials of their
union would listen to them when they had already
made up their minds. It was a carve-up from
beginning to end.

Our job in the research department was to work on
a policy statement called Labour's Challenge to
Britain. Privately, Aneurin Bevan was so appalled by
the final draft that he considered resigning from the
party's National Executive Committee (the NEC).
The six Bevanites on the NEC wanted more
nationalisation and more economic planning. They

got their way over chemicals and the renationali-
sation of steel and road transport, but lost out in
their wider aim to increase the economic powers of
the state. By this time, however, Bevan was losing
interest in such matters and turning his attention to
foreign affairs. It was clear the party was split and
that the next election would make Attlee Prime
Minister again or push him into retirement. Either
way, I had to get a job in the House of Commons if I
wanted to be closer to the action.

By great good luck, two MPs needed secretaries
and were willing to share me and thus halve the cost,
an important consideration at a time when MPs had
to finance their offices out of their own pockets. If the
whole House of Commons had queued up for my
services, I could not have chosen two better employers than Barbara Castle and Geoffrey de Freitas.
Barbara's reputation as a leading Bevanite and a
fearless debater was already established, while
Geoffrey, a rich land-owning lawyer on the right of
the party, had already served as a minister. I worked
happily for them both.

Politically on different wavelengths and from
different social backgrounds, they got on well
together because they respected each other's point of
view and knew it was genuinely held. They both
enjoyed life to the full, were well travelled and hated
bigotry and intolerance. Geoffrey's career had
peaked before Barbara got into her stride, but that
made no difference. They were gregarious
intellectuals in a party where sober suits and tribal
loyalties still held sway.

They had served together on Britain's delegation to the United Nations general assembly in New York, when Geoffrey was in the Attlee Government and Barbara was Harold Wilson's Parliamentary Private Secretary (PPS). Geoffrey was quickly rewarded with a minister's job, but Labour's defeat in 1951 and Wilson's rise to the leadership in 1963 blighted his chances at the same time as they enhanced Barbara's. She became a household name, but he never begrudged her success. He believed in a 'broad-church' Labour Party and despaired of Labour MPs who did not.

Geoffrey recounted an amusing story about their work together on the British delegation at the UN in 1949, which showed why they hit it off. Barbara was put on a committee charged with drafting a convention to outlaw prostitution, which brought her into contact with the formidable Eleanor Roosevelt, widow of the wartime President.

The Home Office took the view, which Barbara shared, that the real villains were the pimps and procurers, and argued strongly to that effect. According to Geoffrey, some American high-school girls watching the debate misunderstood Barbara's stand. They thought she was defending prostitutes and berated her for it. So he took her for a drink and told her she had been chosen to serve next on a committee drafting a drugs convention. 'Thank heavens,' she exclaimed in a clear English voice that turned heads in the hotel lobby. 'Prostitution is over. Ernie [Ernest Bevin, the Foreign Secretary] will put me on narcotics now.'

Labour's long years in opposition after 1951 saw Barbara blossom into an influential, headline-winning member on the NEC, while Geoffrey's fortunes waned. Barbara, an inveterate note-taker all her life, dictated her accounts of party meetings to me, whetting my appetite for whatever would come next.

Wilson admired her enormously, but had no time for Geoffrey. When I worked for them, Labour leaders had little patronage to bestow in opposition, so that did not matter. Both Barbara and Geoffrey were immensely busy and happy to delegate as much work to me as I could manage. It was an ideal introduction to the place that was to become the centre of my life.

In the 1950s Labour MPs' secretaries worked in ill-equipped offices in Westminster Hall, the historic heart of the Palace of Westminster, where dead sovereigns lie in state and many scenes of English history have taken place. My early days as a Members' secretary in the House of Commons were enormous fun, but our working conditions were primitive, to say the least. Members today don't know how lucky they are!

When I started working for Barbara Castle and Geoffrey de Freitas I was in the 'Labour Room' with other secretaries. Although we were all members of the Clerical and Administrative Workers' Union (Parliamentary Branch), we were never recognised by the Serjeant at Arms and our circumstances never improved. We each had one shelf and two drawers of a filing cabinet and were warned in no uncertain

terms not 'to expand'. Each Friday afternoon Mary
Frampton, a senior member of the Serjeant at Arms'
staff and a formidable stickler for the rules, would
come round to check that we hadn't 'expanded'. Woe
betide the girl whose papers had strayed on to
another desk. Mary Frampton worked in the
Commons for 40 years and made headlines in 1978
by serving a writ on Sir Charles Villiers, then head of
the British Steel Corporation, ordering him to supply
a select committee with sensitive financial information. He agreed 'forthwith'. Miss Frampton was
not a person to be messed around.

In those days there were only four telephones in
the room, all in booths at the far end. Long-distance
calls had to be paid for by the Members, and so we
only called the local newspapers in our Members'
constituencies once a week. Nor was there any
question of privacy. Members would come and sit on
the edge of our desks to dictate their letters or, in
cases of extreme confidentiality, take us out into the
corridor.

There was a huge sense of camaraderie among the
Members' secretaries. Although we were in the
'Labour Room', Gillian King-Hill (who worked for
a Tory Member) sat with us and we all mucked in
together. We were slightly in awe of Peggy Hughes
because she worked for two Cabinet ministers –
Hugh Dalton and Kenneth Younger. She never
seemed to know where the Post Office or the
Transport Office or the Table Office (in those days
secretaries could table motions for their Members)
were, which was just fine by me. I loved the whole

feeling of the building and its traditions so much that I would happily collect her post or book travel arrangements just so that I could walk across Westminster Hall. I just felt privileged to be there.

We all ate in the canteen at the end of Westminster Hall and Barbara Castle gave me one shilling and ninepence for egg and chips when I worked late for her. We shared the canteen with the police who worked at the House, and they were always very kind to me. One of the Good Luck telegrams I treasured came to me from my policemen friends during my first campaign to get into Parliament.

My job was to handle Barbara's and Geoffrey's correspondence and to help them chase up ministers and Government departments on behalf of their constituents. Barbara had been a wartime civil servant and was tenacious at badgering Whitehall. I learned a lot from her, tackling everything that came my way. All the time, I was learning how Parliament works, from the bottom up.

That was how I met Jo Richardson, who became my lifelong friend. There were about twelve of us in our office, all politically active outside the House. Jo was Ian Mikardo's secretary, and later his indispensable partner in his East-West trading company. She was the doyenne of Labour secretaries, ran our trade-union staff federation and worked tirelessly for left-wing organisations such as the Keep Left Group, the Tribune Group, the Tribune Brains Trust, the Campaign for Nuclear Disarmament (CND) and the 2nd XI (the Bevanites second division). At that time Jo lived with her mother and brother in north London and her home was always open to me.

Working alongside Jo and typing policy drafts for the Keep Left Group, I saw the tensions developing in the party. Founded by Richard Crossman, Michael Foot and Ian Mikardo, the group's purpose was to think about the long-term direction of the party, co-opt experts for research work and publish its findings. The group produced more than seventy papers between 1947 and 1951, which formed the basis of official party policy in the following years. But that did not save it from condemnation by its critics as a rebel conspiracy, especially when Bevan became more closely involved. Barbara produced a paper on Labour's problems in government and one pamphlet, printed by *Tribune*, sold an astonishing 100,000 copies. Which party, never mind a small party group like Keep Left, could arouse that degree of interest today?

Jo and I differed over the years about the party's direction, but our friendship never waned. All the time I knew her, she took twenty to thirty painkilling tablets a day because of her rheumatoid arthritis. Other drugs were useless because of their side-effects, but she never complained and never stopped working. She was six years older than me and had stood for Monmouth in 1951. Like me, she fought five elections before winning a seat, but it took her a lot longer – twenty-three years – before she entered the House as MP for Barking in east London in 1974, the year after I won West Bromwich.

From the start I enjoyed working in the House of

Commons and often stayed late. Moving around the House was much more restricted in those days and we worked under tighter rules. I became an officer of the staff unions' federation, which gave me another opportunity to see how the House worked.

Barbara and Ted Castle, her husband and a journalist like her, always supported me when I fought elections, right up until I won West Bromwich. But Barbara did not believe in positive discrimination for women, even those she knew well. I had told her I wanted to become an MP so I assumed she had supported my name's inclusion on the list of available candidates circulated to constituency parties – the B List. Months later I looked at it and found that she had not. She said that Len Williams, at that time the national agent, 'wouldn't have it and I didn't want to push it'. When I became a candidate, Barbara was a great supporter, but she regarded me as a back-room girl while I worked for her. I had to make my own impact on constituency parties looking for a candidate. Breaking through the gender barrier made me all the tougher, as it had Barbara. She was always conscious of my well-being. She woke me up with a telephone call one night to apologise for forgetting to pay my wages of three pounds ten, worried about how I would manage.

There was only one 'Barbara' in British politics. She capped her celebrity status by becoming Wilson's first Secretary of State and became an icon of the left. Geoffrey's story, on the other hand, all too common in politics, is one of great but unfulfilled promise. But I was a beneficiary. He and his wife

Helen influenced me greatly, especially after I started working full-time for him in the 1955 general election. They remoulded me. They believed in me and gave me a confidence I never knew was there. Geoffrey's majority was slashed at Lincoln, but he had a charmed life when it came to elections. He fought and won ten parliamentary contests and was as extraordinary in his way as Barbara was in hers.

Geoffrey and I came from opposite ends of the spectrum: socially, culturally and financially. I joined the Labour Party from the womb; he signed on as an act of conscience. He became a socialist at school when the unemployed Jarrow Marchers tramped from Durham to London in a disciplined demonstration that stirred public opinion. Educated at Haileybury, Attlee's public school, and at Cambridge, he trained as a barrister, did social work in the East End of London and volunteered for service when war broke out, ending it as a squadron leader in the Royal Air Force.

He experienced just how close to defeat we came. In his diary for 22 June 1940, he recorded patrolling an unidentified coastline of England with sixty RAF servicemen carrying just three rifles and twelve rounds of ammunition between them. At the height of the invasion alert, the Army took over his beat armed with a solitary machine gun and an order commandeering his rifles and ammunition.

Attlee, who had been a major in the First World War, had soft spots for his old school and the armed services and made Geoffrey his Parliamentary Private Secretary soon after coming to power in

1945. Geoffrey was among the huge intake of new MPs in Labour's landslide victory. Attlee's patronage gave him an enviable head start, which extended to the Prime Minister once showing him top Cabinet papers with the words: 'Study these well. You will never have another opportunity like this.'

Geoffrey told me how Attlee asked him if he was taking his children to see the ceremony of Trooping the Colour on Horse Guards Parade. When Geoffrey replied, 'Sorry, sir, I'm too busy', Attlee told him to drop the children off at No. 10 and he would take them.

John Colville, Attlee's private secretary at 10 Downing Street, recalled the Prime Minister asking him what he thought of de Freitas. 'Charming and highly intelligent,' said Colville. 'Yes,' replied Attlee, 'and what's more, he was at Haileybury, my old school.' Colville, who had served Churchill in the same capacity, noted in his diary: 'I concluded that the old school tie counted even more in Labour than in Conservative circles.' He, like Churchill, had been to Harrow. Churchill, however, had never referred to it.

But there was far more to Geoffrey than the old school tie. Within a year he was made Under Secretary for Air and visited Tokyo, where he met General MacArthur, and Taiwan, where Chiang Kai-shek was his host. Attlee then moved him to the Home Office and he would undoubtedly have gone on to greater things had Labour won a full second term in 1950. Sadly, Geoffrey never held office again. His critics blamed him for accepting a knighthood from a Conservative Government when it appointed him British High Commissioner in Ghana in 1960. This was unfair of them. He merited his title and there were sound reasons for giving it. He was dealing with Kwame Nkrumah, the charismatic leader who led his country to independence. Geoffrey's knighthood showed Nkrumah that Britain's first envoy to the former colony was highly regarded. The two men got on well and Geoffrey went on to become British High Commissioner of the short-lived East African Federation.

On his return to Britain, he was nominated for Kettering, a safe Labour seat that Wilson wanted for Peter Shore, who had followed Ginsburg as party research secretary. Geoffrey's punishment was to be kept on the backbenches for the rest of his career, a fate he accepted without bitterness. He had a wide range of interests, especially in Europe, a happy family life and he was financially independent. He married Helen, the daughter of a prominent Chicago lawyer and Democrat, after proposing to her on a bench in the Champs-Elysées. Adlai Stevenson, the Democratic presidential candidate against Eisenhower in 1952 and 1956, attended their wedding.

Geoffrey and Helen owned a 150-acre dairy farm at Bourn, near Cambridge, when I first knew them. Geoffrey left me alone to organise his Westminster office and political diary and we got on famously.

Geoffrey commissioned L. S. Lowry to paint an urban scene to commemorate his link with Lincoln, but persuading the celebrated painter of northern life to agree was a difficult business. Lefevre, the gallery

that represented Lowry in London, feared he might
fall down the Commons steps when he came to tea
because he was too vain to wear spectacles for his
short-sightedness. It was right and their first meeting
was not a success. But Lowry was unhurt and came
again, this time wearing his glasses. He promised to
paint a street scene 'when the good weather comes'.
When it did, Geoffrey showed him around the town
and took him to the waterside, where there were old
brick houses, and workers passing by – a natural
Lowry scene.

We awaited the result and were not disappointed.
It showed Lincoln's waterside with workers leaving
the factories, a railway track, a man riding a bicycle,
people walking in front of terraced houses on the other
side of the river and Lincoln Cathedral in the background. In the middle distance, he showed the power
station with its chimney stack. The picture hung over
Geoffrey and Helen's mantelpiece until his family
presented it in Geoffrey's memory to the Usher
Gallery Trust in Lincoln in 1996.

I had my own mishap when Geoffrey put me
behind the wheel of his limousine and told me to try
driving. I drove straight into the front door of his
house in Cambridge. Unabashed, he paid for me to
be properly instructed and I never (cross fingers)
crashed again. My close and happy relations with the
whole de Freitas family had a transforming effect.
My horizons widened. I was ready, or so I thought,
for the great leap towards becoming a parliamentary
candidate and an MP.

Len Williams disabused me. All I asked was to be

put on the party's B List of parliamentary candidates, but Len was unhelpful. 'Ee, lass, get some age on your shoulders,' he told me. I was now in my mid-twenties. How old did he think I should be before I fought a seat? I refused to be brushed off like that by an old man with a closed mind. I was more convinced than ever that we had more than enough people with age on their shoulders running the show. Len's reward for his years of party service was to be made Governor-General of Mauritius by Harold Wilson.

All I wanted was to be a backbench MP doing a good job for my constituents. Nothing was going to stop me. The Tories were recruiting younger candidates; so should we.

My opportunity came when the party looked around for a candidate to oppose Captain Charles Waterhouse, the right-wing Tory MP for South-East Leicester. I was chosen in July 1956 to fight the seat and got an immediate taste of what lay in store. 'Yorkshire lass of 26 chosen to oppose Tory,' wrote the *Leicester Evening Mail*. 'A parliamentary candidate's vital statistics are usually the last general election figures, but Miss Boothroyd has others that are also worth quoting: 38-28-40.'

Nobody thought to enquire after Captain Waterhouse's measurements or to describe his appearance. But there was more to come. I was 'a dark-eyed young woman' according to the local paper. Since this was true, I could hardly complain; it was better than being a rheumy-eyed old man. If the newspapers wanted to write me up as 'well worth whistling at – dark-haired, big-eyed, shapely and intense', as the *Daily Herald* did, I had to accept it.

However much I tried to make serious political points, the editors of women's magazines and women's pages saw me in a different light. One such 'soft feature' began with a question that had never entered my head: 'How does an attractive 26-year-old woman politician stop men looking at her ankles long enough to get them interested in her party line?' All I could think of in reply was: 'I don't know what I can do. I suppose I'll have to wear brogue shoes and thick stockings.' What else could I say?

I shared a flat with two other girls, worked from 9 a.m. to 7 p.m. in the Commons and loved going to the theatre on Saturday nights. I was 'fancy-free' and told an interviewer: 'like most women I want to get married and have a family. I don't see why I shouldn't be able to combine that with politics. Many MPs do so very successfully.' I never did. Politics and Parliament became the centre of my life in a way that I could not have managed as a wife and mother. I had a choice, and I exercised it.

In 1957 I had the unexpected opportunity to visit Russia. It was the year after Khrushchev denounced Stalin's reign of terror, but followed it with his own in the brutal crushing of the Hungarian uprising. East–West suspicions were running high and the Cold War made this chance to see behind the Iron Curtain all the more exciting for a young parliamentary hopeful.

Harold Davies, the veteran MP for Leek, asked me if I would like to work my way as a secretary and travel organiser for a Labour group visiting North Vietnam via Moscow and Peking (as Beijing was then known). Geoffrey de Freitas, as ever, said 'Go' – and I jumped at the chance. Four other MPs had signed up for the tour: Lena Jeger, Ian Mikardo, John Baird and Bill Warbey.

Of all the people I met, Ho Chi Minh and Chou En-lai remain in my memory as men of foresight and a certain sophistication. Untutored as I was about their revolutionary struggle, I was conscious that they and their people were making world history, regardless of what we in the West thought about them. The more I learned, the more anxious I became about the dangers of misunderstanding each other and jeopardising our future.

I wrote a diary throughout my trip, and an American journalist I met in Moscow encouraged me to keep it as a permanent record. One entry states that many young people I met were 'angry that they should have been bequeathed the responsibility for seeing that there is actually a future at all, by their elders who at times appear intent on destroying not only their enemies, but their friends and even themselves'. I also noted, 'The children are the best dressed, best fed, best everything.' Their parents and other older people looked deprived by comparison, poorly clothed, their faces starved of colour. But I had little real time for reflection. I was too busy absorbing the sights and sensations of travelling halfway round the world in the days before jumbo jets whisked passengers non-stop across continents.

Just getting to Moscow from London meant changing flights at Amsterdam and Prague, where our passports were taken from us for three hours, even though we were in transit.

The gleaming TU-104 that took us on to Moscow was different from anything I had ever experienced. It had no seatbelts and we sat on large, swivelling club chairs in a private compartment whose fittings would not have been out of place in a Victorian sitting room. Three unsmiling stewardesses looked after us, but the food was good: smoked salmon, steak, chips and gherkins, black bread and lemon tea.

I had always wanted to see Moscow with snow on my boots – and I was not disappointed. We stayed at the old Tsarist hotel, the National, from where I could see Red Square, Lenin's tomb and St Basil's Cathedral. I longed for sleep, but the Vietnamese Embassy had other plans. At 11.30 p.m. they gave us a four-hour dinner of caviar, cold meats, chicken legs, rice, fruit, vodka and wines. I resolved to eat only half a spoonful of each course from then on.

The next day I realised that I had taken care of everyone's passport but my own and that I needed an endorsement from the British Foreign Office to allow me to visit China and North Vietnam. Rising before the others, I implored a friendly taxi driver to take me to the British Embassy as fast as he could, by pointing at my passport and repeating the word 'diplomatic' in a stage French accent. He cottoned on, but retaliated by shouting excitedly all the way in his own limited English, 'I love you, I love you, one two three four.'

That night we were given a box at the Bolshoi Ballet next to Molotov, Malenkov and Khrushchev, Stalin's old stooges, who later clashed – leaving Khrushchev the winner. Sir Patrick Riley, the new British Ambassador, gave drinks for us the next day. Lady Riley spent a long time showing me around the embassy, which had once been a millionaire's town house, complaining about the colour scheme, the furniture and the reluctance of the Ministry of Works to spend any money putting it right. She seemed to think I had some influence in such matters; I thought it best not to disabuse her.

I was deeply affected by the poverty I saw in the streets off the main thoroughfares and noted: 'The real basic needs of human life are ignored. Whatever the achievements of the Soviet Union, it has been at the cost of starving many people of everything that we take for granted.' I was also unimpressed by our visit to Lenin's tomb, where Stalin's embalmed body lay alongside. I found the scene 'barbaric' and the bodies 'horrific'.

We flew east in stages, first to Kazan, then to Sverdlovsk in the Urals and on to Omsk and Novosibirsk in Siberia, where we changed aircraft. I wrote:

The thaw has started – airfield shin-deep in mud. Burly Russian porters wearing white pinafores over their coats make a human chain and carry me to a battered old bus. They insist on my not

showing my knees, which is impossible, and all I
am concerned with is not being dropped in the
mud.

After further stops at Krasnoyarsk and Irkutsk, we
crossed into Mongolia and landed in Ulan Bator,
where we met a group of Yugoslav medics, one of
whom was reading *Tribune*. Four hours later we
arrived in Beijing, where laughing Vietnamese
diplomats gave us a boisterous welcome and Harold,
Lena and I received huge bunches of lilies and
carnations. They told us that the train journey to
Hanoi would take four days, but I did not mind.
Beijing's lively atmosphere was more to my taste
than Moscow's. My diary recorded: 'Streets are
colourful and busy with hundreds of bicyclists and
rickshaw boys. It's all terribly exciting. I can't help
thinking how lovely Chinese children are.'

Our rail journey south was aboard a Hungarian-
built train, which was wide, clean and extremely
comfortable. Lena and I chatted and wrote. Bill
Warbey read Chinese tracts and Mik, John Baird
and Harold Davies played high-stakes cribbage,
which won Mik IOUs for £7 million, which he later
commuted to two pints of bitter back home.

Outside we saw how hard both people and animals
worked to develop the countryside, with little
equipment and no signs of cranes: stones and rubble
were carried in baskets slung over the shoulder. New
China was being built before our eyes on a million
bamboo poles. At that time, the Yangtze had no
bridges and divided the country in a very real sense.

We crossed the river by sampan, in the company of piglets carried in cages across the shoulders of farm workers. On board our train again on the other side of the river, a panorama of paddy fields and more poverty unfolded. An English-speaking professor told us that nobody starved, but it was hard to imagine how people survived on what little we saw them growing. I noted:

> Every few hours at wayside stations, our train stops, passengers alight, a radio blares music and an exercise instructor appears. The Chinese fall into line and do the routines. It's a great lark. It's the rainy season and rather like an English summer with full-blown roses and azaleas everywhere.

The rail gauges were not compatible at the Vietnamese border, so we had to change trains again for the final lap. A delightful young official, who had been at the London School of Oriental Studies, joined us. He had chaired a meeting for Harold Davies there. We celebrated with drinks worthy of the country's colonial past: Martini, French wines, three-star cognac and champagne for the toasts. In Hanoi a tremendous reception awaited us, with a welcoming party from the ruling Fatherland Front, great bouquets of flowers and interviews with the local and Australian press:

> We stay in two private villas on the lakeside, Lena Jeger and I in one, the men in the other. My very

large bedroom is filled with roses and gladioli. I
have balcony and sitting room, sunken bath of
green marble and shower. My clothes are
unpacked by boy and girl who seem to be
allocated to me. Ironing is done and mules are
placed at my bedside. Cosmetics are on the
dressing table, complete with spray perfume.
Toothbrush and paste are waiting . . . wish I could
get down to basics!

An early night, but no rest because a large
tropical creature walks across my room and I am
warned I must sleep under a net because of
mosquitoes and flying spiders. I leave light on to
frighten intruders and am still awake at 3.30 a.m.

I have slept under mosquito nets many times since,
but it was a strange experience that first time.

After two days in the tropics, however, I fell ill and
a doctor gave me the first of a series of daily
injections. When I protested that I was robbing poor
people of precious drugs, he said: 'Don't worry. This
is American stuff captured by the Vietnamese from
the French at Dien Bien Phu.'

'God bless America!' I replied, after which I was
ordered to bed, where I watched a lizard, which I
called Croaky Jo, eat mosquitoes on the bedroom
wall.

Once I had recovered, I joined the group and some
socialist intellectuals for dinner, which ended with a
singsong. Mik treated us to the 'Red Flag', Harold
sang in Welsh, Bill Warbey offered 'John Brown's
Body' and I gave a snatch of panto music that I

remembered, about almond eyes and oriental lights being low.

We met Ho Chi Minh for breakfast in his exquisite garden in an arbour surrounded by bougainvillea. He showed us his rare plants and flowers, recalled his days as a commis-waiter in London and talked of his country's future. He showed no anti-Western bias and spoke warmly of Sir Anthony Eden's diplomatic efforts to bring peace to Vietnam. He did not live to see its reunification, but he had no doubts about North Vietnam's victory, which the communists marked by renaming Saigon Ho Chi Minh City at the end of the Vietnam war.

I needed further injections when we toured the countryside around Hai Long Bay, and returned to Hanoi in an ambulance, being fanned all the way. After recovering again, I attended an evening reception in Ho's garden, at which Russia's President Voroshilov was guest of honour. He told me that he had met British communists before I was born; I thought it had not done them much good.

Back in Beijing we spent two hours with Premier Chou En-lai, who spoke in Mandarin, even though he corrected his interpreter's English translation. He was relaxed, friendly and expansive and I made a detailed note in my diary. According to him, China wanted greater contact with the British, especially with the colony of Hong Kong. China had proposed a direct rail link three years before but nothing had come of it, even though the Governor of Hong Kong had agreed with the proposal. China also wanted official representation in Hong Kong, but had been rebuffed on that, too. 'And I ask why,' Chou said, without anger.

He regarded Chiang Kai-shek, the Chinese nationalist leader holed up in Taiwan, with equal composure. Refusing to condemn him as a rebel, Chou commented: 'I have cooperated twice with him and I can cooperate again.' He never did, of course. And while Hong Kong was returned to Chinese sovereignty in 1997, Taiwan still remains apart.

Ordinary Chinese people whom I encountered impressed me just as much as their leaders. 'These people have the character and determination to win through,' I wrote after meeting a waiter who taught himself English every night with the aid of a tattered textbook. It was a judgement that subsequent visits to China confirmed.

The 1955 Parliament, with its comfortable Conservative majority, ran on until 1959, but Captain Waterhouse had had enough. He resigned, leaving his successor an 11,000 Tory majority to defend and denying me the chance to hack away at it gradually for another two years. The by-election was called for November 1957. I had barely had time to find my way around. But I would have loved the chance to fight Waterhouse. An unbending Tory, who clung to Britain's imperial past, he led the Tory rebels who opposed negotiations with Colonel Nasser about the future of the Suez Canal, which the Egyptians had wrested from Anglo-French ownership.

I warned against 'a mad military adventure in Egypt' and deplored the 'nineteenth-century gun-

boat mentality of the Suez Group in the Conservative Party'. When Anglo-French forces
attacked Egypt with Israeli collusion, I denounced it
as an action the world would not soon forget. The
atmosphere in the Commons during the Suez crisis
was electrifying. Speaker Morrison was forced to
suspend the House because passions ran so high and
taxi drivers picking up fares refused Labour MPs
who opposed the invasion – Geoffrey among them. I
favoured giving the canal international status under
United Nations auspices, but Sir Anthony Eden's
recklessness ruled that out and he resigned as Prime
Minister.

Captain Waterhouse realised that his days were
also up and quit to concentrate on his business
activities in Central Africa. I had many Tory friends
but he could never have been one of them, regardless
of our age difference. I supported the Movement for
Colonial Freedom and wore the black sash at
demonstrations in protest against apartheid. Jo
Richardson and I were photographed walking away
from South Africa House in Trafalgar Square after
the police had prevented Fenner Brockway, the
veteran anti-apartheid campaigner, from leading a
procession in Whitehall. All the same, Waterhouse
did me a favour. By-elections attract national
publicity, and I would have been ignored fighting a
safe Tory seat in a general election.

Herbert Bowden, Labour's Chief Whip and MP
for neighbouring South-West Leicester, gave me a
VIP send-off at Westminster. He endorsed me,
saying: 'I have known her since she came to work in

the House of Commons some four years ago and the experience she has gained in Parliament will be invaluable to her as a Member. She states her views quite fearlessly.'

This gave the Tories an easy pot-shot. John Peel, their candidate, said that Bowden's comment might have misled some voters into believing I had actually been an MP, which was nonsense. His heart was not in the stunt, however, and he declared me to be 'a very charming young lady' after meeting me in the hotel in which we were both staying. 'I think he is a very charming young man,' I responded. Win or lose, I would be heading back to the Commons in one capacity or another. There was no point in making enemies gratuitously.

Mum supported me, as she did in every election afterwards. It was her fifty-third birthday and I went to the station to greet her with a big hug and a bunch of chrysanthemums. We posed for photographs. I was learning how the press viewed politics, always looking for an eye-catching angle. They reported that I felt on 'top form', which was nice, but a reporter from the London *Evening Standard* wrote I had 'a Kensington modulated voice', which was rather a surprise. He thought I created the alarming illusion of a 'belle of the Young Tories' at the microphone.

True, I was living in South Kensington at the time, but I was astonished to hear that I had gone native. The man from *The Times* had no doubts about it. He too detected a 'Kensingtonian sophistication' of a kind associated more with Tory garden parties than

with Labour rallies, but he was more impressed with
my seventeen-hour daily schedule.

House of Commons secretaries telegrammed me:
'Here's hoping we will lose a secretary and gain an
employer – Wage slaves of the Parliamentary Staff
branch.' Another message from Nye Bevan and
Jennie Lee wished me a 'a bumper vote'. And
Barbara Castle and Jim Griffiths, Labour's deputy
leader, came up to speak for me – all to no avail. The
charming John Peel won comfortably and I had to
console myself with almost halving the Tory
majority in a 6 per cent swing to Labour.

Personally, it was a worthwhile effort. The
Manchester Guardian commended me as 'an attractive and indefatigable candidate' who had inflicted a
severe blow on the Tories. The result even attracted
the attention of the *New York Times*. It pondered the
implications for Harold Macmillan, Eden's successor as Prime Minister after the Suez debacle. Uncle
Mac, as the press called him, turned out to be a wilier
operator than his foppish style indicated, as I learned
when I made my next attempt to win a seat.

I tried my hardest to return Peterborough and
North Northants to the Labour fold in the 1959 general election. It had been Labour from 1945 to 1950,
but once again I had little time to nurse the constituency. The previous Labour candidate resigned
at short notice so I had to move fast. I won the nomination on the second ballot against six men. Harmar
Nicholls, the sitting Tory MP, was entrenched and
more presentable than Waterhouse. Jo Richardson
and I snatched a holiday on the Italian Riviera

before the election was called. Even there, she found an issue to campaign about in the sacking of twenty-five Birmingham office girls working for the AA, who had gone on unofficial strike. We took time off sunbathing to lobby British motorists on their behalf. Jo never admitted defeat, however hopeless the cause.

When the election began I stressed my position at the centre of the party. I called for every child to have the same standard of education as the grammar schools provided and rejected unilateral nuclear disarmament on the grounds that it would make Britain totally dependent on the United States. I also called for fair treatment for immigrants from the West Indies and Africa. 'Britain is on trial. If we fail, it is not we who will suffer, but our children and grandchildren,' I said. That, and my opposition to immigration controls at that time, made me an easy target for bigots.

The party decided that Peterborough was a key battleground and Hugh Gaitskell, our leader, spoke for me. George Brown also enlivened the campaign by having a row with the manager of Peterborough's Bull Hotel, where I was staying. George objected to a Tory leaflet that the management had placed on the hotel notice board. After a fist-shaking encounter with an unrepentant manager, he stormed out, insisting that I checked out too. He helped me to pack, complaining loudly as we left that I had not received the common courtesy expected from a commercial enterprise. Life was never dull for long with George around.

I presented myself to the local press as a town girl who looked forward to enjoying country life in the lush, rolling meadows of middle England. I wore sensible shoes and a tweed skirt. I had never campaigned in such beautiful countryside – all 160,000 acres of it. I acknowledged the rising prosperity of the 1950s, but argued for it to be considered in a wider context. Nobody could question the benefit that women derived from the washing machine, I argued, or the way television widened our horizons. But rising living standards did not mean we had to lower our moral values. 'The disgrace is that Britain should tolerate second-rate schools, bad housing, inadequate hospitals and the plight of old people. They are moral issues as great as any in the last fifty years.'

In one week I visited sixty villages in a car cavalcade, to show I meant business. I really believed I could win by impressing voters with my high-octane mixture of enthusiasm and total conviction. The press called my charging around a three-day 'grand prix', starting at 10 a.m. and finishing at 8.30 p.m., with an hour off for a sandwich lunch at a pub. Villages with names from ancient times withstood our assault with polite indifference and occasional displays of friendly encouragement. Slipton, Lowick, Aldwincle and Woodnewton on the first day; the villages beyond Oundle on the second; and the Clopton and Barwell area on the third. It was described as the most extensive tour ever undertaken by a parliamentary candidate. I introduced myself on the loudspeaker, while party workers canvassed with leaflets and offered to introduce me to anyone interested. An old-fashioned approach, but I met some surprising people that way. One woman told me she had worked as a maid to a local landowner when she first had the vote and he had told all the servants to vote Tory, so she had never given it a second thought since then. One chap working in his garden was so outraged at my saying hello that he shouted: 'There's enough trouble in this world without the likes of you coming here.' When I protested that I was not plotting a bloody revolution, he got even madder, so I beat a hasty retreat.

There was an 83 per cent turnout on election day. As the results came in overnight from the urban areas, the tide against Labour was irresistible. Britain was becoming a consumer society and the Tories were seen as its advocates. Harmar Nicholls won his fourth successive victory and all I could do was promise to breathe down his neck until the next time. A Tory of the old school, he gave me a warm response: 'I could not have had a better opponent than Miss Boothroyd ... I know it is no real satisfaction to her, but I would like to tell her that I lost twice before I won, so I can sense some of the feelings she must have. But she has the ability and skill, and I hope that in another constituency she will use them successfully. Her mother, who is here, can be very proud of her daughter.'

Gracious as Harmar was, I knew that Labour faced a tougher struggle to regain power than some people in the Labour Party realised. We were victims of our own success in creating the welfare state and

First photocall

My new Whitsun dress

Taking to the road

Mum as a flapper in 1927

My Edwardian father

'I do like to be beside the seaside . . .' Blackpool, 1933

A family outing

Fronting the Swing Stars: cheering
up the troops

The Yorkshire Labour League of Youth Magazine 3d

March 1953.

EDITORIAL

Recent trends in American
foreign and domestic policy have
indicated that reactionary elements
are now firmly entrenched in the
Eisenhower administration.

The decision to withdraw
United States warships from
Formosa, thus freeing the Chinese
Nationalist forces for an attack
on the mainland was but the first
intimation that Eisenhower's
inaugural 'Peace' address, was
merely hypocritical cant. President Eisenhower would have us
believe that he made the decision
purely on the grounds that it was
irrational for the U.S.Navy to be,
in effect, protecting Communist
China from attack whilst Chinese
volunteer forces participated in
the Korean war. He stated that
the American government had no

carefully trained and supplied with
arms by the American Military Administration. Is it perhaps that
President Eisenhower is too much of
a soldier not to employ an army
nearly 600,000 strong?

Mr. Dulles' attitude towards
France and Britain over the European Defence Community Treaty has
been taken to the extreme.
During his recent European tour,
he echoed official American sentiment when he stated that "if the
bulwark of a united Europe did
not materialise, the United States
would have to consider what alternative policy to adopt". The
implication of the words 'alternative policy' was made clear by
Dr. Adenauer when he euphemist-
ically commented that "it would
hardly be to Europe's advantage".

A politically incorrect
Beauty contest, won by No. 583.
Filey, 1949.

Politics and fresh air on Haworth
Moor with The League of Youth

Stepping out in breezy Blackpool, 1950

On the campaign trail with
Helen de Freitas at the wheel
during the 1956 South-East
Leicester by-election

Harold Wilson in
Dewsbury Town Hall

In Bournemouth with
Mum after my father's
death

Peterborough – the 1959
General Election. Second time
unlucky.

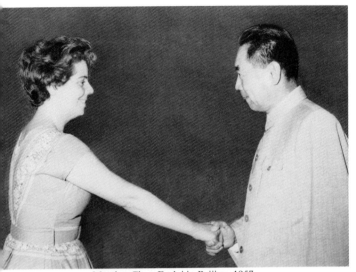

Meeting Chou En-lai in Beijing, 1957

Hanoi, 1957. Admiring Ho Chi Minh's garden. Harold Davies, MP,
is on Ho's left.

Jo Richardson, Mum and Geoffrey de Freitas during the Nelson and Colne by-election, 1968

Catherine and Harry Walston playing dominoes with Father Thomas Gilbey on Rat Island, 1963

Barbara Castle and Harold Wilson at the time of the Bevan controversy, 1955

Under police surveillance at an anti-apartheid protest outside South Africa House. Jo Richardson is on the right.

On holiday with Jo Richardson on the Adriatic Coast, 1952

The world at my feet. Stepping out on Capitol Hill, 1960.

full employment in peacetime. Addressing local
supporters after our defeat, I set out the challenge as
I saw it. We had made it impossible for any
government to return to the inhumanity of the 1930s,
but there were no votes in gratitude. 'Most people
vote against things that they don't like, not to change
things,' I said. 'In 1959, there is no widespread
grievance. Over large parts of the country there is
material contentment.' But Labour was a party of
change and wanted to build a new society. If it
stopped being that, there was no reason for its
existence. The question it faced was whether
prosperity was blunting the country's sense of moral
indignation. I left the question hanging in the air, but
the answer was pretty obvious.

Back in London, I returned to my work with
Geoffrey de Freitas and life resumed much as before
– apart from one curious episode. It involved a
Russian diplomat called Anatol Strelnikov, whom I
had met at a Labour Party conference. He was one of
thirteen officials at the Soviet Embassy to share the
rank of Third Secretary, the lowest embassy status.
We seemed to have interests in common and a similar working-class background and we soon became
friends. He wanted to know how the Labour Party
made its policy and I saw nothing suspicious in that,
at least at the start. It was a good chat-up line, but
there was no romance. I had no secret information to
give anybody anyway.

I found Strelnikov charming, as did Geoffrey,
whom he also cultivated. He probably thought my
work for Geoffrey and my own parliamentary

ambitions made me a worthwhile contact. Diplomats
have to justify their existence and there was nothing
covert in his interest in the Labour Party. He had,
after all, attended our party conference. It was only
after he had taken Geoffrey to lunch several times in
the spring of 1958 that Geoffrey became uneasy. He
decided to check him out with his Whitehall
contacts, taking care not to alert Strelnikov.

On 5 May 1958 Geoffrey wrote to Strelnikov
saying that he had very much enjoyed meeting him
for lunch and looked forward to seeing him again.
On 19 May Geoffrey thanked him for an invitation
to lunch the next day at Margarita, a Spanish
restaurant at 17 Cork Street, W1. He then wrote to
the Foreign Office asking if they knew anything
'unusual' about his attentive Soviet host. Was he, in
other words, a known (or suspected) spy?

Geoffrey wrote on first-name terms to David
Ormsby-Gore, Minister of State at the Foreign
Office in Harold Macmillan's government. He
explained our contacts with the young Soviet
diplomat and why Strelnikov puzzled us:

Confidential
Dear David,

    Anatol G. Strelnikov
    Soviet Embassy

During the past six months or so, my secretary
Miss Betty Boothroyd of 21 Gilston Road, SW10,
has been seeing a good deal of Anatol Strelnikov,

a junior member of the staff of the Soviet Embassy. During the last month, I have met him twice and I liked him so much that I have invited him to visit me at home in Cambridge with his wife when she returns to England.

My secretary and I have never met him when we have been together and when we compare notes we are very puzzled by him. I find that his views are not representative of a Russian of his age and education. On the other hand, my secretary finds that he is very representative. Miss Boothroyd has visited the Soviet Union and has met a number of Russians. I have not been there but I know two or three Russians fairly well – UN delegates, air attachés, etc. This much is certain: we both find him charming and interesting and he is anxious to see more of us.

We are wondering if your people know anything unusual about Strelnikov and if so whether there is anything that could be passed on to me confidentially, or better still, to both my secretary and me. This is a small matter to bother you with, but we have both been so puzzled by this young man that I feel compelled to write to you. I shall try to have a word with you in the House when we return. I hope you have a break at Whitsun.

Ormsby-Gore's 'people' in secret intelligence duly called me in for a chat. Far from expressing any interest in Strelnikov, however, they turned the conversation to the Labour Party's Tribune Group, the parliamentary gathering of left-wing MPs to which Ian Mikardo and other friends of mine belonged. Three or four of them needed keeping an eye on, I was told. Would I do that for them? I was astonished. Geoffrey and I had asked for guidance about a young Soviet diplomat and their response was to try to recruit me to spy on the Tribune Group. My answer was a categorical no, and I never had any further dealings with them.

I seemed to be in demand on both sides of the Iron Curtain. It was time to draw a line under the whole business. Geoffrey and I did so as politely as we knew how. Unaware of our concerns, Strelnikov pushed his luck in an audacious move that forced me to write to him on 12 June 1958, disabusing him:

21 Gilston Road,
London SW10
12 June 1958

Dear Tony,
    I am enclosing the ring. It was very kind of you to give it to me. I am sure you understand that the giving of jewellery in this country is a very difficult matter and, on thinking it over, I am sorry to say I cannot accept it.
    I do appreciate your kind gesture,
    Yours sincerely,
    Betty Boothroyd. With certificate of posting.

Eleven days later Geoffrey cancelled a lunch with Strelnikov arranged for 2 July, but left the door open

to him to accept an earlier invitation to visit the de
Freitas family in Cambridge on 27 July. Whatever
Strelnikov's intentions were, he realised the game
was up.

He replied coolly that the cancelled lunch was 'a
pity' and did not commit himself to the family visit. I
never saw him again. If he was a spy, he completely
misjudged Geoffrey and me. Strelnikov may have
thought that if I handed over policy documents that
he could easily have obtained from Labour Party
headquarters, confidential information might
follow. If so, he was wrong. Whatever his aims, the
Russians had more important people than me in
their sights, as subsequent scandals would show.

CHAPTER THREE

American Adventure

═══

We have the capacity to make this the best generation in the history of mankind, or make it the last.

John F. Kennedy

JOHN F. KENNEDY made his bid to become the thirty-fifth President of the United States at exactly the right time for me. I felt I needed a new inspiration, and when he summoned his country to a new destiny, he unconsciously summoned me too.

Everything I knew about Kennedy appealed to me. Young, fresh and progressive, he made Europe's elderly leaders seem even more out of touch. My generation needed a new voice to express our aspirations and JFK provided it. We did not have to check his birth certificate to know that he was the first American leader to be born in the twentieth century. His vigour and idealism contrasted sharply with the tired politics on this side of the Atlantic. It was time for Western politicians born in the Victorian era to move over. I had admired Harold

Macmillan's 'winds of change' warning to South Africa's ruling whites who clung to their abhorrent apartheid system, but his droll Edwardian mannerisms were from another world.

I wanted to experience Kennedy's charisma close up. I wanted to help him if I could. Who knows, I might be on the winning side for once and come back energised and better able to change the face of British politics. Geoffrey was all for it. The Democrats had friendly relations with Labour and I had got on well with the Americans I had met when I worked for him at Nato parliamentarians' meetings. So we wrote to the Democratic Party National Committee in Washington, DC and to every Democratic senator fighting for re-election, offering my services.

I had already met three of Capitol Hill's most powerful Democrats at Nato meetings – Lyndon Johnson, Kennedy's running mate; Estes Kefauver, who was running for re-election in Tennessee; and Wayne Hays, who was campaigning for another term in Ohio. Such transatlantic experience is commonplace in today's easy relationship between Washington and Westminster, but it was rarer then, especially at my level. I needed an immigrant's visa to work in the States, even though I had no intention of settling there. Although I was offering my services free to the Democrats, I had to earn a salary after the election if I was to stay there six months, as I planned. Optimistic and willing to take a chance, I counted on my House of Commons background to open doors. All the same, I bought a return air ticket – just in case.

I arrived in New York on 26 September 1960, the day of the first television debate of the election between Kennedy and his Republican rival, Vice-President Richard Nixon. It was watched by more than 70 million viewers across the nation. For me, the main difference in the style of American politics stuck out a mile. After the cut-and-thrust of Westminster, their formality and lack of passion seemed strange. A moderator introduced the men and said they would each make opening statements of eight minutes, would answer questions from journalists on an agreed area of policy and would then make closing statements of four minutes. The voters were thus deprived of judging them in direct confrontation, but I could hardly criticise that. British MPs shunned television coverage of their debates for another twenty-five years.

Kennedy spoke first and immediately justified my enthusiasm. He recalled Abraham Lincoln's declaration that the question before America was whether it could be half-slave, half-free. A century later, the same question confronted the world and the outcome depended on the kind of society they built in America – and how strong they were. Kennedy believed they were falling behind industrially and socially and pointed to the country's 50 per cent unused steel capacity, its uncompetitive economic growth and the fact that four million Americans depended on federal food aid. He had even seen children in West Virginia who took some of their school lunch home in order to feed their families. 'I don't think we are meeting our

obligations towards these Americans,' he said. But
his opponents – he did not mention the Republicans
by name – had opposed every piece of social
legislation for the past twenty-five years.

Watching him on television in my hotel room, I
knew I had been right to come. There was nobody in
British politics like him. I had £200 in my pocket and
I was ready to go. I flew first to Flushing, Ohio, to
work for Wayne Hays. All I knew about him was
that he was an influential Democrat standing for re-
election to the House of Representatives and that he
was well known in Nato circles. My friendship with
his secretary, Elaine Heslin, whom I had met at Nato
meetings in Paris, was the decisive factor in my going
to the Midwest. For an honorarium of a few dollars
a day I did dogsbody jobs around his office and
immersed myself in Midwest politics.

'When you get the chance of a lifetime, you don't
ask questions,' I had told a Fleet Street reporter
before flying out. 'They can ask me to lick stamps or
make the tea. I'll be quite happy. I shall be looking
for pointers and ideas which I might be able to use in
future campaigns.' My hosts had other ideas,
however, and decided to exploit my novelty value.
They asked me to speak to women's groups on Hays'
behalf, something nobody would dream of asking an
American to do in a British election. I revelled in the
whole thing.

Hays held his seat without difficulty, but became
increasingly unpopular in Washington and was
eventually disgraced when the House of
Representatives Ethics Committee caught up with

him in 1976. His undoing was an assistant who worked for him on the House Administration Committee, who told an interviewer, 'I can't type, I can't file, I can't even answer the phone.' When she explained what she actually did for Hays, it was something the taxpayer should not have been paying $14,000 a year for. He resigned, leaving Washington in disgrace.

My next secondment couldn't have been a bigger contrast. I caught up with Estes Kefauver, a big, slow-moving Southerner who was campaigning for Kennedy in Ohio, as he flew from one campaign engagement to another hundreds of miles away. 'I have a pilot. You can come if you can navigate,' he joked.

'You're on,' I replied, and off we went. I took advantage of every opportunity that came my way and of Americans who helped me like that. In England, my approach would have been regarded as presumptuous. In the United States, seizing your chance is a vital part of the American way.

Kefauver was as widely loved as Hays was heartily loathed. Jack Kennedy admitted learning from him during the previous Democratic Convention in 1956, where they were rivals for the vice-presidential nomination. Kennedy had lots of appeal, but Estes had a core of personal support that even Kennedy could not rival.

'I remember a wonderful Maryland delegate and his wife,' Bobby Kennedy recounted after Estes beat his brother to become Adlai Stevenson's running mate. 'They were entirely friendly. They liked us. But

Kefauver had visited them in their home. He had sent them Christmas cards. We couldn't shake them. Believe me, we've sent out lots of Christmas cards since.'

MPs do this kind of thing too of course, but seldom with the American passion for keeping friendships in good repair and making new contacts. Congressional members also differ in their campaign styles. Estes saw his main role as motivating party workers and raising party funds by speaking to $100-a-plate diners. His direct contact with voters was limited to shaking hands in places where he knew they would be.

Candidates in Britain are still expected to join their workers as they canvass street by street, finding out where their local support is and what the voters think. American politicians have much bigger national constituencies and cannot do that, so they rely more on television advertising, telephone canvassing and rallies to get their message across. Estes showed me that just saying hello to people as they went about their daily business could be as effective as the British tradition of knocking on doors.

He worked his way through a supermarket – a new kind of shopping experience to me – greeting everybody in his Southern drawl: 'Hi, I'm Estes Kefauver. Glad to meet you.' Nobody bothered him with policy questions, and he did not hold the shoppers up by engaging them in conversation. His aim was to meet a large number of people. They called it 'pressing the flesh' and I did a lot of it when

I returned to England. 'Hi, I'm Betty Boothroyd' became my standard greeting. For me, American folksiness came easily. After watching Kefauver, I pressed the flesh every inch of the way – as a candidate, an MP and as Speaker.

But Estes was a man of principle as well as a popular personality. Routinely denounced as 'too liberal for Tennessee', he confounded his critics at every election. The joke after his 1960 Senate victory was that nobody would promise to vote for him on the day before the election and nobody would admit to voting for him on the day after. All the same, he won 65 per cent of the vote by being his own man.

He died after a heart attack on the Senate floor, aged sixty, just three years later. A wonderful tribute to his memory explained something of what he meant to the people of Tennessee, where Franklin D. Roosevelt's 'New Deal' had transformed people's lives and Estes, like FDR, was denounced as an agent of the 'pinkos and communists'.

This commemorative account by Theodore Brown Jr and Robert B. Allen described his funeral in terms that any world statesman would envy:

Thousands of Kefauver's 'little people' – white farmers with tieless red necks, blacks, laborers, housewives, school teachers, young people, old folk struggling on canes, Democrats and Republicans alike – converged in the narrow, stifling country seats of Madisonville, along with many of Kefauver's Senate colleagues and Vice-President and Mrs Johnson, to participate in

funeral ceremonies for one of Tennessee's most
beloved favorite sons ... Favored with dark,
heavily clouded skies, they clogged all streets
leading to the First Baptist Church here, where he
lay in state, awaiting their chance to bid farewell to
one of the few of the nation's political leaders
whom they felt they had known personally.

My campaigning with Estes Kefauver was the perfect
prelude to working for Kennedy as he entered the
last phase of his campaign. By mid-October I was a
member of the army of Democrats, journalists and
staffers who followed him around. It gave me the
opportunity to observe him away from the public
spotlight. I reported my impressions to the *Yorkshire
Evening Post* in my first dispatch on 20 October:

Everything associated with an American election
campaign is noisy, colourful and exciting, like the
15,000 people who had been waiting more than
three hours to give him a traditional Ohio
welcome when he arrived in the football stadium
at Salem. It was bands, streamers and pretty drum
majorettes all the way.

I travelled with Kennedy's team of political
advisers, newspapermen, public relations officers,
cameramen, secretaries and what-have-you in a
caravan of cars for the 65 miles between
Youngstown and Salem. A second caravan of
buses containing typewriters, cameras and
equipment followed.

The road was crowded with cheering supporters

carrying banners. Even with a police escort we managed no more than 10 miles an hour.

In these circumstances one sees a different Kennedy from the man who talks from platforms. He seems shy, even alarmed, by the closeness of so many people. Hence the hesitation to shake hands. But his audiences think of him as a hard-hitting fighter out to win. Generally, he seems so sure of himself, so confident of the gospel he is preaching, that one critic likened him to a door-to-door salesman.

When addressing enormous crowds he is relaxed but earnest – a man with no time to talk nonsense. To a country accustomed to thinking of its politicians as long-winded, he is a novelty.

By the time we reached Pittsburgh, Pennsylvania, my enthusiasm knew no bounds:

As I begin to write this I looked up and asked a man: 'What day is it?' He was a middle-aged man, one of John Kennedy's aides who had been with the election team from the start. He replied: 'Never mind the day – what month is it, September, October or November?'

Electioneering, American-style, is an ordeal made up of fatigue, occasional hunger and thirst, and almost constant noise and hullabaloo . . . the bus I travel in carries no drinking water and it can get very hot and dusty. By mid-afternoons, our leather-lined throats are croaking for water. I became desperate one day. As our motorcade arrived at a town's main square, I jumped out and ran back two blocks to where I had seen a sign: Jim's Bar. I dashed in and asked the bartender for the largest container he had to be filled with water.

He was a little surprised but filled an enormous jar with water and ice cubes and would not take a cent for his trouble. Back on the bus, we drank it straight from the jar even though it tasted slightly of relish, for that is what it had previously contained.

Back in New York, Kennedy was hailed by a milling mass ... the enthusiasm of cheering, jumping, laughing crowds is infectious. I find the endless sea of faces enthralling. They are a complete cross-section of America.

I was an eager convert to everything Kennedy represented and was dazzled by him personally. 'He's slim, erect and the contrast of a sun-tanned skin against well-whitened teeth accentuates his natural good looks,' I gushed. A girl cannot be more bowled over than that. More Americans than I had guessed, however, were less impressed and he won by the smallest whisker, polling 49.7 per cent of the popular vote to Nixon's 49.6 per cent.

In Ohio, where victory looked certain, he actually lost to Nixon by 273,000 votes in the greatest upset of the election. It was a lesson that crowd sizes can be deceptive and, as an astute commentator remarked, that quiet people also have votes.

It was calculated that if 4,500 Kennedy voters had switched to Nixon in Illinois and 28,000 had done the same in Texas, both states would have moved into the Republican camp, giving Nixon the White House. But he did not challenge the result and I had the heady sensation of being part of the winning team. I watched the election results in Ohio and prepared my next move – to Washington, DC and, hopefully, a job watching the Kennedy Administration in action.

I got a room in Washington at the YWCA, where I enjoyed comforts worthy of a four-star English hotel. That year was the first time my mother and I had spent Christmas apart and I thought of her a lot, even though we were constantly in touch. She never reproached me for my absence and I knew that cousins in Yorkshire would keep an eye on her, but that was not the same as my being at home. I was more affected by not being able to see her at Christmas than I had expected and I think of it still.

I was soon swept up in trying to find a job in Washington in time for the transfer of power at President Kennedy's inauguration on 20 January 1961. The omens were good as I watched the boisterous inauguration parade and thrilled to his call to Americans: 'Ask not what your country can do for you – ask what you can do for your country.' I still have my copy of the limited de-luxe edition of the Official Inaugural Program, No. 412, with my name in gold lettering on the cover and a handwritten inscription inside: 'To Betty Boothroyd, With Very Best Wishes, John Kennedy.'

As he took the oath, even the Yorkshire volunteer who had fetched iced water shared the belief that something tremendous had happened. The Inaugural Program described his achievement as a triumph of 'sheer intensity, stamina and coolness under fire'. It stated that 'every speech, every debate [and] every act of courage had counted' during the campaign – and I remembered that. I was introduced to Kennedy later at a congressional reception in the White House, but my sponsor was not a Democrat, as I would have expected. It was an extraordinary Massachusetts Republican, admired by Kennedy and respected on both sides of Congress: Silvio O. Conte.

Meeting Silvio was an amazing thing. I soon found that there were no jobs around Washington for an ambitious immigrant who had worked as an extra for a few dollars expenses a day in an election cast of thousands.

I had thought of applying to Senator William Fulbright, who had a great reputation in Britain for promoting the exchange scholarship programme for UK and US academics that bore his name. I assumed that his domestic policies were as progressive as his international outlook and was astonished to discover I was wrong. Fulbright belonged to the old tradition of Southern Democrats who opposed civil rights for black Americans. Along with most of them, he signed the Southern Manifesto in 1956, protesting against the Supreme Court's historic judgement outlawing racial segregation in the South.

Only three Southern senators did not join Fulbright in opposing the Supreme Court judgement. One of them was Lyndon Johnson and another was Senator Al Gore Sr of Kentucky, the father of Al Gore, Democratic candidate for the presidency in 2000. It was said that Fulbright could have been Kennedy's Secretary of State but for his attitude to racial issues.

Weeks followed without work or income as Washington filled with Democratic appointees. I began to think I was never going to get a job. The British Embassy offered me one but, grateful though I was, I had come to America to work for Americans. I wanted to understand their system of government and return home better qualified to become an MP.

I knew I would not become destitute. By this time I had made some good friends and Ian Mikardo had given me the name of a relative living in New York to turn to in any emergency. Mik thought I had made a mistake by going to America. He wrote to his relation telling him to give me money if I needed it and that he would repay him. It was typical of Mik's thoughtfulness, but I got through without bothering his family or anybody else.

Elaine Heslin and Melba Congleton, another girl I had met on the campaign trail, saw to that. They were senior congressional aides and became my lifelong friends. Back in Washington, they moved heaven and earth to find me a job and made sure I was never lonely. British newspaper correspondents also invited me into their social circle. Thanks to Elaine and Melba, whom I called my 'golden girls', I found work in the end with Silvio, a remarkable first-generation American who was happy to give me a chance, despite my Democrat and Labour credentials and the communist-bloc visas on my passport. If he could overlook all that, I decided, I could overlook his being a Republican. What mattered more was that he had a strong sense of social justice and was willing to give me a break.

Working for Silvio Conte from Massachusetts turned out to be one of the best moves I ever made. He hired me as an office help and I ended up as an assistant specialising in overseas aid and European policy. 'Sil' Conte was an unabashed liberal, proud of his Italian roots and fearless in his views, which often contradicted the official Republican line. He did not care a jot about my being on the left of British politics and when I eventually won a Commons seat, he and his wife Corinne were delighted. I could not have worked for a finer man or known a better advertisement for the American way of life.

He liked my English voice, so I began by cheerily answering the office telephone, sometimes forgetting the deference expected of me. When Henry Cabot Lodge, President Eisenhower's campaign manager in the race for the 1952 Republican nomination, called and said who he was, I thought he was pulling my leg. 'And I'm Jackie Kennedy,' I retorted.

I trawled the Massachusetts papers for personal news that would give Silvio the opportunity to write a congratulatory letter and send a small gift. A birth notice would merit an autographed baby book, a wedding announcement a cookery book, while a new Round Table chairman would receive a book about the Constitution of the United States. Nobody missed out. It was part of the Conte technique for keeping in touch.

I graduated to showing his constituents around Capitol Hill because he thought they would enjoy my English accent as much as he did. And they did, despite my having to explain the famous painting that hangs in Congress of British soldiers burning down the White House during the war of 1812. A photograph taken of me at the time shows me sweeping down the steps of Capitol Hill and loving every minute of it.

Silvio knew an enthusiast when he met one and I was soon researching speeches and keeping him up to date on European affairs. He was punctilious in dealing with letters from constituents and my House of Commons training served me well in helping him. The letters I typed can still be found among the Conte files in the University of Massachusetts. They bear the reference initials SOC/bb.

He was 'cordially yours' to every correspondent, but his replies varied according to his interest in the issues raised and the sort of person he was dealing with. I soon learned how to draft what he wanted. To a constituent who wrote denouncing President Kennedy and American aid, he cooed: 'I want to thank you for letting me have your views on these matters and I hope you will continue to write to me from time to time for, despite our differences on some issues, a useful exchange of opinions is always conducive to reasonable thought.'

To the chairman of a federal commission who lobbied him to support American citizens claiming

$300 million in damages from enemy countries in the Second World War, he was politely non-committal: 'The documents you enclose with your letter will form part of my weekend reading and I shall give them close attention at that time.' Who could complain about that?

Not everybody was treated with kid gloves. He wrote to the editor of the *Berkshire Eagle* in Pittsfield, Massachusetts, complaining that it had misrepresented his position on foreign aid. In a covering personal letter that I typed, he ridiculed the 'cockeyed lie' that he was opposed to foreign aid, but added that he hoped that he and the paper would be able to 'get together so that we can discuss these matters further'. He always took care not to burn his bridges.

A student's pencilled appeal relayed by a mother in Adams, Massachusetts, was handled with the same immaculate care. Her daughter wanted Congressman Conte to brief her for a high-school debate about the use of nuclear weapons in a war with Russia. 'I am on the affirmative team,' said the girl.

I returned a reasoned explanation of American policy that limited the possibility of nuclear retaliation to three scenarios: a Soviet miscalculation about America's resolve to defend itself; Russia's belief that it could win a nuclear war; and a pre-emptive Soviet attack prompted by fear of an American attack. We never heard whether the girl won the debate, but she could not complain of lacking good information.

My original six-month leave of absence soon passed, but Geoffrey did not object to my staying on. I was learning a lot and had every intention of returning home. By then, I was earning more than an MP, but I still calculated the price of everything in pounds and shillings to make sure I did not lose touch with reality. I began drafting some of Silvio's speeches and he was delighted when one about the need for strong overseas aid was applauded from the public galleries.

Silvio's constituents sent him to Washington seventeen times, three times with bipartisan support and eight times unopposed, a record that no British politician could rival – not even the Speaker. He did it by being a man of deep convictions, a great character and an expert on issues that mattered most to him: health, education and the environment. It was said he could never resist a parade or a stunt. He wore a pig mask to oppose 'pork-barrel' spending by Congress in favoured constituencies. On St Patrick's Day he carried a shillelagh and called himself Silvio O'Conte.

But he was nobody's pawn. He gave the casting vote that allowed President Kennedy to get his legislative programme through Congress against Republican opposition and he was greatly admired by the Kennedy family. So I worked for the Kennedy cause in Washington after all.

Silvio died in 1991, the year before I became Speaker. Senator Edward Kennedy said of him that the secret of his success was 'that he took most issues seriously but he never took himself too seriously'.

Like everybody I worked for on my way to the Speaker's chair, Silvio encouraged me, and he and his wife Corinne took me into their family bosom. I spent weekends with them in their homes outside Washington and in the Berkshires, in his New England constituency. We had a natural affinity. His father was laid off work for long stretches in the Depression. He was a 'moderate' when moderation was unfashionable in his party. He called his party's extremists 'apes'; I called mine 'headbangers'. I learned from Silvio more than I knew at the time.

He gloried in being what he called 'a minority within a minority within a minority', a reference to his being an Italian in the Irish-run state of Massachusetts, a Republican in a Democratic House of Representatives and a liberal in a conservative party. My minority status was to be a woman in a male-dominated political system, a moderate in a party undermined by extremists and a stickler for the rights of Parliament against ministers of both parties who found this irksome.

I could easily have stayed in the States and become an American citizen. Instead, I returned to England in time for Christmas 1961. Britain was my home and the place where my unfulfilled ambitions lay. America was wonderful to me, but I did not belong there. More than ever, I wanted to be a Labour MP.

Leaving Washington for the last time with my immigrant's visa, I headed for Chicago and the West Coast, which I had not yet seen. Everywhere, somebody known to friends or colleagues met me – nobody networks like the Americans and I was a beneficiary. I had such a good time partying in Chicago that ·I lost track of what day it was and missed my train for the next leg of my journey to Mexico. I spent the time waiting for the next Chieftain train writing Christmas cards in my hotel room.

After Mexico, I met up with Elaine and Melba in Las Vegas, where we saw Frank Sinatra's show at the Desert Sands Hotel. Elaine enjoyed herself working the one-armed bandits, but the gambling side of the city's attractions bored me. As they flew home, I finished my coast-to-coast tour in Los Angeles, from where I returned to London.

Melba retired to Florida, and Elaine and I visited her when I became Speaker. We took photographs of each other on the pier and wanted a group shot, so Melba asked a local resident to take one. He was happy to do so but as he looked at me, he exclaimed: 'You're the one who don't wear the wig!' Such is the power of television.

I have visited the United States many times in different capacities, but always as a friend. When I became Speaker, my own special relationship with America took on a new dimension, which I hope is not yet finished. I am not starry-eyed about it. On the contrary I believe that, special though our relationship is, it should never be exaggerated or taken for granted.

When I returned to the States as Speaker in 1993, my hosts on Capitol Hill showed me a handwritten report of the first Congress in 1789 and Donnald Anderson, the clerk of the House of Representatives, asked me to sign a copy of Erskine May's great work, *Treatise on the Law, Privileges, Proceedings, and Usage of Parliament*, the bible of our parliamentary procedure. I was happy to do so. We can admire each other's traditions without any loss of pride in our own.

I have always defended the Commons against charges from overseas that it is a bear pit in which the loudest voice wins the day. At times, it can sound like that, but our spirited exchanges are part of our robust democracy – what R. A. Butler, who served under Winston Churchill, called 'the noise of democracy'. I believe that silence in the Commons is neither golden, realistic nor democratic. Legislators in other countries who read their speeches without challenge or interruption are 'all such goodies', I said on returning to the United States as Speaker. Thankfully, nobody asked me if I was referring to Congress! How Silvio would have laughed.

The fact that so many Americans are interested in how the Commons works, and watch it regularly on the C-Span channel, illustrates its international appeal as a real forum, where people's concerns can be expressed without fear or favour. 'We're not Madame Tussaud's waxworks. We're human beings,' I told one interviewer. My job as Speaker was 'a cross between train-spotting and bungee-jumping', swinging from numbing boredom when the House is half-dead to wild excitement when it erupts into open warfare.

Congressional members have a much easier time than MPs. They treat each other with studied courtesy and insert newspaper editorials and articles into the Congressional Record to register views with which they wish to be associated. An academic observer from the University of Pennsylvania wrote during my Speakership of how 'after one week of positively banal proceedings on the floor of the US House of Representatives, I take solace in the fact that on Sunday evenings I can cuddle up to the latest antics from the House of Commons'.

He described my role as 'the pugnacious arbiter of the spectacle' and marvelled at the 'unique admixture of rumblings of assent and dissent that makes the House of Commons such a special body'. In his view, the British system won hands down for its parliamentary procedure, decorum, net entertainment value, audacity and the scoring of cheap political points.

I declared my own American influences when President Clinton visited Westminster in November 1995: 'Just as you studied British politics as a Rhodes Scholar at Oxford University, so I studied American politics as a congressional assistant on Capitol Hill, a rather unusual role for a resolute British subject.' It was a formative experience that gave me a new outlook on the world and one that I would not have missed for anything.

CHAPTER FOUR

The Walstons

_Poverty is apt to strike suddenly like influenza,
it is well to have a few memories of extravagance in store
for bad times..._
Graham Greene, _Travels with My Aunt_

I RETURNED FROM THE United States in December 1961, without a job or anywhere to live. Geoffrey de Freitas had gone to Africa as British High Commissioner to Ghana, and London was lacking career opportunities for an ambitious young woman set on becoming an MP. Politics was not the profession it has since become, with its legions of special advisers and parliamentary consultants. So I went on the dole until I found something that matched my qualifications.

Jo Richardson, bless her, solved my accommodation problem by allowing me to share her flat, thus sealing our lasting friendship. Returning to a humdrum commercial job with my experience would have been foolish, and my network of friends cast around for an opening with a political flavour to it.

George Brown came to the rescue when he heard that Lord Walston, a newly ennobled Labour peer and an old friend of his, was looking for a personal assistant. I jumped at the opportunity.

The problem was that Harry Walston was in the West Indies, where he owned a large estate, and I had never met him. All I knew was that he was a millionaire land-owner, had a distinguished record of service to the Labour Party and was a cultivated man with a deep knowledge of art, agriculture and European affairs.

George doubted whether I would get on with his American wife, Catherine, but in that he was mistaken. Harry's long-serving secretary, Mrs D. R. Young, interviewed me in the Walstons' apartment in Albany, Piccadilly, and told Harry, 'I don't think she will do.'

'Hire her all the same,' he replied. George's recommendation must have mattered more than Mrs Young's doubts. She had worked for Harry since he was director of agriculture in the British zone of occupied Germany after the war and stayed with him when he returned to London.

Mrs Young must have been an exemplar of discretion, for she worked for the novelist Graham Greene as well as for Harry, and took their secrets to the grave. Graham's affair with Catherine had more or less spluttered out by 1960, but their relationship remained close until the end. Greene's involvement with the Walston family was an extraordinary relationship that Mrs Young probably thought would be quite beyond my comprehension. Harry and Catherine were living in 6 St James's Street, above Locks the Hatter, when Greene – already a successful writer – moved next door to be close to Catherine. Harry knew about the affair, but accepted him into the family circle, as did their children.

I found Harry to be a shy man, but I liked Catherine from the start. Her family said she got on well with only two women, of whom I was one. Diana Crutchley, the Catholic wife of the printer to the Cambridge University Press, was the other. Why Catherine and I hit it off is hard to say. Our social and religious backgrounds were complete opposites. We just gelled, as the Americans say.

Catherine came from New England and had a personality that bowled over everyone who knew her. From the outset she treated me almost as part of the family and we developed an enormous bond of respect and love for each other. Victor Gollancz, the publisher, was a great friend of hers and wrote in adoring terms that might have raised eyebrows in some quarters, but was totally natural in the Walstons' circle.

He described her in one letter as 'incomparably fascinating Catherine' and chided her in another for writing to him as 'Dear Victor'. He signed it 'Yours, with more than mere love', which she rewarded with a greeting to 'Most enchanting Victor'. Comparing the quality of different cigars, she told him that the wrapping on some she had bought in Dublin was 'distinguished by its quality of almost Graham Greene sordidness'. She promised him something better from a visit she was about to make to

Afghanistan and wondered if 'caviar would be better or a Persian lamb handkerchief'.

It was a way of life I had never encountered before: exuberant, unconventional, lavish, open and yet more complex in its personal relationships than anything I had known. That may explain why I hated the 1999 film of Greene's novel, *The End of the Affair*, depicting his failure to persuade Catherine to break with Harry. Harry was always the one she went home to and would never abandon. She married him at eighteen, had six children and said of him during her tempestuous years: 'We have become very loving friends, almost twins – brother and sister. Certainly I could not live with him without his compassion, his fondness, justice, humour, willingness.'

Harry's grandparents were American Jews who had emigrated from Vienna. The family name was Waldstein. Harry's father Charles had adopted the Anglicised version of Walston in 1912 when anything Germanic was unpopular. The Battenbergs, Prince Philip's family, later changed their name to Mountbatten and the royal family dropped Saxe-Coburg-Gotha in favour of Windsor for the same reason.

It was said that King George V encouraged Charles Walston to become a naturalised British citizen during a shooting visit to his estate. Whether or not any encouragement was needed, the King subsequently knighted him for his public services and he fitted easily into the British establishment as a land-owner, a fellow of King's College, Cambridge, and

Professor of Fine Art. He bought Newton Hall, a Queen Anne-style house near Cambridge, with money given him as a wedding gift by his wife's father, a New York textile magnate. It became the centre of a liberal intelligentsia that Harry perpetuated.

Harry was born at Newton Hall and lived there until he married in the mid-1930s and built Thriplow farmhouse nearby. The Army moved into Newton Hall during the war and stayed until 1951, when Harry moved back. It had thirty-two rooms and a chapel. It was ideal for the military, but far too big for modern living.

Harry and Catherine had moved their London home from St James's Street to Albany, the eighteenth-century block of apartments in Piccadilly, by the time I worked for him. The Walstons lived in Apartment K3 along the ropewalk, later moving to A14 at the front. Greene followed and lived in C6. Edward Heath and Lord Clark, the art historian, were also tenants with whom I exchanged 'good mornings' as I commuted from my Hammersmith flat.

Lord Beaverbrook's Express Newspapers dubbed Harry a 'socialist millionaire', but he did not mind the tag. He thought it odd that rich people were assumed to be Tories. Sir Stafford Cripps, Attlee's Chancellor of the Exchequer, had been very rich, and Labour leaders enjoyed Harry's hospitality without any qualms.

His friends knew they could use his Cambridgeshire home as a congenial meeting place. George

Brown enjoyed its intimacy and held a weekend brainstorming session there in 1965, when he was Deputy Prime Minister. He summoned Sir Donald MacDougall, his economic adviser, Tony Crosland, Secretary of State for Education, and Roy Jenkins, Aviation Minister, to discuss the mounting sterling crisis.

Newton Hall has been described as the Cliveden of the left; a socialist salon presided over by a wealthy couple on the fringes of politics. It was not like that at all. Harry was no Lord Astor and Catherine had nothing in common with Nancy Astor, apart from her American spirit of independence. Catherine expected friends invited for weekends to help with the preparations for meals – which meant sitting around the kitchen table with Mrs O'Malley, the cook, and kitchen staff splitting peas, topping strawberries, filling butter dishes and generally helping out. One old man, a retired under butler, Fred, came for the company and lent a hand. Harry believed that wealth imposed obligations and he was happy to fulfil them. Had he lived, Hugh Gaitskell might have made him his Agriculture Minister, although they would probably have fallen out over European union, which Harry supported.

His farming knowledge and expertise in land use were widely acknowledged. The Queen made him a Commander of the Royal Victorian Order for his services as a Commissioner of the Crown Estate. Yet his views about land ownership were more radical than the Labour Party's. He believed that every farmer should become a tenant and that the nation's land should be owned by a trust, on the lines of the Crown Estates.

He also advocated a capital gains tax of 60 per cent and the imposition of inheritance tax on estates above £10,000. 'In that way you will get great distribution,' he said – an undeniable fact, but one that sounded eccentric coming from him.

His radicalism did not deter him from being an active member of the House of Lords, enjoying its proceedings and entertaining on a grand scale, both in London and at Newton Hall. A London housekeeper served lunch in Albany and he normally dined at one of his clubs or in the Lords. I handled his correspondence and researched his many interests. I was nowhere near as well paid as I had been in America, but it was great fun and an entirely new world.

Weekends at Newton Hall were tremendous social affairs. Visitors came from all walks of life – royalty, politics, entertainment and the arts. After a few years Catherine insisted on my joining the Walstons for their six-week winter holiday in the West Indies. Harry owned a 3,000-acre banana and coconut plantation on St Lucia, one of the Windward Islands, which we reached by air via Antigua or the Paris–Martinique route. We could have lived in a rather run-down French colonial house on the estate, but Catherine preferred spending most of February and March getting totally away from civilisation on Rat Island: three acres of rock with just a few old goats, 400 yards offshore.

We lived there in a disused quarantine station that

Harry leased from the local administration. Harry himself would have preferred to stay on his plantation, where there were 350 workers, but he indulged Catherine's love for her Caribbean hideaway. The quarantine station had been built to take sick passengers from the great liner ships that berthed in Castries, St Lucia's capital. It comprised eight very basic rooms, which were allocated between first-class invalids (who had their own rooms) and second- and third-class invalids (who were required to share).

We enjoyed it because it was so primitive. We walked barefoot everywhere, taking care to wash the sand from our feet in bowls of water on our return from the beach. The building's concrete floors, cast-iron beds and lumpy mattresses were a complete contrast to the comfort of Albany and Newton Hall. Before electricity was installed, oil lamps lit the quarantine station and communications with the outside world depended on one unreliable telephone. Mustique, the luxurious Caribbean resort that attracted more famous personalities, was everything Rat Island was not – but we would not have swapped. Our tropical escape offered the most valuable commodity in the world: privacy.

Everyone read books, snorkelled, played Scrabble and consumed vast quantities of alcohol. Catherine's sister Binney, a psychiatrist, stayed there sometimes with American friends. We used the old hospital's cubicles as bedrooms, the veranda as our sitting room and the rear porch as our dining room. Staff came over from the mainland to run the laundry and kitchen and a patois-speaking boatman lived in a small shack nearby and ferried us across. I swam to the mainland and back – about ten minutes each way – most mornings before breakfast. At weekends we sailed on Harry's yacht, *Dodo*, a sixty-five-foot-long sixty-tonner. Catherine had crossed the Atlantic on her once with her captain, John Barkel, and his wife Carol. Summer found us cruising in the Mediterranean.

After Catherine's death in 1978 Harry's maquis plantation was broken up and sold. A foreign sale was prohibited under St Lucia's new laws, and so Harry Atkinson, the estate manager, local people and the island's public authorities bought the land. Harry made nothing from the deal but supported the government's policies and believed the local people should own the land. St Lucia has remained one of my favourite places, and the Rat Island years were a fabulous period in my life, full of happy memories.

Catherine was enormously good to those she liked and difficult to those she did not. I was in the first category; Sophie Brown, George's long-suffering wife, was in the second. Unlike George, who believed that nothing was too good for the working class, Sophie did not enjoy the Walstons' hospitality. She never made Harry and Catherine out, commenting that they were not what she meant by socialism. Catherine's behaviour did nothing to quell her doubts, and Catherine herself almost went out of her way to make Sophie feel uncomfortable. She found Sophie gauche and shy – and showed it. Sophie's conclusion was that Catherine was snobbish and grand. It was a total mismatch, which was a pity.

George also paraded his proletarian credentials when he felt like it. He once told Catherine: 'I'm only a lorry driver's son, not rich like you.' But she could not have cared less about people's origins, and he loved the ambience at Newton Hall. Evelyn Waugh described the family's lifestyle in a letter to Nancy Mitford as 'a side of life I never saw before – very rich, Cambridge, Jewish, socialist, high-brow, scientific farming'.

Harry was Jewish on both sides, but had no faith and 'married out' when he met Catherine. To their children, they appeared somewhat distant, having little time to spare for them as they travelled the world in search of fulfilment. Harry was even something of a mystery to them. His second son Oliver once described him as 'rather boring, an emotion-free zone', who 'never got angry, or sad, or shouted'. Catherine, by contrast, appeared to them irregularly in a perfumed cloud of Mitsouko 'detectable a quarter of a mile away' and seemed stupendously generous with everything 'except her time'.

Children have their own unique perspective; mine was different. Harry would ask me on a Thursday if I was doing anything at the weekend and would invite me to join them if I was not. Catherine urged me to live close by so that she could see more of me. Perhaps she regarded me as an ally in her constant delight in bringing people down to earth. Despite, or perhaps because of, her unconventionality, the British establishment took her to its heart.

Her generosity was unquenchable. She loved buying things and treating friends and staff. On her regular stays in hospitals, she bought Fortnum & Mason sweaters for the nurses. She thought nothing of buying me shoes and sweaters when she went shopping in the West End. She remembered my mother, too, and would tell me to buy a nice plant from the florist next to Albany to take home to Dewsbury with me. Mum was also invited to Newton Hall at weekends and loved it.

Catherine would have been happy for me to have a permanent suite at Newton Hall and to spend every weekend with them but I preferred to come and go. Her four sons were at school – David, Oliver and Bill at Eton and James at prep school – and I watched them grow up. I also stayed with her family in the States many times on our way back from the Caribbean. I am still in touch with them and like to think of myself as still a part of the Walston family.

She had an American's love of gadgetry, although she did not always understand it, and was a fast and accurate typist. Once, after lunching with Madame Prunier in St James's Street, she insisted on buying two IBM electric typewriters she had read about – one for her and one for me. Electric typewriters were still a novelty in Britain, although I had used one in Washington.

We went to the shop to find that the model we wanted was for display purposes only and there was a six-month waiting list. 'We'll take it now,' Catherine decreed, and her order for a second one settled the matter. She was determined to get her own way. But even she could not immediately have the tropical version of the model that she wanted. That came later.

Each year we went with Rose, the housekeeper, and other members of the staff to Dublin, where Catherine had an apartment in Fitzwilliam Square. She was very taken with the country and with the Catholic Church, and they with her. She had converted to Catholicism at the start of her affair with Greene, who was of course himself a Catholic. Rose and some staff stayed in the five-star Shelbourne Hotel, while Catherine and the rest of us shared the flat.

Sadly, she was not at all well for much of the time I knew her. She drank too much and had all sorts of breakdowns and illnesses. Messages would arrive that she had collapsed in Venice or somewhere in South America, and Harry would arrange to bring her home. She broke her hip falling down some steps at Dublin airport and was on crutches for a year before the doctors discovered that the bone needed resetting. Harry was always there when she needed him. They spent much of their time apart, but their marriage survived everything. They were happy and relaxed in each other's company and she always sat next to him at dinner, never at the other end of the table.

Practicalities did not concern her. The Shah of Persia and Queen Farah stayed at Newton Hall for a weekend during their visit to England in 1965 and Catherine wanted him to see some of her art collection, which she kept in the Albany apartment. Without a care for the risks involved, I was sent to London to get what I could and returned with a fortune's worth of art in the boot of my battered old Ford: some Henry Moore drawings, a Stanley Spencer and a Lowry. Mercifully they arrived undamaged, but the insurance company would have had a ready excuse for not paying up if they had been. Catherine had recognised Moore's genius and bought many of his works at comparatively low prices long before he was widely known.

Her art collection was broken up after her death, while her vast correspondence with Greene went to Georgetown University. Her political sympathies, such as they were, were shaped by her American upbringing and, while she supported me actively in the two parliamentary campaigns I fought in the 1960s, she did it out of friendship, not political conviction.

Little things about the way ordinary people lived struck Catherine as odd as we canvassed the streets. She was surprised, for example, to see how people hung their curtains with the pattern visible to passers-by and not to themselves. My explanation that working-class people did it to make their houses look as attractive as possible from the outside struck her as extraordinary. But party workers liked her cheerfulness and her willingness to help with the chores of committee-room work; they regarded her as a 'character'. She hid her lack of real interest in British politics well.

Harry had no party allegiance when they married

in 1936, but stood as a Liberal in Huntingdon in the 1945 general election. He switched to Labour during Attlee's Government and contested Cambridgeshire in 1951 and 1955 and Gainsborough in 1957 and 1959. Five failures in a row did not depress him, as it would have done me, although I did have to endure four.

Hugh Gaitskell was a friend and recognised Harry's services to the party and his unfulfilled talents by sending him to the House of Lords as a Labour life peer in 1961. This enabled Harold Wilson to make him a junior minister at the Foreign Office in 1964 and a Board of Trade minister in 1967, so he answered questions on departmental matters in the upper house. Such are the vagaries of British politics.

At first I was regarded with suspicion by some in Harry's circle, simply because I had worked for Barbara Castle and was a friend of Jo Richardson, both fiery left-wingers. They overlooked the fact that I had worked much longer for Geoffrey de Freitas than I had for Barbara. I soon convinced them I was no firebrand.

As a youngster I really had been one. I believed passionately in socialism, in a better future for all and, like most young people, saw no reason to compromise my beliefs. But, as they say, travel broadens the mind, and my increasing exposure to other countries and political regimes had a profound effect. Gradually I began to realise that there was no point in keeping my socialist heart pure in permanent opposition.

America and my time spent with the Democratic

campaign had a significant impact on me. I had always believed in the power of political oratory to move voters and was puzzled, at first, by the American tradition of 'gold-plate' dinners aimed at the already 'converted'. 'Why waste your time on confirmed Democrats when there are undecided people out there to be won?' I argued. I soon saw, however, how effective these campaigns could be. Every Democrat voter at a party function was so enthused by their contact with the hierarchy that their commitment to the party doubled and they went on to become highly effective ambassadors for the cause. This, to me, was politics in action. Ideals, yes, and commitment, but tempered with real pragmatism.

At this stage in his career, Harry needed a political as well as a social secretary and I fitted the bill. His life changed a lot during the years I was with him. His circle of friends and informants widened and his wealth and talents enabled him to play a catalytic role, which Labour leaders found useful.

I was as eager as ever to find a winnable seat, despite Labour's long years in opposition. I came close, by being shortlisted in 1962 for Huddersfield West, a textile constituency just down the road from Dewsbury, but was beaten into second place by Ken Lomas, who went on to become Tony Benn's PPS, but never really liked the Commons.

I was fortunate in that my frustrated ambitions made no difference to my relationship with the Walstons. They swept me up and were supportive of everything I did, just as the de Freitas family had always been. Harry enjoyed politics and believed passionately in the democratic process. He would have made an excellent MP and wanted me to fulfil my own ambition to be one.

'What can I do to help?' he asked when I stood as a Labour candidate for Hammersmith Borough Council.

'Do some canvassing,' I said, and off he went in his Aston-Martin.

I won my ward and served for one term, from 1965 to 1968; but local government was not for me and I retired from the council at the next election.

I came close to winning the nomination for Plymouth Sutton in 1965 but was beaten by David Owen, who went on to become Britain's youngest Foreign Secretary of the twentieth century. He recalled my doomed effort in his memoirs: 'The strongest challenge came from an extremely attractive candidate, Betty Boothroyd. She spoke far better than I, as many of the General Management Committee [of the local party] teasingly reminded me over the years, but I was the local boy.' Not only that, but his parents were well-respected public figures; his father was a GP and his mother a JP. 'A few of the delegates were patients of my father's or knew my mother and no doubt they gave me the benefit of the doubt,' he remembered. They undoubtedly did and they were right to do so. Local loyalty counts, the world over, and David's family roots helped him to hold his Plymouth seat against strong opposition. I wished I had been as favoured when I tried for a Yorkshire nomination.

By the time I did become an MP, David had risen through the ranks and was an obvious candidate for Cabinet office. To what extent the Labour Party's history, not to mention the Liberal Party's, would have been altered had I been selected for Plymouth Sutton instead of him is a beguiling thought. Would there have been a Limehouse Declaration from his London home to launch the breakaway Social Democratic Party?

Another imponderable is how I would subsequently have fared against Alan Clark, the right-wing Tory and celebrated diarist, who won Owen's Plymouth seat in 1974 after David had moved to safer ground. Boothroyd versus Clark would have given the newspapers something to write about.

As it was, Plymouth was another entry on my list of rejections, but I was still better placed than most Westminster hopefuls to find fresh opportunities and I remained optimistic. Working for Harry meant being in touch with people and events at the very centre and keeping my political antennae sharp. But old hands at MI5, it appeared, thought I was too well placed to succeed, for a girl who had declined their invitation to spy against fellow party members.

I had all but forgotten about the Strelnikov business and the weird encounter with the security services after Geoffrey de Freitas and I had reported our concerns to the Foreign Office. But MI5 had not. Sir Roger Hollis, its director-general, sent Wilson what must have been a selective account of what had happened, because he asked George Wigg, his loyal watchdog whom he made Paymaster General, to talk to Harry.

The upshot was that Harry was told I should no longer go to the Foreign Office and that his working arrangements with me should be purely private. He and I made light of this, but there was no doubting that somebody in the security services harboured a grievance against me.

Had I been a real suspect, they would surely have told Harry to get rid of me. They would not have allowed a Foreign Office minister to employ a personal assistant whose loyalty was considered dubious. Nor would I have been allowed to stand as a Labour candidate and subsequently to become a regional whip in Harold Wilson's 1974 government. It was a weird business but I had not heard the end of it.

I shared my thoughts about Harry's move to the Board of Trade with his son Oliver, who was then working in the States. Later he became George Brown's special adviser, inherited the Thriplow estate and turned into an even more successful grain farmer than his father:

Foreign Office
13 January 1967

Dear Ol,

Like you I didn't send Xmas cards this year. By the time I'd got through 600 for HW I couldn't stand the sight of them. If I had sent any, you would have got one – being on the overseas list, like. Am using up the old notepaper as fast as possible. A bit sad in some ways, but I think the boss will enjoy the Board of T. At least there will be real people to entertain in this new job, rather than Japanese Princes. I haven't had a letter from the boss since the switch so don't know how he feels about it, but looking on the bright side, it will be a job he can really get his teeth into . . . When No. 10 called up to ask the telephone number of Rat Island I almost fell apart at the thought of the PM and the boss talking together after three rings on the Rat Island telephone. Anyway, I pulled myself together just in time to suggest they call the Administrator. I had visions of the boss not getting a job at all and me really having to work for my pay cheque.

By this time Catherine's carefree lifestyle had rubbed off on me a little. Unlike her, however, I had to watch my living expenses, although the bank manager sometimes wondered about that. My letter continued:

Your apartment sounds in good shape: I'd love to see it sometime. You almost had an unexpected guest a couple of weeks ago when Wayne Hays offered me a seat across the Atlantic on the Presidential jet. I took it up until I found the return fare would cost me £80. But to have joined the jet set at the Presidential level would have been a dining-out story for 12 months.

I've been in my new flat for about a couple of

months and it really is great. It's on the 8th floor top, front, and has a fabulous view of London: two lifts (one for me and one for the F[ortnum] & M[ason] delivery man), polished wood floors AND CENTRAL HEATING. Two bedrooms, lounge and all mod cons. Needless to say I'm living well above my income and the bank manager has sent me a polite but firm letter this morning . . .

Glad St Lucia was nice for you all – and that you eventually got there: that'll teach you to mess about with Albany [travel service] reservations. After Athens CW [Catherine Walston] was a good deal better than I had seen her for a long time and was marvellous about sticking only to Retsina: in fact she was a much nicer, less moody, even-tempered person than previously. But I'm afraid it may not last for long and the old problem will always be there, but let's hope the setbacks occur less frequently. I hope she comes back in the same good form . . .

Be sure to give my love to Lesley [Oliver's first wife] and save a bit for yourself.

Betty

I was wrong about Harry enjoying the Board of Trade. He resigned later that year and never held ministerial office again. He became chairman of the Institute of Race Relations and immersed himself in his farm and other interests. His political network remained extensive and well connected and he made new, sometimes surprising, contacts in Africa. George Brown still confided in him, and in his last weeks as First Secretary came up with a startling proposal that has remained secret until now. He proposed that I should be his personal barrier against the civil servants he so hated. Harry did not want to stand in my way, but I had no such ambition. George's position in the Government had become a matter of constant speculation and I did not intend to do battle with his private office at the Department of Economic Affairs.

I had known George for years. We got on well because we both said what we thought. I knew his qualities as well as his weaknesses and he knew I was a fighter, like him, and loyal to the Labour Party. But I baulked at walking into a Whitehall minefield, despite George showing me how he proposed to partition his offices overlooking St James's Park, with me as his buffer against the outside world.

Wigg monitored everything going on in Whitehall and told Wilson about George's crazy plan, although there was no need. He was soon to leave the Government himself. As for George, Wilson ended his misery in the DEA by making him Foreign Secretary a few weeks later, which only accelerated the self-destruction of his career and eventually left him outside the Cabinet, soon to be outside Parliament and the Labour Party.

Wigg's paranoia continued until the end. Three months later he secretly proposed to Wilson that any letter addressed to the Soviet Embassy in a House of Commons envelope should be opened by the security services and its contents noted. Copies of letters judged to be innocuous were to be destroyed, but others were to be kept. Ignoring all the rules of parliamentary privilege, he saw no reason why MPs should be spared MI5 surveillance, whether or not there was any reason to suspect them. In his opinion, any contact with the Soviet Embassy was enough to warrant suspicion.

His justification for this bizarre attitude was that the Russians could exploit the loophole in the security services' surveillance by acquiring supplies of House of Commons envelopes and avoiding MI5's censorship. Sir Burke Trend, the Cabinet Secretary, was privy to this proposal, but there would have been uproar if MPs had known.

Wigg resigned ten days after his note to Wilson, to give the Racecourse Betting Control Board the benefit of his inside information. Wilson's in-tray must have been rather duller after that. Amongst other things, Wigg told him that *Private Eye* was influenced by communist fellow-travellers and that China had armies ready to attack Thailand; and what had been discussed in the editorial conference of a national newspaper. Tony Benn described Wigg as 'completely crazy' at the time and Barbara Castle called him 'Harold's Rasputin'.

He caused me no harm, but while Wigg busied himself with trivia and fantasy, Soviet agents in Whitehall were feeding valuable information to Moscow. Wilson voiced his suspicions about the political bias of the security services and the Thatcher Government was later concerned enough to put them on a proper legal footing for the first time.

Wigg had his own brush with authority in 1976 when the police charged him with kerb-crawling around Marble Arch. The charge was dropped after Chapman Pincher, a Fleet Street contact, told the court that Wigg drove around the area not to pick up women but the first editions of the morning papers.

In 1968 Pretoria's apartheid regime allowed Harry Walston to visit Nelson Mandela during his long exile in prison on Robben Island. I helped prepare Harry's visit and heard on his return how moved he was by Mandela's dignity, recognising his special qualities much earlier than most people. 'Mandela showed no bitterness,' he wrote. 'He did not revile his jailers nor rail against the government that had incarcerated him.'

He was also relieved to find the freedom fighter well treated and noted this in the prison visitors' book, thus giving the regime an easy propaganda point. Johannes Vorster, South Africa's Prime Minister, had no illusions about Harry's views. He invited him to Pretoria because he knew Harry had good contacts with the Labour Government and wanted to broker a British deal with Ian Smith's rebel regime in Rhodesia. Nothing came of that, but Vorster credited Harry with setting in train events that led to Harold Wilson's abortive attempt at reconciliation with Smith on board HMS *Fearless* at Gibraltar.

Harry was on especially good terms with Robert Mugabe, who at that time advocated partnership between blacks and whites in the campaign for Zimbabwe's independence. But he would have deplored Mugabe's drift into dictatorship and subsequent incitement to violence and hatred.

Harry expressed himself forcefully during his South African visit in a lecture I helped prepare, which he delivered at the University of the Witwatersrand in Johannesburg in August 1968. Before an audience of 2,000 students and academic staff, he made the case for resistance to apartheid in reasoned but – in South Africa's 1960s climate – almost revolutionary terms:

> An individual citizen may use force if it is the only means of preventing the unjust governor from using his power unjustly. If one is in a minority in a true democracy, force should not be used to thwart the will of the majority, though passive resistance can be justified if the majority connives at or supports unjust laws. But against a tyranny, which does not represent the will of the people, and which is unjust, arbitrary, despotic, force may be the only answer.
>
> Those who live in a country whose government enacts unjust laws, which are contrary to the will of the majority, are faced, as you well know, with a series of hard decisions. Some may decide to co-operate with the government, hoping that by remaining in positions of influence they can moderate some of the extremes of injustice that would otherwise take place.
>
> Others will decide that violence is the only means of eradicating the evil. In between are a whole range of possible courses – passive

resistance, non-co-operation, preaching and practising as individuals what one considers to be right, in defiance of government edicts, fully aware of the consequences and prepared to submit to them. These decisions can only be taken by each individual himself. No one but he can say he has taken the wrong one.

Like Harold Macmillan, Harry believed that the winds of change were blowing through Africa although, sadly, he did not live to see them sweep apartheid away. His final words were a rallying cry to white moderates who wanted to build a new future: 'It was with men and women such as you in mind that Byron wrote: "Yet Freedom! Yet thy banner, torn, but flying, Streams like the thunder-cloud against the wind."'

Harry put Newton Hall on the market that year with a price tag of £65,000–70,000. The children had gone and it had become far too large for him. It had twenty-eight bedrooms and staff were difficult to find. He commissioned Sir Leslie Martin, the architect of the Royal Festival Hall on London's South Bank, to design a new home in Thriplow village. The result was a smaller modern replica of Newton Hall, built around a large, square, galleried hall, which served as a new meeting place for Labour moderates and later, when Harry joined the SDP, for Social Democrats.

Harry had enlarged the estate by buying land at low prices during the Depression to test his theories about the suitability of East Anglia's thin soil for mechanised cereals farming. Today's Green activists would have deplored his practices, but he rejected the view that people have no right to mould the environment to their needs. His Jersey herd was one of the most successful in the country, but he switched from milk production to cereals and pioneered the complete mechanisation of sugar beet.

Catherine's enthusiasms, when she was well, complemented his. She would zoom into Albany to suggest that we all went to the opera that night. Tickets would immediately be bought for a performance at Covent Garden and the staff would be treated as well.

Catherine wanted me to live nearby, but Harry knew that I could not afford to do that on my income and proposed a generous and ingenious solution that suited all of us. It required my capital investment as well as his and left me with a wonderfully recon-structed timber-beamed cottage on his estate. The beams came from a demolished cottage that Harry stored on the tennis court of his brother-in-law, Sir Patrick Browne. Harry paid £7,000 for the shell of the new cottage and I paid the same amount for the internal work and fittings. I still live in my rural retreat and look forward to spending many more years of my sixty-six-year lease doing so.

Harry remarried in 1979, a year after Catherine's death. The new Lady Walston was Elizabeth Scott, the former wife of Nicholas Scott, Conservative MP for Chelsea. Harry died twelve years later and by extraordinary coincidence was buried on the same day, at the same hour, as Graham Greene's life was being remembered at a service in Westminster Cathedral. Only then did Greene's long affair with Catherine become public knowledge.

Politically, my Walston years were hard ones in which to be a Labour candidate and the Tories defeated me twice: in a by-election at Nelson and Colne in 1968 and in the 1970 general election in Rossendale. Harold Wilson's Labour Government took office with high hopes in 1964, but was soon enmeshed in industrial strife and runs on the pound. I reduced the swings against Labour in my two fights, but my loyalty to the Government did not endear me to voters. Worse, I encountered my first direct experience of women who cannot stand other women breaking out of the domestic rut.

I had a taste of this in the by-election for the Lancashire seat of Nelson and Colne. Once again the prospect of a woman candidate made the headlines. 'Labour May Choose Woman As Candidate' announced the *Lancashire Evening Telegraph*. The report that followed was not hostile, but it did show I was still swimming against the tide of sex discrimination. That year was the golden jubilee of women's suffrage and Wilson wanted me to reinforce the twenty-six women MPs in the House of Commons.

Sydney Silverman, a colourful left-wing Labour MP, had held Nelson and Colne from 1935 until his death, bequeathing me a majority of 4,577: far too small for comfort. Labour had just lost Dudley, a safer Labour seat in the Midlands, and I faced an uphill task. Barbara Castle, George Brown and Tony

Benn, a rising star, all came to speak for me. Unexpectedly, I was also favoured with the extended presence of Emmanuel ('Manny') Shinwell, the veteran former Defence Secretary from Attlee's post-war Cabinet. The reason, it turned out, was that the party leadership found him a nuisance and seized on my by-election campaign as an ideal opportunity to get him out of London.

Ladbroke, the bookmakers, were so sure of a Tory win that they refused to offer odds on it. My opponent, David (later Lord) Waddington, was well known locally as a thirty-eight-year-old barrister and the son-in-law of a former Tory candidate, so everything was stacked against me. The press described Waddington as 'well-heeled, well-dressed, well-educated, probably good at his job and certainly good-looking'. The same paper added that 'his style suggests a divine right to legislate for us and he is confident that Nelson and Colne can't and won't do without him'.

The Tories were so confident that they drafted in Alec Douglas-Home, the former Prime Minister, who stayed on in Edward Heath's shadow cabinet. He advanced the curious notion that the people would rather place their trust in the Lords than in a Labour Government. When I rejected that as nonsense, he accused me of being 'touchy'.

I spoke to packed meetings and had a good reception in the constituency's five Pennine towns: Nelson and Colne, Brierfield, Barrowford and Trawden. But I refused to trim. Asked if I would promise to live in the constituency if I were elected, I replied that I lived in London and could not afford to live in two places at once. Inviting comparison with Waddington's well-to-do background, I added that my car was 'just about falling apart'.

Nor did I pretend to be a left-winger in the Silverman tradition. Indeed, I resisted the division of Labour supporters into different camps. 'I am a card-holding member of the Labour Party and that's enough classification for me.' I urged the party to get away from its 'cloth-cap' image, and Mum injected her own dose of common sense into the campaign by endorsing me in an uncompromising fashion: 'When I hear people complaining today, I remember the time when there was really something to complain about. Though prices were low, we were often out of a job. We then had real problems in making ends meet and buying the essentials for a decent family life. People who want opportunities for the young, employment for the breadwinner and security for the elderly have only one way to vote – that's for Betty.'

To complete my break with the old orthodoxy, I denounced the level of taxation on the working class as the 'worst imposition' they faced. 'The first principle of socialism has always been free choice,' I said. Nobody pulled me up in the middle of a by-election, but it was obvious to anybody who listened that I was a revisionist who believed that Labour needed a different approach and a new image.

It did me no harm in the long run. The press portrayed me as a woman with what the *Sun* called 'insouciant gaiety'. Another commentator described me as a 'solid, comely wench' walking the corridors of power and being on first-name terms with everybody who mattered in Whitehall and Westminster. The truth was that I was still working at it and needed more time – and a break.

'I'm backing Britain and I'm backing Betty' sounded fine as slogan, but the good folk of Nelson and Colne had other ideas. They declined my invitation to rededicate themselves to the principles of social democracy and chose a right-wing Tory instead. The swing against Labour was 11 per cent and it was our eleventh by-election loss since 1964. I scored points for what *The Times* called my 'sincerity and enthusiasm', but I was still the loser. I said goodbye to Nelson and Colne declaring, 'This is where Labour's fight back has started.' It was the best gloss I could put on it.

The fact was there were shadows over the Nelson and Colne by-election that I could do nothing about. Devaluation was still a sore in the government's side and Barbara Castle's proposals to reform labour relations by her far-reaching proposals, which she called (on Ted Castle's advice) 'In Place of Strife', had upset the trade unions. They won the fight to preserve their exemption from legal restraint and we lost. What Barbara failed to achieve in 1970, Thatcher accomplished a decade later in a way the unions were powerless to prevent. How different the outcome would have been if Barbara's weak-kneed Cabinet colleagues had stuck by her.

Locally, the issue of capital punishment also dogged me. I was questioned about it on the doorstep and was forced to declare myself, like

Sydney Silverman, an abolitionist. In 1965 he had successfully introduced a bill abolishing the death penalty for certain categories of murder and its provisions were due for renewal in 1970. The Moors murders had happened in 1966, not far away from the constituency, shocking the whole country, but especially the North of England.

The Moors murderers escaped hanging because of Silverman's bill and feelings ran high during the by-election. They did not make the headlines, but they were there all the same. Waddington's pro-hanging views chimed with the electorate's and he went on to become Home Secretary, Leader of the Lords and Governor of Bermuda. All the Tories who trounced me did well – I must have been lucky for them. That was little consolation to me, despite warm words from the party leadership for my efforts. Barbara Castle wrote comforting me:

Dear Betty.

It was sweet of you to write and thank me for my help but really it was you who should be thanked. You put up an absolutely magnificent fight and I think the result was a great credit to you that you reduced the swing against us so markedly at such a terribly difficult time for the Party.

I do hope you hang on to Nelson & Colne because I am sure you will build up a great following there and could win it at the general election – if any of us are winning any seats by that time!

Love.

Barbara.

Her caution was perceptive. The Nelson and Colne party decided that I had fluffed my chance and chose Douglas Hoyle for the forth-coming general election, from a new shortlist of four trade-unionists – all men. Little good it did them. Douglas fared no better than I in 1970 and had to wait until 1974 to win the seat, by which time I was already in the House. Waddington and I returned to London at the same time, he to take his seat and I to work for Harry Walston.

The party's fundamental problems were now clear to me. Wilson had talked of us being the best party to take Britain into the new scientific age. He enthused about Labour ushering in a new era of prosperity brought about by 'the white heat of the technology-led revolution'. The reality was that we were still perceived as old-fashioned and class-based and I was tired of it. I longed for women to make their voice heard more in politics and said so in an interview in Harry's Albany apartment a year later.

It was supposed to be another of the many soft-focus interviews I had given over the years, but I was having none of it. The female reporter who interviewed me saw an easy news angle in a Labour hopeful meeting her in such exclusive surroundings. 'There I was,' she gushed in her report, 'sipping tea from a golden cup and talking politics in the home of Lord Walston.' And not with him, but with 'his secretary, Miss Betty Boothroyd'.

I told her precisely what I thought about the conventional view most women had of politics. 'Women haven't learned to use their emancipation,'

I said. 'As long as they've a husband, a nice house, a car outside and the kids doing well at school, they don't care who's governing them.' Some women were also inclined to be bitchy. 'When they see a woman like Barbara Castle, an outstanding political leader, a brilliant example of her own sex's potential, they still don't admire her or feel drawn to the movement that has given that woman her head.' Some women, I went on, 'look up to Liz Taylor more than Barbara Castle' and it was time they thought differently.

'In my very early days as a young socialist, I used to go round canvassing in the North, and if I went during the day and asked the housewife how she intended to vote, her reply was inevitably "Sorry, my husband's not at home." At least we have now progressed to a stage where women are thinking independently of their husbands. But there has always been a tendency among women, both here and on the Continent, to vote for the party of the right rather than the party of the left.

'Women are by nature conservative, and scared of change. They like things left as they are. They don't like upheaval and they don't like the thought that Labour believes in making great industrial changes. Tories in the past have always seemed more polished and suave. They have had snob value, an air of having possessions, which appeals to housewives desperately trying to catch up with the Joneses.'

In 1970 I tried again to convince the voters that they needed me to represent them. It was my fourth attempt to become an MP and my second in a

Labour-held Lancashire constituency. This time, I found myself being parachuted in to fill an unexpected vacancy. The general election campaign had already begun when Tony Greenwood, a member of Wilson's Cabinet, announced he was quitting as MP for Rossendale to join the Commonwealth Development Corporation. His local party was preparing for their annual gala when he deserted his post, and it was dumbfounded.

They needed a candidate fast and chose me from an emergency shortlist of nine. That gave the wife of a local company director the chance to show what emancipated women were up against.

She wrote to the local paper to complain at my audacity. Miss Boothroyd, she said, had 'escaped from her industrial background into a different world. She did not marry and try to raise a family as most Rossendale housewives have ... she had an exciting life.' The implication was clear: how could I relate to the needs of Rossendale women – or anybody else for that matter – who had not 'escaped' from the sort of lives their parents had? My response was terse: 'I believe North Country people will accept a woman for what she is.'

I lost Rossendale all the same and Edward Heath became Prime Minister. My unemancipated critic was doubtless pleased. Heath had a working majority of thirty and I was a four-time loser. The Rossendale party lost little time in dispensing with my services in favour of Michael Noble, a Burnley councillor, who won the seat in 1974. Barbara Castle wrote to me saying she thought it an 'absolute disgrace and a scandal' that I had been turfed out, and sent her own and Ted's 'shocked sympathy'.

It was typical of Barbara's combative spirit that she saw me in a new light after four election defeats, followed by the heave-ho from local parties who did not take kindly to losing. When I worked for her, she never saw me as having political potential but after Rossendale, she urged me to fight on. 'I do hope you will not give up the battle to get a constituency where you can win next time,' she wrote. 'Once you have got over the prejudice and got a foothold in the House, I know you will never look back.'

It was a cheering letter at a dark time. If anybody had predicted my becoming MP for one of the safest seats in the country before the next general election, I would have said they were mad.

CHAPTER FIVE

An MP at Last

——

*. . . the Commons remind one of a flock of birds settling
on a stretch of ploughed land. They never alight for more
than a few minutes; some are always flying off . . .*

Virginia Woolf

NOT EVERYONE IN the Walston circle supported
my political ambitions. Michael Behrens, a
Tory banker and regular guest at Newton Hall,
wrote to me at the start of my campaign in the 1973
West Bromwich by-election:

Darling Betty

We shall all think of you from now on and
produce strength and courage by our prayers,
although privately hoping both for your sake and
the country's that the electors are not stupid
enough to choose you!

This time, however, Michael – and not I – was on the
losing side. Edward Heath had come to power with a
mandate to take Britain into the European

Community, which he did, and to transform the country's economic prospects, which he did not. By 1973 he had abandoned his programme for radical reform in the face of rising unemployment and industrial strife, led by the miners. Labour's revival was evident everywhere and my chance to take part in it came when Maurice Foley resigned as MP for West Bromwich to take a post with the European Commission. I applied for the vacancy and got it, with his support.

I had worked for Maurice in his by-election campaign there ten years previously, and he and I had worked with Harry Walston on race-relations issues and had produced several publications. Maurice had recommended me for West Bromwich East, a new seat created by redistribution, but the chance to win a by-election a year earlier was irresistible. I was determined that it would be my last campaign if I lost again. I had had enough failures. I felt qualified for the *Guinness Book of Records* for the number of seats I had fought and lost. This time, however, I was in the right place at the right time. Before Maurice originally stood for West Bromwich, I knew more about its football fame than its place on the map, but years of jumping into my car to help in other people's elections finally paid off.

Sceptical journalists pointed out that I had fought Labour seats before – and lost them. Nelson and Colne and Rossendale had both had 4,000 majorities, just like West Bromwich. They did not go so far as to predict my losing it against the national trend, but they hedged their bets by raising the possibility of a triple duck, and nobody was more aware of that possibility than I. I fought as hard as if I were facing a 4,000 Tory majority. I rang Barbara Castle for help: would she mind if I asked Ted to be my campaign press officer? His experience as a former Fleet Street executive on the *Daily Mirror* and ex-editor of the *Picture Post* made him ideally suited. My only worry was that he had not long before had a heart bypass operation. Barbara's view was that 'if you can give him somebody to do the running around, it will be the making of him', and she was right. Ted Castle was a tremendous help in shaping my campaign around the theme of Heath's failure to control prices.

West Bromwich, then a booming metal-bashing town, is on the edge of the Black Country, five miles down the A41 from Birmingham, and we took to each other from the start. Queen Victoria is said to have ordered the curtains of her railway carriage to be closed when she passed through the town on her way north because of the smoke pouring from its factory chimneys. Pollution remained a problem when I first went there, but the spirit of its people was unbroken and we created a partnership that endured for twenty-seven years.

I liked its no-nonsense vitality and friendliness. Unemployment was virtually non-existent and there was plenty of work for women, which brought many households two pay packets. West Bromwich had been loyal to Labour since 1935, and it would have taken an earthquake to shift its allegiance, although past form was no guarantee of success, as my forays elsewhere had shown.

A vicious racialist tinge to the by-election wrecked the usual civilities across party battlelines. Martin Webster, a prominent official of the National Front, stood on a platform of phased repatriation for ethnic minorities and all-out opposition to Europe and the Third World. The Tory candidate was a jovial estate agent and there was an independent Labour dissident, of whom little was seen. The best story-line for visiting national reporters was obvious: 'Poll town fears race tension.'

There was some cause for this. We were near two constituencies where right-wing Tories had rattled good race relations by raising the immigration issue in a chilling fashion. In Wolverhampton, Enoch Powell peered into the future and saw 'rivers of blood'. In Smethwick, Peter Griffiths, the Tory candidate, so outraged Labour MPs by his rhetoric that he was labelled a parliamentary leper when he finally became an MP.

My Tory opponent admired Powell and did not mind who knew it. 'He stands for the maintenance of the culture of the indigenous population,' he said. Even so, Powell declined to speak for him and the Tory split on race was impossible to hide. Roy Jenkins, Brian Walden and Michael Foot came to support me and my worry was not about winning the argument, but about getting our people out to vote.

'What is lacking is dynamic support within the constituency,' noted the *New Statesman*. 'She fears her vote-shy supporters more than she fears the Tories.' It was right. 'I believe Miss Boothroyd will win,' wrote Peter Patterson, George Brown's biographer. 'But I was just a little alarmed by the haunting memory, as I left West Bromwich, of those vulnerable, anxious eyes.' All I could do was give it my best, hammer home the message about rising prices under the Tories and rely on my party workers, who had taken over a former police station for our headquarters, complete with de-lousing bath.

I won with a bigger majority than Ted Castle or I dared hope. I was home and dry by 8,000 votes on a 9 per cent swing to Labour. Squeezed by my support on one side and the National Front on the other, the Tory vote slumped, leaving the pundits with plenty to write about the racist threat to Ted Heath after his principled stand against Powell. Jo Richardson had written my speech notes to cover any eventuality when the result was announced. I had a 'win-well' speech, a 'win-badly' speech and ones for 'lose-well' and 'lose-badly'. As the Labour votes piled up on the counting tables, I discarded the last three.

I had finally made it, noted the *Wolverhampton Express & Star*, 'after years of toil and heartbreak'. Toil, certainly, but never heartbreak. I had always picked myself up and prepared for the next round. All the same, it was a giddy sensation. I became the twenty-seventh woman MP in the 1970 Parliament. Mum, standing by my side, told a reporter something I had never heard her say before: 'I'm proud of her.'

I was naturally ebullient and listed the qualities an MP needs as good health, an enquiring mind, inexhaustible energy and a very thick skin. 'I've got the first three, but I haven't got a hide like a rhinoceros,' I added. 'I don't think many women have.'

'It's my old mum who's made me,' I told the *Birmingham Evening Mail*. The woman interviewer must have had winning ways, for I told her I spent my weekends washing clothes, lazing around, making supper for a friend who lived along the corridor – Jo Richardson – and sitting and giggling for hours with her as we talked about old boyfriends.

Inevitably, the marriage question arose. Yes, I explained, proposals of marriage had come up, but never at the right time. 'I have reached the age when I would like some bloke to come home to, somebody to tell me to keep up the fight or to stop making a fool of myself.' But the truth was that I had immersed myself in a career in which my schedule was always hectic. If someone wanted to date me, they had to take pot luck, and few men are willing to do that. It was not that I was opposed to the idea of getting married, although I saw many failures around me. I envied the companionship that happily married couples enjoyed, but marriage requires sacrifices too and I was never in the sacrificial mood.

Why do people seem to feel that you need a marriage or a mortgage before you're a whole person? People have been asking me for forty years why I've never married, and I've always given them the same reply: it's never been on the agenda. I could add that it's none of their business, but to a certain extent when you become a public figure you become public property – although I find it very irritating that the questions of marriage and age more usually come up with women than with men. I remember one

woman standing up at the party meeting when I was
selected as a candidate for West Bromwich. 'You
won't be any good to us,' she said. 'You've never
been married, you've never had children and you've
never run a home.' 'Well, then,' I replied, 'I'll have all
the more time for you, dearie, won't I?'

Entering Parliament under my own colours at the
age of forty-three, after twenty years as an onlooker,
thrilled me to the core. My maiden speech was well
received on both sides and I applied myself to
becoming a good constituency Member and an
enthusiastic supporter of the Labour Opposition.
We had plenty of targets as Heath fought his
increasingly desperate battle with the miners and
time ran out before the general election. Even so, I
was glad to be made welcome by Tory as well as
Labour MPs.

Janet Fookes, Conservative MP for Plymouth
Drake, wrote commending my maiden speech for its
diction as a lesson to some of the men. Barbara
Castle also relished the impact I appeared to have
had on 'the chaps':

Betty dear –
   Well done! I envied your poise – far greater than
mine when I made my maiden all those years ago.
Your voice has a most attractive resonance and
you sounded completely at home . . . when you
have found the subject you want to make your
own, there will be no holding you.
   Bless you,
   Barbara.

Consumer rights appealed to me as a subject about which I could express myself forcefully. It covered everything from prices to trading standards and meant a lot to ordinary people struggling with inflation and trying to raise their living standards. It was the ideal topic for my maiden speech during an Opposition debate condemning the Government's inability to control prices. 'My roots are working class and I have earned my living since I was seventeen, so I can claim some authority to speak for ordinary working people,' I said.

The cost of a plot of land on which to build a house in West Bromwich was £3,000, twice what it had been three years before. The average price of a new house in the Midlands had also risen steeply, from £4,800 to £8,200, and the lesson of my by-election was that voters felt that society was unfair. 'They know they live by the rule of law, but feel that there is one law for the well-off and another for those not so well-off.'

In February 1974 Heath's failure to negotiate a settlement of the miners' dispute sent me back to the hustings for the second time in nine months. In the general election I fought the new constituency of West Bromwich West, where I had a runaway victory with a bigger majority than the Tory vote. Even so, I fretted about the party's decision to put all its efforts into winning the other new seat created by boundary revisions in the town – West Bromwich East. With my luck, I feared being kicked out of the Commons just after arriving and I panicked. That was when Mum made her classic comment that my losing was of little consequence compared with my being her daughter!

Somebody at party headquarters must have sensed my insecurity because they sent James Callaghan, our shadow Foreign Secretary, to canvass for me. There was no need, of course. The party was quite right to support Peter Snape's campaign next door. He won by 5,000 votes over two opponents who had stood against me the previous year – the Tory estate agent and the National Front's Martin Webster. Although the NF candidates came bottom of the polls in both seats, their 6,000 votes showed how important it was to create good race relations. Even Labour clubs operated a 'whites-only' membership policy at the time. Peter and I thought alike on the dangers of extremism on the left and the right and worked together effectively to defeat both.

Harold Wilson's narrow victory over Heath ended the miners' strike but not the country's economic troubles. Healey became Chancellor of the Exchequer and the new Government committed itself to a national referendum on British membership of the European Economic Community, the old 'Common Market'. On this, Peter Snape and I disagreed. He was anti-Market; I was, and remain, convinced of the benefits of close links with Europe.

I returned to America in June 1974 for the first time in my new capacity as an MP. I was selected for the British delegation to the North Atlantic Assembly in Washington, where I met Henry Kissinger. He had just returned from a marathon round of talks in the Middle East, but switched effortlessly into comparing the effects on the American and European economies of the OPEC-induced oil crisis. 'He is a giant of a man – his adrenalin seems to flow at twice the rate as the rest of us,' I noted.

My mood changed when I returned home to a stream of complaints from constituents about uncaring local officials. The sight of women in tears about their desperate housing needs made me furious and I accused council officers of treating people as if they were numbers. They were made to travel long distances for interviews, kept waiting in corridors and then told to come back months later. I saw for myself what I already knew from my early days as a Commons secretary: much of what an MP does is unrelated to parliamentary duties. People turn to their MP in despair, whatever the cause.

Occasionally I allowed myself a speculative glimpse of the future. Writing for a local paper in July 1974, I predicted that whichever party held power in 1980 was likely to be there for a very long time – even a generation. That proved to be an exaggeration but the Tories did hold on for eighteen years, five of them under my Speakership. My forecast was based on the expectation that North Sea oil revenues would free us from foreign creditors and that the Government would continue to hold a 51 per cent stake in newly discovered oil beds. I was wrong on both counts, but right about one party being on top during the 1980s.

It took me a year to settle into the routine of being an MP. At the start, I volunteered for anything that came along. It was just like the old days when I ran errands for other secretaries. In time, I learned that the only way to develop a disciplined workload was to say 'no' sometimes.

For years, the most important man in my life was a Tory MP – Barney Hayhoe, the Member for Brentford and Isleworth, a state schoolboy who went to a Polytechnic, served his time as a toolroom apprentice and became Minister for Health. He was my pair. Without our arrangement never to vote in a division if we agreed to let the other have the evening off, I would have had little time of my own.

Our association began even before I won West Bromwich. He asked me to be his pair a few weeks before my by-election and when I protested that I was not sure I would win it, he said: 'Don't worry about that. Just say the word.' Barney and I never let each other down. Our friendship was an example of how people from different sides of the fence may not share the same views, but hope for the same ends.

Harold Wilson's decision to call an October election in 1974 meant my third fight in sixteen months. My message to the voters was that employers, unions and the Government needed to keep in step, that the Exchequer should have a proper share of North Sea revenues and that, while I favoured public ownership of building land, the mixed economy was here to stay.

My majority soared to nearly 15,000 and Wilson's position was made secure by a further swing against the Tories. My backbench days were over. Rejecting my feeble protest that I had not had enough time to make an impact on the House, Bob Mellish, the Government Chief Whip, recruited me to his team as a regional whip, which meant that I became a junior member of the Government. I was the first woman Labour MP to join the whips' office while the party was in office.

Bob, whom I respected enormously, told me he knew I was a very feminine woman, but it was toughness that mattered in the whips' office. 'Tough?' I replied, 'I chew tobacco for breakfast.' To him, loyalty to the party and the Government came first and other considerations a long way behind. He entered the House in 1946 after wartime service as a Royal Engineers captain and served his Bermondsey constituency for thirty-six years. Sadly, he resigned the Labour whip in his last year, when much to his distaste the left wing had the upper hand. His old party did not mourn his death in 1988, but Michael Cocks, his successor as Labour's Chief Whip, Gwyneth Dunwoody and I went to his funeral and Tam Dalyell gave the address, at the family's invitation.

As a whip, responsible for keeping our numbers up in Commons divisions, I was prevented from speaking in the House, but that did not stop me expressing elsewhere my views on Midlands issues or saying what I thought about party discipline if the need arose. When Bob threatened to resign after fifty-eight left-wing Labour MPs rebelled against the Government's defence policy, I said: 'If Bob goes, I go.' He stayed on for two more gruelling years.

Being a whip, in the days before the 'modernisers'

changed the rules of procedure to make life easier, taught me how governments managed the Commons and got their programmes through. We were the first to arrive and the last to leave. In 1975 I reckoned that I was never home before midnight. I was responsible for ensuring the attendance of thirty-two Labour MPs from Birmingham and the Midlands, but, despite my baccy-chewing boast, I was not always as tough as I should have been. I was sometimes a softie, sending new MPs clearly under stress back home to their families when the rulebook said that I should have kept them at Westminster.

One of my flock proved the exception to all the rules. The Right Honourable John Stonehouse was a classic example of a man whose career promised much, but whose flawed character brought disgrace. He had been a Midlands MP for sixteen years when I entered the House and had served in Wilson's 1964–70 Government in six ministerial posts, including Aviation Minister. By the time I became a regional whip, his life was going off the rails. He developed a split personality and acquired two bogus passports to match it.

I returned to the Labour whips' office in the Commons one November lunchtime in 1974 to find a letter on my desk from a West Midlands MP. That morning I had been on duty making sure we had a quorum to see a Government bill through its line-by-line approval in committee. We were on full alert in case of Opposition ambushes. Bob Mellish had instructed us to refuse any Labour MP asking to be excused voting in divisions. An excuse was normally granted only after 'pairing' with a Tory, who had his party's permission to be absent.

The letter was from John Stonehouse, the Member for Walsall North, the constituency adjoining mine. It read: 'Dear Betty. Thank you very much for allowing me to pair today. I am most grateful. John.'

I was amazed. I had done no such thing. What was he playing at? It was after 1 p.m., but Bob, a liquid luncher, was still in his office and I showed him the letter. 'Get me his wife,' he ordered and I put him through to Barbara Stonehouse, whom John had married when he was an adult student at the London School of Economics. They had three children.

'Where is he?' demanded Bob. 'He must return at once.'

'He's gone to the airport,' she replied. 'He told me he's going to America.' But she knew nothing about his flight arrangements or his precise destination. She assumed it was on business, which rang true, for Stonehouse was a commercial banker as well as an MP and had widespread interests.

Bob was furious. Within minutes the whips' office was in overdrive. The British Airports Authority was asked to track Stonehouse's movements and, if possible, hold him before he left the country.

But Stonehouse had gone, never to speak in the Commons again. His last parliamentary question had been to the Home Secretary, asking 'whether he will review the arrangements for preventing drowning accidents'. The next we heard was that his clothes had been found on the shore at Miami Beach in Florida on 21 November.

An air and sea search was made, but there was no trace of him. Had he, by curious irony, been drowned? His wife believed so and, as the weeks passed, pressed for a death certificate to be issued. 'I can do nothing without it,' she told me. 'I can't even draw any money from the bank.'

But missing MPs, let alone Privy Councillors, are not lightly written off and from the outset there were doubts about her husband's mysterious disappearance. Tony Benn wrote in his diary: 'Nobody knows whether he has been abducted, kidnapped, killed, drowned or simply disappeared – astonishing.' I could offer his wife no quick solution. 'No body means no death certificate,' I reminded her. Other women would have broken down in these circumstances, but Barbara showed no signs of grief. Her stoicism amazed me.

I also spoke to another woman affected by the mystery of Stonehouse's whereabouts – Sheila Buckley, his Commons secretary. It seemed likely that she had not been paid since he flew off, and I asked her how she was managing and whether I could help. As a former MP's secretary myself, I was concerned for her. We drank tea on the Commons terrace. She was a good-looking twenty-one-year-old. She did not work at Westminster, as most constituency secretaries do, but was based in Stonehouse's West End office, where he ran the British Bangladesh Trust and other companies.

She said that, in fact, she had not been paid for a couple of months, which made me wonder how she managed to pay her rent. 'We must try to help you,' I

offered. 'What about taking another job?' Bruce
George, another West Midlands MP, was looking for
a secretary: what about working for him? 'Shall I
speak to him? You know the area and the local
authority. Your knowledge could be quite valuable to
him.'

'I am only valuable to John,' she replied, looking
me straight in the eye. I did not know what to make
of that, but it was clear she was not interested in
another Commons job, so there was nothing I could
do for her. She fooled me completely. All the time she
knew that Stonehouse was living under two aliases
and was simply waiting for her to join him. She was
the best liar I ever met.

I never believed that Stonehouse was dead. I
suspected his wife of collusion, but not Sheila
Buckley. Barbara sparked my suspicions by being so
matter-of-fact and seemingly devoid of grief. We
learned later that her husband had taken out a large
life-insurance policy, payable to her – all that
prevented her from collecting it was a death
certificate.

His faked drowning never rang true. He was a
strong swimmer and his discovery in Australia, where
police bizarrely suspected him at first of being the
missing Lord Lucan, led to a sixty-eight-day fraud
trial in which his runaway motives were laid bare. He
was exposed as a 'sophisticated and skilful confidence
trickster' whose company reports were saturated with
'offences, irregularities and improprieties'. He fled
Britain with £48,000 to finance his bogus new life,
using passports taken out in the names of two dead

constituents. He had personal debts of £375,000 and his companies crashed owing £200,000.

Even so, he refused to resign his seat and received his MP's salary until his conviction in 1976. He left his constituents unrepresented for two years while Bruce George, Geoffrey Edge and I did our best as the neighbouring MPs to look after them. When he was under arrest in Melbourne, I sent Stonehouse a telegram saying 'Immediate resignation imperative', and a Commons select committee called for his expulsion. But he hung on and a few Labour MPs were misguided enough to suggest that he should be allowed to return to the Commons to explain himself.

I had never heard such nonsense. 'I don't want to hear any more explanations,' I retorted. Stonehouse claimed he had had a mental breakdown, but I dismissed that as part of 'a calculated plan'. The jury at his trial evidently held the same view.

He was jailed for seven years on eighteen charges of theft, fraud and deception and released after three. Buckley was found guilty on five charges and was given a two-year suspended sentence. They married and had a son. Stonehouse died, aged sixty-two, after turning his hand to thriller writing.

Few Labour MPs rose so fast and fell so catastrophically. While Bob Mellish and I were searching for him, Stonehouse had already left for Miami, carrying John Le Carré's novel *Tinker, Tailor, Soldier, Spy* to read on the journey. A career that held great promise burned itself out in escapist fantasy.

CHAPTER SIX

Mayhem and Militant

The constitution of the Party, adopted in 1918, had been
drafted by people of goodwill. What was not foreseen was
that the time would come when some of the goodwill
would evaporate and that the constitution and its
provisions would be used by people with ulterior motives.
Michael Cocks, Labour Chief Whip 1976–1985

M Y MOTHER DIED in 1982. She had spent quite a
lot of time with me in London after her
retirement. When her health began to fail, I went
home to Yorkshire as often as possible. The lovely
Michael Cocks, later Lord Cocks of Hartcliffe, was
Opposition Chief Whip and gave me as much time as
possible to be with her. We had wonderful friends
who took her to and from hospital, but I became so
stressed and so torn between my mother and the
demands of Westminster that I seriously considered
giving up being an MP to care for her. Labour's
strength was threatened by rebel Social Democrats
and the Trotskyist Militant Tendency. My duties had
increased with my promotion to Labour's National
Executive Committee in 1981.

I did not speak to anyone about my worries but they were often in my mind. My mother, however, had no doubt where my duty lay: she wanted me to fight the Trots. In her quiet, understated way she had made me what I was by her unfailing loyalty and love. She never pushed me beyond what I felt I could do, but always believed I could do anything that I set my mind to, if the Fates were kind. For the first forty years of my life I took more brickbats than bouquets, but her faith in me never wavered. She had an inner strength that was quite amazing, considering the hard life she had led.

I remember every detail of our last days together. Had I not been recalled by Michael for an important vote in the Commons that Tuesday night and a difficult meeting of the NEC next day, I would have stayed with her. But Mum said: 'No, you go. I'll be all right until you come back. You'll be back on Thursday. It's only a couple of days. I'll be fine.'

That evening in London I went with other NEC moderates to Denis Howell's flat in Dolphin Square to prepare for the meeting. Then we voted in the Commons at 10 p.m. We seldom arranged to miss votes by pairing with Tories, because the left might have spotted our collective absence. By 11 p.m. I was back in my flat.

Next morning I went directly to the NEC meeting in Walworth Road. I had been there only fifteen minutes when I got a message to ring Mum's hospital. They had tried to reach me in the Commons the night before to tell me that Mum had died during the late afternoon. I left immediately for Yorkshire. I don't think I ever regretted not being with her when she died. I gave her as much as I could, she knew that. She was a totally unselfish person, wholly committed to the Labour Party and to me. She wanted everything right by both of us.

I contacted a Catholic priest and described the kind of cremation service she had suggested. He took the view that since she had been born, raised and married as a Catholic, she should be regarded as having died one, but I disagreed. I thought that would be hypocritical. She had not raised me as a Catholic, or gone to church since her wedding. Nor had she asked for absolution when she was seriously ill.

We settled on a simple service. I showed him the eulogy I had written, but he thought I would be unable to get through it and so I gave it to Jean Megahy, a close family friend, to deliver. In it I recalled how I had pushed Mum around Thriplow village in her wheelchair towards the end. We sang some bright hymns and the priest said a prayer in the crematorium, as I wished.

Geoffrey de Freitas also died that year after a long illness. He and Helen had stayed in my home at Thriplow in Cambridgeshire a few months previously, prompting Helen to send a round-robin to friends about his progress:

Betty Boothroyd lent us Thriplow and we felt we were among old friends. Our Cambridge doctor was at hand and encouraging, the weather was lovely and the bucolic setting, the neighbouring

field of white Charollais heifers so beautiful in the
moonlight with their chumping, chuffing noise,
birds galore and watching spring come in.

At the memorial service Eugene Rostow, a close
American friend, paid tribute to Geoffrey as an
upholder of the 'liberal, decent, richly textured
culture' that binds English-speaking countries and
Western civilisation together. He called it a 'miracle
of history', which could be improved, but above all
needed cherishing and protecting.

To lose my mother and Geoffrey in the same year
was a double blow. In their different ways they both
believed in me, encouraged me and stood by me.
Despite her own mourning, Helen de Freitas was
conscious of this. She told her children that they
would have to be my family now, and she and I
became closer than ever. I fought on, knowing that
Mum would want me to see the Trots off, and the
party that she and Geoffrey had loved restored to
health and vigour.

Trotskyist infiltration had been known about for
years, but our leaders had been reluctant to confront
it. Their inactivity was regrettable but under-
standable. Labour governments struggled throughout the 1970s and 1980s with deep-seated economic
problems and great industrial turbulence. Harold
Wilson and James Callaghan were aware of the
ultra-left's operations, but thought it more important to maintain party unity as best they could than
to declare war on 'the Trots'.

There was another vital consideration. The

Conservatives were never as fragile during the Wilson and Callaghan governments as Labour was during Margaret Thatcher's ascendancy. We nearly collapsed in 1983 when we polled fewer than 8.5 million votes, whereas the Tories never won fewer than 10 million votes when they lost to us in the 1960s and 1970s. Our problems gave the Trotskyists, who were well financed by their supporters, a golden opportunity to worm their way into every level of our organisation, including the NEC.

As a cloak for their operation as a separate organisation with its own aims and agenda, they presented themselves as a fringe group of radicals, whose interpretation of Labour's core beliefs was as legitimate as ours. They propagated their revolutionary views in their weekly tabloid, *Militant*. When Neil Kinnock denounced them as 'a maggot in the body of the Labour Party', they posed as persecuted innocents – and some on the left believed them. I did not and wanted them expelled, no matter how long it took.

It was no sinecure, therefore, when the NEC appointed me to join a committee of inquiry into Trotskyist control of the Liverpool district party and city council, whose antics had created a national scandal. But I was glad to serve. The life-and-death struggle that followed marked an important turning point in Labour's fortunes. Before the Liverpool inquiry, the battle against extremism hung in the balance. After it, the hard left was finished as a threat to our constitution and the NEC worked with the leadership, instead of against it.

My disdain for the parasitic activities of the Militant Tendency, as they were known, was on record long before Neil declared war on them. So was my despair at the strategy of those on the traditional left, who believed the party had lost power by betraying its socialist principles. To them, the fact that a clique spawned in the Russian Revolution was intent on subverting our party, which prided itself on being more Methodist than Marxist, was an unproven irrelevance.

Long before the NEC finally decided to act in the winter of 1985, a few far-sighted party officials knew better than that. Reg Underhill, the national agent, raised the alarm in a report that gave chapter and verse of the extent of Trotskyist infiltration in 1975, but his report fell on stony ground.

Left-wing advances in the party during James Callaghan's minority government and the impact of Margaret Thatcher's right-wing populism encouraged Militant's leaders to raise their profile. They hired Wembley Stadium and the Royal Albert Hall for their annual conventions and flaunted themselves as Marxist revolutionaries riding the tide of history.

They were helped by new rules for choosing Labour candidates at general elections, which forced sitting Labour MPs to submit themselves for reselection by local party activists, who were not always representative of the broad membership or Labour voters. Hailed as a move towards greater party democracy, this enabled the hard left to seize their chance to turf out Labour MPs who stood in their way, regardless of their service or popularity.

When my local party decided to confirm my candidacy without a re-selection battle, there was uproar. The pretence of greater democracy was exposed by the left's refusal to allow the party's mass membership the opportunity to choose the party's candidates and elect its leaders. I argued for a 'one-member, one-vote' system of choosing candidates; the hard left wanted Labour MPs to run the gauntlet on their terms.

As soon as we lost the 1979 election to Margaret Thatcher, the hard left agitated against Jim Callaghan's leadership, and I resented that. I knew he wanted to retire and appealed for him to be allowed to go with dignity and honour when the party was in better shape. 'Had he won the last election, those now calling for his resignation would have been in the forefront in the whip-round for a bronze statue,' I told my local party.

The hard left planned to purge the party of everything that Callaghan and I, and others like us, represented. Total schism was prevented only by Michael Foot's authority as our new leader. Aneurin Bevan had been his mentor and nobody on the left could denigrate Foot's socialist instincts or impugn his motives. He also commanded respect in the centre of the party for his efforts to sustain the Callaghan government against enormous odds.

My hostility to the hard left, and the fact that I held a safe seat, made me an obvious target. A local councillor was nominated to run against me and *Tribune*, the left-wing paper that supported mandatory re-selection, reckoned that my chances –

and those of others in jeopardy – were 'slim'. When I fought back by turning to West Bromwich's Labour clubs for support, the left complained about my not playing the game: I was able to go to loyal people they could not reach, and they could do nothing about it.

My resistance made national news and forced Militant on the defensive. It showed that keeping your head down is seldom a good idea when major issues are at stake. That was not my style – and the gamble paid off.

I declared myself a 'militant moderate' and accused Tony Benn of wanting to pack the parliamentary party with zombies. By a majority of 23:21, my constituency committee decided to endorse me without putting me through the hoops that the hard left had lined up. Chris Mullin, later a minister in Tony Blair's Government, wrote an aggrieved article in *Tribune* saying that I had broken the rules. The NEC, however, found in my favour.

I was reselected and was never challenged again. It proved that moderates had as much organising ability as the other side, if only they put their minds to it. It also showed how narrow the margin often is between success and failure. Another two votes for the left could have undone me. Speaker Boothroyd would have been a pipe dream.

It was a hazardous time to be a Labour moderate, so we formed the Campaign for Labour Victory (CLV) to organise nationally. Tony Benn observed me in action with David Owen at one of our meetings in Exeter in March 1980:

Betty made an awful speech about how we need radical policies but we cannot be too far ahead of public opinion; that there's a great attraction to private investment in public industry and perhaps we should consider giving people a share, a divvy, in the nationalised industries and so on. She said: 'We want to create a society on the basis of consumer democracy. We have got to strike the right balance between individual and collective rights.' She was critical of the NEC for presiding over a declining membership.

My 'awful' ideas are now the common ground of politics, but our fight-back was weakened by the defection of four leading members of James Callaghan's Cabinet who believed in much the same things as we did. The Gang of Four – Roy Jenkins, Shirley Williams, David Owen and Bill Rodgers – attracted twenty-five Labour MPs and one Tory to their breakaway Social Democratic Party (the SDP) in 1982. They and their Liberal allies went on to win 25.4 per cent of the national vote in the 1983 general election – only 2 per cent less than Labour. Yet they owed everything to the Labour Party, just as we did. The difference was that they had given up on the party and we had not. Nor would we.

The hard left hailed their defection as proof that the Wilson-Callaghan era had nurtured traitors and that all moderates were suspect. Militant supporters moved into positions of influence in many constituency parties and called for our heads. They were an obnoxious lot with their ranting delivery, jerky arm movements and streams of disjointed logic. We had a simple choice: we could stand and fight or let them take over. I vowed to resist them to the end. I owed it to my parents' sacrifices and to my innermost beliefs.

While I did not agree with them, I understood why the Gang of Four had walked out. The human frame can only withstand so much. They found un-endurable the punishment inflicted on them by extremists who detested belief in social democracy. I would have fitted into the SDP, and they would have liked to enrol me.

None of my friends who left the party discussed it with me, but I never thought of them as traitors and there was no bitterness between us. Shirley Williams was a heroine of mine and I had enormous respect and admiration for her. 'The party I loved and worked for over so many years no longer exists,' she wrote in her letter of resignation in February 1981 from the NEC. There was an uncomfortable degree of truth in that, but her departure gave me an unexpected opportunity. I inherited her seat on the NEC at a critical time in Labour's civil war.

I did so as runner-up in 1980's annual conference elections to the national executive. If a vacancy occurs between party conferences, the 'also-ran' with the most votes fills the gap. My luck was in.

After her resignation Shirley briefed me in her London flat about the way the NEC worked. She was still a Labour MP at that time and told me that I was unlikely to inherit her place on the executive's main committees. She was right about that, but not for long. A year later we moderates were on our way back. We re-formed at the 1982 party conference and called ourselves Labour Solidarity, after the Polish Solidarity movement led by Lech Walesa. We may have been latecomers to factional infighting but we were catching up.

We urged the party to reflect on why the Tories had won under Margaret Thatcher. I hated what Tory policies were doing to British industry, especially in the West Midlands, but turning Labour into a dogmatic party of the hard left was not the answer. Instead it needed to reconnect with its traditional voters and win the centre ground.

We were more successful than we dared hope when we picked ourselves up from the floor in 1979. The left failed to unseat many moderate MPs and we did spectacularly well in the NEC elections in October 1982. We broke the hard left's grip by making five gains. I held my seat with strong trade-union support and Gwyneth Dunwoody swelled the anti-Militant ranks. The change in the balance of power was decisive. A left-wing majority of 20:9 became a hairline advantage of 15:14. The terminal dangers facing the party were far from over, but we had edged away from the abyss.

The changed mood showed itself during the Falklands conflict when Mrs Thatcher ordered the sinking of the Argentine warship, the *Belgrano*. At a meeting of the NEC International Committee in May, Tony Benn proposed an immediate truce. He feared an extension of the conflict to the Argentine mainland and the possibility of nuclear escalation.

Michael Foot replied that he did not believe Margaret Thatcher had wanted the war and that the British people did not think so either.

Eric Heffer, Benn's ally, began shouting. We were heading for disaster, so I moved 'previous business', the procedural device for closing the debate. Gwyneth seconded me and we won by eight votes to four. Tony noted that it was the first time in his twenty-three years on the NEC that a motion was allowed to prevent a vote on an issue already under discussion, but I had no regrets. My personal view on the Falklands was that the United Nations offered the best prospect for a settlement, but the party was in danger of committing suicide and the infighting had to be stopped.

I voted against Tony's bid to become deputy leader of the party later that year. We had a balanced leadership with Michael Foot as leader and Denis Healey as his deputy. Dropping Denis would have sent a clear signal to moderates on the centre left that they were not wanted. His survival, by less than one percentage point, in the leadership elections at Brighton was a turning point in the party's recovery. I was delighted; it meant that the party was on the mend after its biggest crisis for fifty years.

Tony proved a valued supporter of mine when I became Speaker, and I acknowledged his seniority and his right to express minority opinions by calling him regularly to speak. But we were at loggerheads in those desperate times. Declaring my support for Denis, I objected to candidates who offered simple solutions to complex problems and who promised to

transform society in a matter of weeks. 'In a
democracy, political life is not that easy. Nor, in a
democracy, is intensity of commitment a substitute
for the wider breadth of support needed to return a
Labour government.' I mentioned no names, but did
not need to.

Michael Foot was exasperated by Tony's decision
to oppose Denis, but there was no time to pull the
party round before the 1983 general election. We
were still out of touch with the national mood and
could never win on a platform of unilateral nuclear
disarmament and isolation from Europe. 'We have
to show a greater readiness to listen to what people
have to say,' I remarked during a speech in the West
Midlands. It was only 'an arrogant minority, who
care more for dogma than for meeting the
aspirations of the people', who thought otherwise.

My own majority was cut by one-third and we
could no longer ignore the revulsion we aroused.
When Michael Foot's resignation brought matters to
a head, I made my support for a new leader
conditional on his standing firm against extremism
of all kinds. I did not know then that Neil Kinnock
and I were to become such close allies that he would
resist my departure from the NEC four years later to
become deputy Speaker. My opposition to the
enemies within the Labour Party was uncompromising.

'I will only support a new leader who wants a total
reappraisal of the party's policies and a leader who
commits himself to making sure that the party
internally is a democratic socialist party,' I said. 'I do

not want a militant faction in the party. They have a party of their own [the Militant Tendency]. What is needed is a solemn commitment from anybody in the leadership stakes that they will get rid of the head-bangers in the party, and by that I mean the extremists and militants.' Neil had come to the same conclusion by a different and more difficult route. He had to break with people on the left who accused him of being a Judas. I lost no sleep when I was called a 'Witchfinder General' by Militant for my role in the Liverpool inquiry. It was an epithet I was happy to bear.

Militant's success in penetrating the party was a textbook case of what happens when a democratic organisation lowers its guard. We had resisted the Communist Party's efforts to affiliate for fifty years and had pursued pro-Nato policies throughout the Cold War. Labour members were forbidden to join communist front organisations, but because the Kremlin had outlawed the Trotskyists we overlooked their revolutionary policies and paid the price.

The Trots detected Labour's blind spot and moved in. They had a textbook term for it: 'entrism'. In the Trotskyist dictionary this meant the covert infiltration of a democratic party in order to undermine it and create the conditions of chaos necessary for revolution. Analysing its failure to make headway in Britain during the 1950s, Militant's chief strategist, Ted Grant, recalled Leon Trotsky's advice to his British followers in 1936 to organise 'a secret faction' in the Labour Party, 'regardless of how we enter'. Liverpool and Merseyside, with its declining industrial base and inbred sectarian politics, proved fertile ground. So too did the party's youth wing, the Young Socialists, which fell to the Militants in 1970.

It was a valuable prize. It gave Militant a seat on the NEC and conferred on it the status of a semi-official organisation. In 1974 the Militant newspaper celebrated its tenth anniversary. By this time the Trots were so entrenched in the party that the NEC refused to take action against them a year later, despite the warnings of Reg Underhill, our national agent.

When Margaret Thatcher won power in 1979 with a programme aimed at the heart of Labour's post-war legislation, the party still shrank from attacking the Trotskyist virus in its bloodstream. The hard left lost its grip on the NEC only in 1982 when Tony Benn was replaced as chairman of the home-policy committee and Eric Heffer lost his chairmanship of the organisation committee. Militant's days were now numbered. I joined both committees and Gwyneth took the chair of the publicity committee.

Throughout, we moderates met regularly and secretly in the London home of Helen de Freitas in Tufton Court to coordinate our campaign. We called ourselves the Beaujolais Group because we planned our strategy over food and a glass of wine. I kept the accounts. It was hardly high living; we ended 1984 with a deficit of £24.05, which was cleared by everybody paying a modest sum.

Before I joined the NEC, John Golding organised

meetings with allies in the trade unions. He was very much a loner on the executive until reinforcements arrived. In 1982 he widened the group to include Gwyneth, Renée Short, Denis Howell, Charlie Turnock, Tony Clarke, Neville Hough, Ken Cure, Sam McClusky and me. John, supported by Neil Kinnock, subsequently became chairman of the NEC home-policy committee. It was the beginning of a fruitful partnership that paved the way for Tony Blair's New Labour Party.

We met to discuss tactics on the eve of every meeting of the full NEC. Sam McClusky, the party treasurer from the seamen's union, usually sat in Helen's spacious rocking chair, but tended not to come when there was something on the agenda on which he could not follow through. We always ended promptly to get back to the Commons for the 10 p.m. divisions so that nobody would notice our absence. Kinnock and Roy Hattersley joined us from time to time, but did not take an active part. It was a very effective alliance, masterminded by John. He reported the results of our deliberations immediately after every meeting to Neil.

Even so, in the 1983 general election five Militant supporters stood as official Labour candidates and, although the NEC expelled from the party that year five members of *Militant*'s editorial board, it took another two years to force the Trotskyists into open battle on a ground of our choosing – Liverpool.

Militant's error was to sacrifice the city's essential public services to their ideological ambitions. They plunged the city into an acute crisis as a deliberate act of policy, calling on other Labour-controlled councils to join them in defiance of the law that required local authorities to balance their books. They called it 'Thatcher's law', although Labour governments had enforced it long before her time. When she refused to bail them out by giving them the £30 million they demanded, their bravado turned to desperation. They were forced to hire taxis to deliver redundancy notices to council workers they could no longer afford to pay.

Masters of evasion though they were, they had no hiding place after Neil Kinnock's attack on them at the annual conference in Bournemouth in 1985. His fury at the 'grotesque chaos' they had created in Liverpool had a devastating effect. I watched from the platform after being primed by Patricia Hewitt, his press secretary (later a minister in Tony Blair's government), that I would rejoice at what he had to say. It would lift my heart, she said. And it did.

His speech placed Militant and their supporters in an impossible position. He spoke for ordinary people who had no time for political posturing, but whose support Labour needed if it was ever to win office again. It was Neil's finest hour, the moment that put Labour on the way to becoming electable, and the beginning of the end for the Trots inside the Labour Party. One incident during Neil's speech added to the drama of the occasion. Eric Heffer, sitting near me on the platform, suddenly stood up and walked off. This was taken as a sign of outrage at Neil's attack on the Liverpool party, but there was more to it than that. 'Where's Benn?' he whispered to me, looking round for support as Neil moved in for the kill.

'Sitting in the hall, as he always does during leaders' speeches,' I replied. Eric took off when he heard that.

But we had to produce the charge sheet before we could sign Militant's execution warrant. That meant examining its operations in Liverpool at close quarters, taking evidence, cross-examining witnesses and putting Militant's loudmouths on the spot. They resisted us with a persistence that Trotsky himself would have applauded, but the more we uncovered the more determined we became to get rid of them.

Alan Bleasdale's television serial *GBH* (crime-world shorthand for 'grievous bodily harm') realistically portrayed the ruthlessness of Liverpool policies in that era and the atmosphere of intimidation and obstruction created by Militant. Local party officials warned us not to drive to the centre of Liverpool, where our inquiry was to take place, because of the danger involved; instead we were told to leave our cars at the railway station. When we finally reported, a party official had his brakes tampered with. We stayed at a hotel in Bootle where the party said we would be safer than anywhere in Liverpool. The hotel staff were friendly and accommodating, feeding us at all hours. There were eight of us from the NEC plus Larry Whitty, the General Secretary, and Joyce Gould, the National Agent.

Our terms of reference were to conduct an urgent examination into the Liverpool party in the light of its 'damaging and deliberately provocative' attacks against the national party and the trade unions. To show its authority, the NEC prohibited the

A winner finally! Celebrating the 1973 West Bromwich by-election with Mum.

Admiring Mum's rosette.

An MP at last. With Mum and friends, including Barbara and Ted Castle, on the Commons Terrace.

Betty **BOOTHROYD**

LABOUR

Three faces of '70s
Labour

James Callaghan

John Stonehouse

Bob Mellish

Militant's last stand at a Wembley rally

The fightback with Denis Healey. Three cheers for Labour!

Admiring British pork in a West Bromwich abattoir, 1980

A hard slog in Strasbourg – the European Parliament, 1976

The tide turns. Labour enters the wilderness with the Thatcher victory of 1979.

Michael Foot

Eric Heffer (left) and Tony Benn

'The Gang of Four'.
From left to right:
William Rodgers, Shirley
Williams, Roy Jenkins,
David Owen.

Neil Kinnock at the 1985
Labour Party Conference in
Bournemouth. 'Labour was
on the way to becoming
electable.'

After I was elected Speaker, 1992

Liverpool party from holding any meetings or
activities until we reported back. Against some left-
wing opposition, we passed the necessary motions by
substantial majorities. Like Neil Kinnock, most
members of the NEC were sick to the back teeth of
Militant, whatever Tony Benn and Dennis Skinner,
his ally, said in their defence.

Charles Turnock, the railwaymen's NEC
representative, whose deep knowledge of the far left
and magisterial grasp of detail proved invaluable,
headed the inquiry. Charlie, Neville Hough, Tony
Clarke of the Communication Workers and I were
anti-Militant from the start, but the rest of the team
were divided. Margaret Beckett, who later became
leader of the House of Commons, and Audrey Wise
MP were opposed to expulsions, while Eddie Haigh
of the Transport and General Workers' Union and
Tom Sawyer of the National Union of Public
Employees (later General Secretary of the party) had
previously voted with the left on many issues,
including Militant. So we were potentially split down
the middle, with four committed anti-Militants on
one side and four who had, in the past, taken a more
tolerant attitude.

The Trots were confident they could see us off and
threatened a massive national campaign if we found
against them. They talked of holding hundreds of
public meetings, backed by 25,000 posters and
100,000 leaflets and culminating in a London rally
attacking the party leadership. But it was all bluster
and we ignored it.

Had Militant's Liverpool leaders played their

hand differently, they might have exploited our differences to their advantage. They were so used to bullying that their antennae no longer functioned. From what we heard, their meetings had more than a whiff of Jimmy Hoffa's rise in the Teamsters' Union in America during the 1950s and 1960s.

Militant's mobsters used the same tactics, shouting down everyone else and abusing anyone who dared oppose them. By the time we arrived in Liverpool, the NEC had ordered a second inquiry into Militant's role in moves to oust Robert Kilroy-Silk, the Labour MP for Knowsley North. Other Labour MPs threatened to support Kilroy-Silk if he forced a by-election on an anti-Militant platform. That danger passed when Kilroy-Silk quit to work in television, but it was an indication of how agitated Labour MPs had become. If there was to be a purge, I knew who deserved to be purged and it was not the mainstream members of the party who had stood by it during the dark days when the SDP had broken away.

Maintaining the momentum of our inquiry was critically important; we had to keep Militant on the defensive. The longer we took, the more vulnerable we became. So we planned two weeks of interviews in Liverpool, which would give us just enough time to present our report at the NEC's meeting in January 1986. We knew that Granada Television was ready to show its own documentary about Militant in the third week of January. There was no time to waste. Militant's interests, of course, lay in delaying us. They argued that the NEC's decision to suspend the

Liverpool party was unconstitutional, illegal and in breach of 'every single principle of natural justice'.

Our arrival in the city was as depressing as the atmosphere that hung over it. The lack of facilities for the inquiry did nothing to lift our spirits and I was appalled. I had given a better tape recorder to a jumble sale than the one installed for our formal hearings.

Militant showed their hand at our first meeting. They feigned surprise when we invited the local party to outline its position. They claimed that they had expected a list of charges and the opportunity to refute them. They harangued us about their supposed achievements and the misguided attitude of the national leadership. They said we should pack our bags and return to London. If not, they wanted an inquiry on their terms, with the right to see all the evidence and to cross-examine witnesses.

They seemed unaware that a number of organisations and individuals had already briefed us about Militant's catastrophic record in running the city and the local party. After our first exchanges, they put it about that we had agreed to their demand that anyone who contradicted them would have to answer for it. We needed to prove our stamina, so we took evidence until 10.30 p.m. one night; we would not be bullied or worn down. As far as I was concerned, we were the real Labour Party and they were the phonies.

Meeting our deadline, however, proved impossible. The local Black Caucus presented 200 pages of evidence and Jane Kennedy, of the public

employees' union NUPE, sent in 150 pages. Jane,
who became a minister in the 1997 Government, was
so bullied at party meetings by ranters around her
that throughout her ordeal she wore a large woollen
overcoat as a morale-booster. She was a model of
courage and conviction. If Militant had won, Jane
and people like her would have been thrown out of
the party.

'Will you face them when we put your allegations
to them?' we asked local people who were brave
enough to stand up to Militant. Those who did
showed how wrong the bullies were, in thinking they
could silence their opponents. Trade-union leaders
reported the problems that Militant gave them on
Merseyside. The party's national student officer told
how Militant supporters had assaulted him when he
tried to check on Labour membership in the local
colleges. The unions were so worried about
Liverpool's maladministration that they asked the
Government to investigate its finances. They were
even more dismayed when they discovered that the
council was negotiating with Swiss banks to borrow
millions in order to return it to solvency. The
prospect of an alliance between Trotskyists and the
gnomes of Zurich took the breath away.

Jack Dromey, an officer of the Transport and
General Workers' Union, told his executive council
that Liverpool's bankruptcy was the result of a
conscious political decision, inspired by Militant. As
the ring closed around them, the Trots finally
realised how precarious their position had become.
When their apologists on the NEC made another bid

to lift their suspension, we defeated them by twenty votes to seven. We were not about to let Militant off the hook.

Arrogance was part of their arsenal. Derek Hatton, their chief spokesman, boasted of how mercilessly he treated people who got in his way and revelled in his reputation as a snappy dresser, a regular nightclubber and a ladies' man. 'People thought twice about taking me on,' he boasted. Tony Mulhearn, his fellow Militant, was called Il Duce because of his cream-coloured raincoat and swagger to match. 'We needed to use every trick in the book,' Hatton said in self-justification after we cleaned out the stables.

Such incidents included climbing on the roof of a special school to intimidate its teachers and frighten its bewildered children, an incident graphically shown in Bleasdale's drama. One moderate union official kept a baseball bat in his car boot because he was frightened for his life. A journalist was thrown down the stairs. A city gardener was driven to a nervous breakdown.

Meetings at the lowest ward level in the city party became nightmarish as the Trots forced votes on matters that were normally nodded through and argued about voluntary jobs that were usually hard to fill. Anything that deterred ordinary party members from turning up was grist to Militant's mill.

They tried their luck in the High Court, where they were rebuffed by a judge who was understandably loath to become involved in Labour's civil war. He did find the NEC's proposed procedure

wanting, but indicated we could continue the
proceedings provided we conformed at all stages to
the rules of natural justice. Thirty interviews and a
mass of documentation awaited us on our return to
the city. Militant's lawyers threatened to go to court
again and the hard left tried once more to end our
inquiry. Again, they were defeated.

Charlie Turnock told us he had corroborated
evidence against forty-seven Militants in the district
party and twenty-seven members of the city council.
The numbers were larger than some on the team had
expected and his news was received in silence. It
exposed the differences among us that had been
evident at the start.

Margaret Beckett and Audrey Wise thought that
going after Militant lay beyond our terms of
reference, Eddie Haigh and Tom Sawyer wanted
fewer names on the list of suspects, and Tony Clarke
favoured a compromise. That left Charlie, Neville
Hough and me wearing the hard hats. We wanted
Militant's Liverpool leaders out of the party before
the 1987 general election. For far too long they had
acted as if they were beyond retribution. The
'international class struggle' concerned them more
than Liverpool's welfare. They had sidelined the
party's normal channels and made life a misery for
those who got in their way.

Evidence of Militant's wrecking tactics was sent to
me in a briefing note on how to subvert school
boards. It instructed Militant supporters to adapt
their tactics to whatever support they could muster.
If they had a majority they were to force everything

to a vote; if not, they were to interrupt frequently on points of order and prevent votes being taken. 'The aim is to act as one while seeming to act individually.' Filibustering was the recommended way to exasperate non-Militants and to postpone decisions until the end of meetings, by which time anyone sensible had probably gone. If that did not work, Militants were to propose other business that required further meetings and to 'pick awkward times'.

School subjects singled out for criticism included remedial teaching, religious instruction, social studies, political studies, constitutional history and anything about America. 'Never be emotional, keep calm, be relentless,' stated the guidelines. That included pestering school heads with telephone calls, casting doubt on the head's morals, stirring up trouble between the staff and the head, probing the head's past for evidence of litigation, and concentrating on a school's weaknesses while ignoring its successes.

Other sections dealt with undermining the confidence of teachers, students and other staff in the way the school was being run. Such subterfuge was an integral part of Militant's approach to politics. Even when the facts were laid bare, there were still people in key positions in the party who were willing to give them the benefit of the doubt. Our inability to produce a unanimous report only encouraged them.

Six of us (along with Larry Whitty, the General Secretary) signed a majority report calling for root-and-branch reform of the Liverpool party under national supervision, and for disciplinary action to be taken against Militant's ringleaders. Margaret Beckett and Audrey Wise dissented and wrote their own report, which contained the classic line that 'no one can expect a 100% perfectly functioning party'. I thought we had heard every argument in the book, but this was a new one.

Joyce Gould had played a crucial role in bringing the evidence together and in seeing that the NEC's decisions on expulsions were subsequently carried out – a difficult task in which her knowledge of party structures helped enormously.

The final scene was played out in the airless board-room of the old party headquarters in Lambeth, a few miles from the House of Commons. The court case meant that the members of the inquiry could not vote on the final expulsion on grounds of natural justice. So we watched the other members of the NEC, as leading Militants got their just deserts.

Gwyneth sat by an open window doing her embroidery during those anguished months of argument and legal deliberations. She had heard the evidence against the Trotskyites many times before and had voted against the hard left's efforts to save them by raising her hand without expression. We likened her to Madame Defarge, the innkeeper's wife in the French Revolution who knitted as the guillotine did its work.

The party conferences of 1986 and 1987 endorsed our report and, although the final tally was not as large as I would have liked, Militants were left in no doubt that they had been rumbled and were not wanted. They subsequently set up their own splinter party and met the dismal electoral fate they deserved. It was a rewarding finale to my years on the National Executive.

By turning against Militant as vehemently as he did, Neil Kinnock showed leadership of the highest order and we backed him to the hilt. Slowly we relaunched the party, helped enormously by Peter Mandelson's appointment as our director of communications. I voted for Peter without reservation. He inherited a penny-whistle media unit and turned it into a formidable operation. The old press office had rickety accommodation, ramshackle communications and a defensive outlook. Even its walls needed propping up with tables. He was exactly what we needed – an aggressive, confident, focused and imaginative professional.

Above all, he was television-trained and knew how to project the party and get it out of the doldrums. He was undoubtedly one of the chief architects of 'New Labour' and his teaming-up with Tony Blair was to pay off in 1997. Labour's opportunities were transformed after the purging of Militant. Larry Whitty's appointment as General Secretary brought another change for the better, by sweeping away years of ineffectual organisation and rivalry between the NEC and the leader.

In 1987 the electorate was still not persuaded by Labour's policies, but we narrowed the Tory majority and prevented the SDP-Liberal Alliance from dislodging us as the main rivals to Margaret Thatcher. Within a few months the Gang of Four fell out among themselves and Labour was no longer the doomed party it had appeared in 1983. It was back in the hands of leaders who believed that the responsibilities of power were sweeter than the futility of opposition.

CHAPTER SEVEN

Call Me Madam

━━━━

> *Ethel Merman, waiting to go on stage for the Broadway*
> *production of* Call Me Madam, *was asked if she was*
> *nervous. 'No,' she replied. 'The audience have paid their*
> *money. They're the ones that should be nervous.'*
>
> Quoted in Laurence Bergreen's
> *As Thousands Cheer, the Life of Irving Berlin*

NEIL KINNOCK'S POSITION was strengthened by Labour's performance in 1987. The hard left was no longer a threat and we had fought a professional campaign. Neil was well placed to begin the next stage of Labour's recovery and I was ready to move on. I had never wanted to be a frontbencher but I did not want to stay in the trenches for ever, keeping guard for the leadership.

Ernest Armstrong's retirement created a vacancy among the three deputy Speakers to Bernard Weatherill and he invited me to fill it. Neil was reluctant to lose my support on the executive but the Speaker – 'Jack' to his friends – made my appointment conditional on my quitting frontline party politics. Neil relented when Gwyneth Dunwoody told him there was a chance that I might be Speaker one day and the party should not stand in my way. He was an outstanding supporter of women's rights and was delighted by my later success.

Reaction elsewhere to the possibility of my succeeding Jack was far from encouraging. *Private Eye*, the satirical magazine, said I had 'all the charm of carbon monoxide gas in an airtight room' and was 'as thick as the proverbial two planks'. I was glad that others better placed to influence events thought differently.

As a deputy Speaker I kept my party affiliation and attended meetings of the Parliamentary Labour Party when I was not on duty, but I could no longer speak or ask questions in the House or vote in divisions. It was the beginning of the parting of the ways.

From the start Jack was enormously supportive. He marked my promotion by giving me a copy of a Victorian cartoon from *Punch* magazine, which showed John Bull carrying a frilly-knickered woman across his shoulder towards the Speaker's chair. The woman was labelled 'the Mother of Parliaments'. The notion of anyone but a man presiding over the Commons in those pre-suffragette days was hilarious. I was determined to provoke no such titters.

When Peter Pike, Labour MP for Burnley, asked me on my first appearance as deputy Speaker how I was to be addressed, I replied, 'Call me Madam' – an injunction that remained in force when I became

Speaker. The line, of course, was Ethel Merman's from the Broadway show of that name. I had subconsciously remembered it and was grateful to her.

My promotion came as no surprise to those who knew the way Parliament works. Eight years before I had become a member of an obscure body that plays a vital part in overseeing legislation going through Parliament – the Speaker's Panel of Chairmen. These stalwarts chair the standing committees that are set up to examine legislation approved in principle by the House and then sent for detailed scrutiny before the final stages of a bill, known as Report and Third Reading.

The Panel of Chairmen is selected from industrious backbenchers from both sides of the House, who can be relied on to chair standing-committee debates impartially and ensure the efficient examination of a bill's contents and proposed amendments. It was a valuable experience for me because it required a thorough grasp of the rules of the House and an ability to listen to weeks of argument, often on technical matters, without loss of concentration or sense of humour.

Some colleagues regard the job as the kiss of death to any prospect of ever becoming a minister – and they are right. To be chairman of a standing committee requires a willingness to spend hundreds of hours every session away from the limelight. To anyone who wants his or her name in the headlines, being a member of the Speaker's Panel is worse than having a low profile; it means having no profile. I knew that, of course, and accepted the consequences. As an ordinary MP, I was as partisan as the next; as a panel chairman, I was strictly neutral.

George Thomas was the first Speaker whom I knew well. He became a deputy Speaker after the 1974 election and succeeded Selwyn Lloyd two years later. He enjoyed chatting and liked having me around. He sent me notes inviting me to 'Come and have a cup of tea at 4.30 when I leave the Chair'. Once, seeing me wearing a yellow outfit in the chamber, he wrote, 'You look like a little daffodil.' When I went to Strasbourg regularly as a member of the European Parliament, I brought him back duty-free Cuban cigars. He was a great cigar smoker. I also saw a lot of him in Cyprus, one of my favourite holiday spots, where we had mutual friends and he knew Alecos Michaeliades, a former Speaker of the Cyprus Parliament, well, and often stayed with him.

After the Commons agreed to its proceedings being broadcast, George's voice resonated around the world on the radio. He also welcomed the first television cameras into Speaker's House and invited groups of MPs to tea parties there. For decades the place was 'off-limits' to most Members, unlike in the Victorian and Edwardian eras when the Speaker held grand levees on Saturdays and guests were expected to wear court dress.

George succeeded brilliantly in restoring the prestige of the Speakership. His role as Secretary of State for Wales at the investiture of Prince Charles as Prince of Wales also made him a popular figure with the royal family. The Queen and the Duke of

Edinburgh attended a state dinner at Speaker's House in 1977, the first time that a monarch had dined there for 150 years.

Few knew about the turbulence of his earlier years in the chair until he revealed in his memoirs his shock at what went on behind the scenes in Parliament. 'There was a side to the Commons that had remained hidden to me throughout my 31 years there. It was as dark as the other side of the moon, and it was as unattractive. At first I was merely shocked by the things I was learning, but in a short while, shock changed to anger.'

He drifted apart from his old friends in the Labour Party over the devolution of power to Wales, which he strongly opposed, and the way that James Callaghan's Government defied him when he was Speaker, observing: 'Whereas the struggle of my early predecessors had been to protect the rights of the Commons against the monarch, a modern Speaker's struggle is to be independent of the Government.' In this, he, Jack Weatherill and I fought the same fight.

George got on well with Margaret Thatcher – some would say too well. She made him a viscount when he retired and he became, like her, an inveterate Euro-sceptic. However, she followed the example of previous Prime Ministers in wanting his successor to be somebody of whom Downing Street, rather than the House, approved. She was thwarted in this by a bold initiative by a Tory backbencher, which led to Jack Weatherill becoming Speaker instead of a No. 10 appointee.

The unsung hero behind this reassertion of

Commons rights was Robin Maxwell-Hyslop, Conservative MP for Tiverton from 1960 to 1992. He was incensed by the way in which governments had fixed the Speakership in the past and was determined to challenge this. He had done so before when Francis Pym, Edward Heath's Chief Whip, walked into a private weekly meeting of Conservative backbenchers in 1971 to announce, 'The Government have decided that Selwyn Lloyd will be the next Speaker.'

He challenged this by proposing my old boss, Geoffrey de Freitas, which forced a vote – only the second since the war. Selwyn Lloyd won it easily by 294 votes to fifty-five, but Maxwell-Hyslop had made his point. The Speakership is the gift of the House of Commons, not a prize to be doled out to a Downing Street nominee, the sort of person whom Maxwell-Hyslop described in a letter to Jack Weatherill as 'a sombre, decayed ex-minister, in the hope that he will remain grateful'.

Determined to prevent another stitch-up when George Thomas retired, the doughty backbencher moved fast to propose Jack Weatherill, whom Margaret Thatcher did not want, before No. 10 realised what was happening. He nominated Jack in a recorded-delivery letter to Jim Callaghan, Father of the House, and at the same time told the BBC's *World at One* programme what he had done.

The Government was caught off-guard, support for Weatherill surged and No. 10's plans to install a placeman were scuppered. The combination of a strong-minded MP who loved Parliament and a candidate for the chair who owed nobody any favours was irresistible. But Jack's independence guaranteed him a difficult life, especially after the 1987 election, when I knew something of what he had to contend with.

By May 1988 reports of a campaign against him of officially inspired vilification had reached the newspapers. The *Independent* said that Jack was 'subjected to an unprecedented level of private pressure following his decision to allow an Opposition debate on social security changes'. An unnamed senior Tory declared that it was time he resigned and warned that the Tories were 'out to get him'.

Efforts to undermine him became so blatant that Neil Kinnock warned off the plotters after they put it about that Sir Geoffrey Howe, Thatcher's former Chancellor and Foreign Secretary, was in line for the job. Kinnock said that 'the Speaker's chair must not be the depository of people surplus to the requirements of the Prime Minister'.

But that was precisely how it was viewed in Downing Street. The aim of the rumour-mongers was plain enough. They wanted to undermine Jack's authority and restrict Parliament's ability to scrutinise the Government's actions. Jack wrote about these 'Black Glove' tactics in his private papers, which he has kindly allowed me to quote. Undaunted, he soldiered on.

He recorded how ministers berated him privately for making the Government's life difficult. They complained, for example, about his allowing the

Opposition to table questions concerning urgent matters, which took precedence over other business. Some ministers tried to warn him off at encounters in Speaker's House. On one occasion Norman Tebbit, who sat in the Thatcher Cabinet as chairman of the Conservative Party, told Jack that the Government was seething with resentment against him and that 'the hounds were in to get me'.

Another entry records that John Wakeham, the Leader of the House, 'blew up' and said that 'most debates were in any event irrelevant and I was merely massaging the egos of backbenchers'. Wakeham remarked that some ministers objected to being kept in the House too long and 'were frequently late for their press conferences', which were important to 'ensure accuracy before the 6 p.m. press deadlines'.

Tension between the rights of Parliament and the Government's media-consciousness were to reach a higher pitch during my own time in the chair, but its roots were already well established before I got there, because both sides are more concerned with 'spin-doctoring' the headlines than with facing the nation's elected representatives. Jack noted:

It seems that the slightest 'opposition' or independence on the part of Members (or even of Speakers) is considered unacceptable. It was in vain that I explained that it was the duty of backbenchers to put any Government 'on trial' and to provide a forum for the justification of policies.

Jack stood his ground against them all, including David Waddington, the Government Chief Whip and my old election adversary. A weak Speaker would have settled for an easy life and let the Government keep the Commons under its thumb. As Thatcher found, it failed to do so in the end, with fatal consequences for her own leadership.

Neil Kinnock believed that the next Speaker after Weatherill should be a Labour MP, because it was customary for each side to occupy the chair in turn and it was 'our turn'. He was wrong about that, as Michael Martin's succession to me as a Labour-sponsored Speaker showed. Jack noted in his papers that I might be a candidate but expected me to be opposed by a Tory. I bided my time, watching the battles on the floor of the House from a discreet vantage point under the gallery. Only in retrospect does the path to my becoming Speaker look clear.

When Bob Mellish nominated me for a seat in the European Parliament in 1975 the prospect of my eventually becoming Speaker would have seemed fantastic. I was one of eighteen Labour members of the thirty-six-strong British delegation who went to Strasbourg as the nominees of our own parties. Two of my former bosses were in the Labour team: Geoffrey de Freitas and Harry Walston, both Euro-enthusiasts. Ted Castle (now ennobled) was another member and Barbara (a lifelong sceptic) followed later as a directly elected MEP.

I shared Bob Mellish's pro-European views, which was why he nominated me. The party was split in the 1975 referendum on Britain's continued membership of the European Community and, although our side won, the trade unions and many Labour MPs remained hostile.

John Prescott, MP for Hull East, John Evans, MP for St Helens North, and Gwyneth Dunwoody represented the defeated wing of the party in Strasbourg. The European Parliament had a curious effect on some of us. John Prescott threw himself with zeal into its multinational activities, whereas I, who ought to have been thrilled to be there, was disappointed by the experience.

John shunned Strasbourg's culinary delights and the comradeship of after-work hours to read papers and prepare speeches for the following days. I recognised the symptoms from the time I first knew him: he was a workaholic. Whatever doubts he had about the European Community, he was determined to know how it operated and how best to make his contribution to it. He devoured policy documents and drove to far-off conferences that many of us considered expendable.

I have always loved travel, but I found the whole business exhausting and of doubtful value. Britain had dragged its feet over signing the Treaty of Rome and we were still feeling our way after finally being admitted. We had much lost time to make up and we could not be too assertive.

I had been a keen internationalist and an instinctive European since I was a young woman. Like Denis Healey, I viewed the English Channel as no more than a tank-trap. I wanted Britain to take a leading role in Europe and to be at the forefront in shaping its destiny. That meant seeing the big picture and not always niggling about the small print. Our sitting on the sidelines while others took the initiative saddened me.

I wanted our point of view to prevail in the directives that came out of Brussels. I believed there was a better chance of that happening if we made our case when they were being negotiated, instead of which we were generally the laggards in the team, opting out of measures that affected the rest of the Community and trying to renegotiate entry terms that we had belatedly agreed. Then, as now, we were equivocal about the whole venture, and even our landslide win in the 1975 referendum produced little momentum. Our sister parties in the European socialist group despaired of us. I wanted closer links with them, but the sceptics in Labour's delegation hesitated. Both mentally and physically, I began to take a beating.

I kept three bags in my London flat at the time: one for one night away, another for two nights and the third for a whole week. I simply moved my washbag from one to the other. The Parliament met in Luxembourg as well as Strasbourg and, to make its workings even more unsettled, its committees often met in Brussels. Being perpetually on the move was not a system conducive to the orderly creation of the new Europe that I wanted to bring about.

With a Midlands constituency like mine, with more than its fair share of problems, I soon regretted the time I spent away from Westminster and worked twice as hard to disguise the fact that I ever left the country. The European Parliament's inefficiency irked me. One day we found ourselves debating a Commission directive that had been drawn up nine years earlier and amended five times without a revised text ever being produced. Such negligence would have caused outrage in the Commons.

We operated in six languages, creating mountains of paperwork. To add to the sense of unreality, our question times and debates attracted a sparse attendance, especially after lunch. The British and Germans would find themselves sitting in the huge semi-circular chamber staring at rows of empty desks. Many members and officials from the European Commission shared the majority's relaxed view. The Commons would be in uproar if a Cabinet minister arrived late for Question Time, but European Commissioners thought nothing of it.

I focused as best I could on issues of concern to ordinary people, especially consumer rights. 'I don't find a burning interest in Europe or what I am doing here,' I told Birmingham's *Evening Mail*. 'It has to matter in the streets of the West Midlands.' I argued for European rules to standardise the labelling of products. I accepted the guarantee of quality that came with leading brand-names like Cadbury's chocolates and Typhoo tea, but how were shoppers able to judge the soup that these two companies made jointly, without further information? I wanted labelling that gave shoppers the precise ingredients in a product and the date by which it should be consumed. Today we take this for granted, but in 1976 the case had to be argued.

My previous work with Harry Walston had given me the insight to contribute, from the consumer's viewpoint, to the vexed debate on farm surpluses. I deplored the food mountains and wine lakes created by the EC's wasteful system of paying growers subsidies to produce goods that the market could not absorb.

I called for alternative work and retraining to help the countryside adapt, a policy now widely accepted, but our efforts went unreported. Most British newspapers have always covered Europe in terms of 'us versus them'. European institutions were (and are) regarded as too remote to matter. I yearned to be at Westminster full-time again. Expressing myself as bluntly as I could, I described the fledgling parliament as 'a dull place compared with the House of Commons' and scoffed at speeches that could not be interrupted because of the consternation that would cause among the interpreters. Jokes were dangerous too. By the time one had been interpreted and understood, the Member who made it had moved on and laughter would arrive disconcertingly late.

I was glad to return to Westminster after nearly eighteen months and leave others to fight the first direct elections in 1978. Back full-time in the Commons, I was chosen to sit on a special select committee to examine a bill to replace David Steel's Abortion Act. The act had been in force for ten years and was due for review. This gave its opponents an opportunity to make it more difficult to obtain an abortion legally, which they opposed on religious grounds. Catholics argued on the same side as evangelical Protestants, and Mary Whitehouse sided with Malcolm Muggeridge, in demanding greater restrictions.

When James White, a Glasgow Labour MP from a strong Catholic area, proposed a more restrictive bill, the evidence convinced me that Steel's act was working well and that it would be a mistake to change it. Inevitably, our committee became bogged down in fruitless wrangling and six of us – me, David Steel, Joyce Butler, Helene Hayman, Maurice Miller and Sir George Sinclair – pulled out, thus depriving the committee of its quorum. Steel's act remains a landmark of social legislation, enjoying wide public and medical support. It ended the sordid injustice of well-to-do women paying for abortions on demand in private clinics and less fortunate souls risking life and limb in the hands of back-street abortionists. We did not advocate a free-for-all. Abortion under the act required the consent of two doctors and consideration of the woman's social and medical conditions. 'I refuse to put the clock back,' I said.

I rejected calls for a return to capital punishment for the same reason. I did not doubt the popular support behind the hangers' lobby, but argued that the death sentence – judicial killing – did little to deter murder. It was hard to find any substantial evidence that it did. Nor was I moved by those who believed in retribution, whether or not it deterred offenders. 'I do not believe that revenge and retribution are the business of Parliament. For me, retribution can never have, and I believe should never have, a place in the deliberations of a parliament in a civilised nation,' I told a Commons debate on the Criminal Justice Bill. To my constituents who differed I said: 'I am not a mandated delegate and this is not a delegated assembly. I owe respect to the people I represent for their point of view. I also owe them my judgement in seeking what is right and best for the country in its entirety. It would not only be wrong in itself, but wrong in the interests of the nation, to reinstate capital punishment on the basis of public opinion . . . It would be intolerable if I were to allow public perception rather than convincing argument to blow me away from the opinions that I hold.'

I also sat on the foreign affairs select committee from 1979 to 1981, which nearly killed me – literally. We had arranged to visit Saudi Arabia, Oman and Thailand, but the Saudis were still furious over ITV's showing of *Death of a Princess*, a dramatic television reconstruction of the execution of a Saudi princess who had committed adultery. They told us we were not welcome.

We went straight to Oman instead, where we boarded a frigate in the Straits of Hormuz to watch the frequent passing Soviet vessels. This involved disembarking from the motor boat by climbing a rope ladder hung over the side of the frigate. It was a considerable climb. I found it difficult and slipped. But for a valiant rugby tackle by Anthony Kershaw, our chairman, I would have fallen between the frigate and the motor boat.

The second near-miss occurred when we returned

to shore on a British-piloted helicopter, with an Omani second-in-command. On our arrival at the British Embassy, the ambassador told us that it had crashed just minutes after delivering us and taking off again. Kevin McNamara and the late Peter Mills were in the group. That was the nearest I ever came to death.

Flying to Moscow on a Thomson package holiday with three other MPs and two wives in April 1984 was not my idea of a break or theirs. But we were no ordinary tourists and our visas had been obtained under false pretences. We were not in the least bit interested in seeing the tourist sights. Our purpose was to make secret contact with Russia's Refusniks, Jews who wanted to live in Israel but had been refused permission.

We were the first official group of MPs to meet them and I was chosen as its leader. They assumed that since I had been to Moscow before, I knew my way around! We were a mixed bunch – Labour's Mark Fisher and his wife Ingrid, David Sumberg from the Tories and his wife Carolyn and the Reverend Martin Smyth, the Ulster Unionist vice-chairman of the Commons all-party committee on Soviet Jewry.

Martin Gilbert, the distinguished historian and authority on the plight of the Soviet Jews, briefed us before we went. He had visited Russia the year before and told us how desperate the situation had become. Half a million Jews had been allowed to leave between 1972 and 1982 but then the gates closed. New regulations were introduced which made it virtually impossible to get away. Invitations from Israel to rejoin parents or children already there became the new basis for applying for an exit visa. All previous applications were declared invalid, leaving 380,000 Russian Jews in limbo.

Pressure against the Refusniks was stepped up in March 1983 when the authorities launched an anti-Zionist campaign and declared that Soviet Jews were 'an inseparable part of the Soviet people'. Those who persisted in wanting to leave the country were hounded from their jobs, harassed by the KGB and denied their religious and cultural freedoms.

The authorities were clearly suspicious about our motives, for when we arrived in Moscow we were interviewed by a Soviet news agency about where we intended to go. Acutely conscious that our contacts faced prosecution if we incriminated them, we stuck to the line that we were just visitors. The Refusniks had taken great risks inviting us to come. Regardless of what the KGB guessed, we were determined to do nothing to make their task easier.

I had been given a list of telephone numbers to ring. On no account was I to use the hotel telephone or the public kiosk opposite it. So Martin and I walked into Red Square and I rang the first number on my list from there. I was told that if the person at the other end showed any hesitation in talking to me, I was to ring off and try the next number. Fortunately, I struck gold at the first try and was given our next set of instructions.

We were to travel by underground next morning to Moscow's Yugo-zapadnaya station in the suburbs, where we would be recognised and taken to meet other Refusniks. I wrote down the name of the station and asked if we could take a taxi, which would be easier than our using the Moscow Metro. 'No, use the Metro' I was told. 'We will find you.' As we were talking, a soldier and his girlfriend turned up to use an adjacent kiosk. I whispered to Martin that we had better make ourselves scarce.

Next morning, as directed, we told our Intourist guide that we did not need her services because we preferred to wander round by ourselves. She was bemused but did not object. Our contact met us as planned and took us on by bus to a drab estate where the streets were covered in slush, snow and ice. There, in a nondescript apartment, its curtains closed against prying eyes, a distinguished Jewish scientist and other Refusniks, all of whom spoke English, greeted us. Our host had been dismissed from his profession and made to do menial work but he was still allowed to receive Western royalties for his published work because it brought hard currency into the country. Many of the others we met had been demoted at work and moved from their apartments to sordid blocks in the suburbs.

We gave them suitcases of warm clothing, coffee, sweets and chocolates, but what mattered to them most was our assurances that they had friends in the West who wanted to help. They had not met any British politicians before and we offered them hope, however frail, of better times. At the end of a long day of talks, one of our hosts drew the curtains back and was not surprised to see two cars parked outside.

The drivers offered to take us back to the city centre. We declined the invitation but it seemed likely we were under observation and they were KGB cars. We returned to our spartan Intourist hotel by public transport.

A week before, 72-year-old Konstantin Chernenko had been elected President in succession to Yuri Andropov, who had died after only 15 months in power. Mikhail Gorbachev, whose reforms led to the collapse of the USSR, was already talked of as the coming man. Other meetings with Refusniks followed in other flats. At one, I met a woman who had travelled from Riga, the Latvian capital then inside the USSR, to plead for her husband who had been arrested. Recently married, they had been refused exit visas and burned their identity papers in protest outside the General Post Office, for which he was imprisoned. I noted her details and comforted her as best I could.

On our return, I was debriefed in my Commons office by a young man whose Israeli connections I could only surmise. He seemed pleased with what I told him and offered me a holiday in Israel to show his appreciation. I replied that I would settle for Israeli intervention if I were ever held hostage. I had in mind the Israeli rescue of Jewish hostages hijacked and taken to Entebbe. My interrogator merely smiled.

There was a happy footnote to our visit to the Refusniks for them and for me. The restrictions on emigration to Israel were eventually lifted and when I became Speaker, my supporters included Martin

Smyth, Mark Fisher and David Sumberg. David became director of the Anglo-Israel Association, which bought 20 trees in my name for the British Park in Jerusalem. Our mission to help Soviet Jewry bound all four of us together in a special way.

By this time I was a member of the Speaker's Panel. We were examining a housing bill when a division was called on an amendment. I looked at the Government and Opposition whips to see if all of their Members were present. Joe Dean, the Government whip on the committee, nodded and so did the Opposition whip. 'Lock the doors,' I ordered. At that point, Joe realised that Frank Allaun, the veteran left-winger and a member of the committee, was outside making a telephone call in the corridor. As Joe ran out to fetch him, the door closed on both of them.

'Let me in! Let me in!' Joe demanded, banging on the door. But the voice vote was already under way and could not be stopped. The Government won, but Joe was so annoyed that he reported me to Jack Weatherill, who oversaw the standing committees as Chairman of Ways and Means.

I went home for the weekend feeling terrible. Joe was an old friend and blamed me personally for his embarrassment. Jack, however, was totally unconcerned. He asked to see me on Monday morning and, before I could speak, said: 'I don't know what you've done. I don't very much mind. I'm totally on your side. Come and tell me all about it.'

Jonathan Aitken, then a rising Tory backbencher, enlivened one committee I chaired by quoting a

French proverb: 'It's a sad woman who has to buy her own perfume.' He was making a political point about the Channel Tunnel Bill. This prompted David Mitchell, the Transport Minister on the committee, to present me with some perfume, with a note attached that read: 'Hope it's not Channel No. 5.'

My appointment to the House of Commons Commission, which oversees the administration of the House, confirmed my rising parliamentary status, and the general election of 1987 was my last as a backbencher. My nomination as a deputy Speaker, with the official title of Deputy Chairman of Ways and Means (which made me No. 3 to the Speaker), was approved by acclamation. It meant that I could still make political speeches in my constituency, and did, especially against Thatcher's poll tax. I told the *Telegraph and Argus* that Nigel Lawson's tax-cutting 1988 budget made me 'hopping mad that so much money can be given to people who have already got it. They give thousands back to the rich but say they can't give anything to the lower-paid or the nurses because it causes inflation.' On my desk, as I gave that interview, was a letter from a pensioner on £47 a week, reduced to £17 after rent and rates. I could say nothing in the House, but was free on my own patch to accuse the Thatcher government of betraying pensioners and allowing them to lose out 'in our increasingly divided society, which so desperately needs to be changed'.

One constituent of mine, a mother with a learning difficulty and severe asthma, was gaoled for twenty-one days for not paying the Poll Tax, despite her having a fourteen-year-old daughter. She weighed only seven stone and the decline in her health so alarmed prison and probation officers that I contacted Peter Lloyd, the Prisons Minister, and she was released.

I noted signs of a rift between Thatcher and Lawson and observed that this was not only undermining the Government's reputation for confidence but was also 'bringing Mrs Thatcher's leadership into question' – which proved to be the case a year later. I spent a lot of time in the chamber watching proceedings and I felt that the chemistry between them was wrong. There was no visible rapport and they weren't working as a team.

The *Observer* tipped me to succeed Jack Weatherill just four months after I joined his team, but I was too busy training myself to recognise MPs to care. I sat on the side benches during debates referring to an index of MPs' names and faces as I watched them in action. My problem in the early days was remembering the names of MPs who intervened in a speech. Somehow or other, with a little prompting from officials, I got through without embarrassment.

The 1987 Parliament had brought in more women MPs – twenty-one Labour and seventeen Conservative. Dame Jill Knight's election as a vice-chairman of the 1922 Committee of Tory MPs was a further advance. Kenneth Clarke welcomed me as a deputy Speaker on behalf of the Government and Gordon Brown for the Opposition when I took the chair for the first time on 9 July.

We worked a rota system. Some days I sat in the chair from 4.30 to 6 p.m. and from 8.30 to 9.30 p.m. When the House sat late or into the early hours of the morning, I did 4.30–6.30 p.m. and 11 p.m.–2 a.m. On other occasions, I did 4.30–6.30 p.m., 8.00–9.30 p.m. and 4.30–7.00 a.m. The tiny bedroom in my office was a lifesaver. During all-night sittings I lay on my bed with my eyes closed and relied on Don Lord, the Speaker's Trainbearer, to call me. He had to stay on duty to remove the Mace at the end of the sitting and place it in the safe. Whatever the hour when we finished, I attended the Speaker's noon conference, but it was an undeniable ordeal.

One debate that I chaired lasted far longer than expected. Unaware of this, the other two deputies had gone home and the Speaker had gone to bed. As one speech followed another into the early hours, Charles Winnifrith, one of the clerks, asked if he should wake up the Speaker. I declined and said I thought I could go on. Sensing my predicament, he remarked, 'You have been in the chair for more than three hours. You are perfectly entitled to adjourn for ten minutes.' I took him at his word. The clerks were as relieved as I was, and the Members present had a laugh at my expense.

One of my first tests was to deal with heated points of order about the Government's decision to take legal action against a BBC radio series dealing with national security, called *My Country Right or Wrong*. The Government objected to the series because members and former members of the security services who had taken part were under a lifelong duty of confidentiality to the Crown.

This aroused enormous comment and the Speaker allowed the Opposition to table a question obliging Sir Patrick Mayhew, the Attorney-General, to make a statement. Heated exchanges followed, with accusations of 'tinpot dictatorship' and 'a dangerous slide into authoritarianism'. Although Jack Weatherill gave both sides ample time to state their case, the controversy spilled over into a later debate that I chaired. By deciding to allow the storm to run its course, I was praised for my sagacity. Often the Speaker's best option is to shut Members up, but there are times when it pays to let them talk themselves to a standstill.

'It's a job you grow in, and I'm just starting to grow,' I said after seven months. Whenever I could, I argued the case for television to be admitted, to bring us closer to the people and to improve some Members' manners. 'It works in the Lords,' I told the Bradford *Telegraph and Argus*. 'I don't think MPs will be conscious of the cameras after a few weeks. If people at home don't like it, there's the "off" button, there's another channel. What I don't like at the moment is seeing still photographs on the TV news, or a picture of Neil Kinnock with only his voice. Why shouldn't people be able to see their own Parliament at work?'

My advice to new Members was: 'Be natural. Pace yourself. Only speak when you have something vital and important to say. Don't be a rent-a-mouth or a rent-a-signature because you will lose your worth.'

At the start of my third year as a deputy, I commissioned Hardy Amies to design something distinctive for me to wear in the chair, which I paid for myself. He created a gown in navy silk faille, with Tudor roses embroidered on the sleeves, and he was as delighted by the reaction as I was. I chose him because he represented the best of British classic design and workmanship. My father would have approved.

The clerks told me later that my 'uniform' raised eyebrows, but nobody objected. Nor could they. Harold Walker and Paul Dean, my seniors in the pecking order, wore morning coat and striped trousers. I was simply ensuring that I did not let the side down, by being formal in a feminine way. If Members thought I would look even better in the Speaker's robes, I was already well prepared. I had a half-dozen legal collars made, of the kind Speakers wear, and the rest of the basic kit: white blouse, black skirt and black stockings. I also happened to have a pair of black patent shoes decorated with imitation buckles. It occurred to me that they just might come in useful one day, so I put them at the back of my cupboard. Was I being presumptuous? I do not think so. I have always believed in taking life as it comes, but in being ready for it.

What I could not do was appear complacent. When *The Times* published an unexplained photomontage of me wearing the Speaker's wig, thus giving the erroneous impression that I had actually posed for the photograph, I complained and they published an apology the next day.

By 1990 my future was a staple item in the press. Joe Haines, writing in the *Daily Mirror*, said that I ought to get the Speakership on merit, but that the Labour Party would have to insist on it or Mrs Thatcher would prevent it. In the event, she had no say in the matter. She had gone.

CHAPTER EIGHT

Elect Me
for What I Am

―――――

The office of Speaker does not demand rare qualities.
It demands common qualities in rare degrees.

Speaker Lowther

NEIL KINNOCK DID A tremendous job of
making the Labour Party electable again, but
our prospects faded when John Major replaced
Margaret Thatcher in November 1990. The Tories
were now able to present themselves in a less
abrasive guise and Labour still looked too much of
a gamble. I held my seat with an increased majority
in the 1992 general election and we had a net gain of
forty-two seats across the country, but it was not
enough and the Tories seemed immovable. I had
visions of spending my remaining years looking at
them sitting on the Government benches.

There was no denying Major's achievement. He
had risen through the ranks from backbencher to
Prime Minister in just eleven years, never

experiencing the frustrations of opposition that I knew so well.

Jack Weatherill had made his mind up in late 1991 to retire after eight years in the chair, and Neil's view was that it was Labour's turn to nominate his successor. He said as much when Weatherill went through a rough patch with the Thatcher Government in 1989 and there were rumours of Sir Geoffrey Howe replacing him. If Weatherill chose to go, said Neil, it was 'our turn' to name the Speaker.

In terms of maintaining the non-partisan status of the Speakership, he had a valid point, but there is no rule or convention about alternating the occupancy of the chair between the two sides of the House. The Tory whips made that clear when they campaigned against my succession. They regarded the Speakership as a legitimate spoil of office and were intent on having it. They had provided seven of the eleven Speakers from 1900 to 1992 and saw no reason why they should not have an eighth. The only Labour Speakers before me had been Horace King and George Thomas and they had been elected by Labour Parliaments. For a Tory Parliament to put a Labour nominee in the chair was as unprecedented as electing a woman.

Weatherill's unopposed election had been a historic assertion of the rights of the House to choose its own Speaker, regardless of the Government's wishes – a breakthrough I intended to repeat. His announcement that he planned to retire at the 1992 general election left the decision on his successor to the new House.

Jack was characteristically generous to his deputies in his farewell speech. 'The Speaker carries a heavy burden and I shall always be in debt to my admirable deputies – the Chairman of Ways and Means, Harold Walker, Sir Paul Dean and Betty Boothroyd – for their loyalty, dedication and friendship.' Paul had been a deputy Speaker for ten years, longer than anybody else since the post was created in 1902. He retired at the election and was made Lord Dean of Harptree.

Harold Walker and I were thus left as the survivors of Weatherill's team, both of us re-elected Labour MPs and both of us ambitious. Only two years older than me, Harold entered the House nine years before me at his first attempt. During my years in the wilderness he served as a minister in three Labour governments and was Jack's chief deputy. There was no question that seniority was on his side and he was a capable and well-liked deputy Speaker.

My advantages were that I was better known outside the House and had a stronger party record as a member of the National Executive. I also had the leader's backing and strong support in other parties. My service to the chair was not to be sniffed at, either. I had presided regularly over the whole House as a deputy Speaker for five years and had chaired many of its standing committees for eight years before that.

The frustrating years of being told I was too young, or not in the right trade union, or the token woman on somebody's list where the decision had already been made were over. Margaret Thatcher had broken the biggest gender barrier in politics when she became leader of the Conservative Party and Prime Minister. With my party's support and a general mood that the House – and not the Government – should decide who it wanted for Speaker, I was well placed. I had been regarded as a likely candidate for the chair for years. While I could neither deny nor confirm it while I was deputy Speaker, there was no rule preventing me from having my photograph taken or giving interviews about my life and how much I enjoyed the hard slog of managing the House of Commons.

I was sad that Harold abstained when the vote was taken, but I understood his disappointment; his service was recognised by a knighthood followed by a life peerage. For me, there could be no turning back. Terry Lancaster, a distinguished journalist and an old friend, agreed to help, advise me and draft my speech accepting nomination. We had known each other since our young days on the left of the party and his professionalism was invaluable.

Any prospect of my succeeding Weatherill without a fight evaporated as the Tory victory in the 1992 general election became clear. Michael Cocks and I knew that despite everything Neil had done to make the party electable again, we had no chance. For us, the encouraging opinion polls and the extravaganza of the Sheffield rally were noises off. The gap was still too wide. I had one of the safest Labour seats in the country, but had lost too many elections to take anything for granted and fought my usual flat-out campaign. As John Major named his new Government, I flew to Paris for a much-needed break.

The Tory party's astonishment at Major's victory revealed itself in their tardiness in putting up a candidate against me. The longer they dillied and dallied, the more serious my chances were reckoned to be.

I might have retired in 1992 and gone to the House of Lords then. Life peerages had been awarded for less service than mine and I would have been a genuine 'working peer', unlike some of those who have donned ermine and subsequently dodged the column. That would have been preferable to becoming a backbencher in the Commons again, if I ran for the Speakership and lost.

I could not have faced that. I had not voted in divisions or made controversial speeches in the House for five years. My heart was with Labour as deputy Speaker, but my duty was to the whole House and I fulfilled it to the best of my abilities. I would not have found it easy to become partisan again, nor would I have enjoyed trying. When I became Speaker the divorce was complete. I was not even allowed to be an individual member of the Labour Party, although I was, curiously, allowed to retain my membership of my union – the General and Municipal Workers (now the GMB).

My sole remaining ambition was to use my experience and convictions about the proper role of Parliament for the benefit of the whole House of Commons, regardless of party. John Biffen, one of the most respected Tory Members of the House, shared my views. He called me before the general election to urge me to run for the Speakership, whichever party formed the Government. As an ex-Leader of the Commons, sacked by Thatcher for becoming a 'semi-detached member' of her Cabinet, his integrity was beyond doubt and his judgement on the Speakership carried weight.

Having him on my side was a bonus. In a House with an overall Tory majority, I stood no chance without some Tory support. Biffen's courage in openly supporting me was an excellent basis for getting that. His case for me was simple: he believed the country needed a Speaker who would represent the interests of the House and protect its rights against the executive. He saw it as a choice between a 'People's Speaker' and a 'Patronage Speaker' – the latter being a Government nominee chosen for services rendered and, possibly, services yet to come. When Sir Russell Johnston, the veteran Liberal Democrat MP, and others outside the Labour Party also urged me to stand, it became clear that the Tory whips would have trouble stopping me.

They were bound to try, of course. As speculation about my candidacy grew, the Tory old guard became more determined to put anybody but me in Weatherill's vacant chair. John Major's view was less clear. It was reported that he wanted a Tory Speaker, but would leave it to the House. He may have recalled Thatcher's failure to block Weatherill's election and decided to steer clear of the whole business.

My personal relations with Major were always cordial after I became Speaker and he abstained in the vote, as did Richard Ryder, his Chief Whip. Ryder's hostility however was never in doubt. It marred our relationship and made the good running of the House more difficult than it need have been for the next three years.

The new Parliament met on 27 April with some notable absentees. Margaret Thatcher, Michael Foot, Denis Healey, Geoffrey Howe, David Owen and Norman Tebbit had all retired. Chris Patten, soon to become the last British Governor of Hong Kong, had lost his seat. Labour was left with only two ex-Cabinet ministers on its front bench – John Smith and Roy Hattersley.

The government's majority of twenty-one over all other parties meant that it could expect to get its legislation through and, unless it lost eleven seats in by-elections, would last the full five-year course, if that was what Major wanted. The other proviso was Tory-party unity. If eleven or more Tories rebelled on a contentious issue that united all the Opposition factions, the Government would find itself in trouble. And so it proved.

My chances of becoming Speaker depended on exactly that scenario. I needed the solid support of the opposition – 315 of them minus me, for I decided I would not vote for myself – plus a dozen or so rebel Tories. Such a coup had never succeeded in modern parliamentary history, let alone one that placed the first woman Speaker in the chair. Undaunted, my closest friends in the Labour Party also rallied round in a way that gives comradeship its real meaning. They urged me to 'go for gold' and I resolved not to disappoint them.

I depended throughout on two faithful people, who accompanied me into Speaker's House: Terry Lancaster and Joan Booth, my constituency secretary. Without their steadfastness, I would have been overwhelmed by the challenge.

Gwyneth Dunwoody was also enormously supportive. She agreed without hesitation to second my nomination from the Labour side, enabling John Biffen to move my election from the Tory benches. George Robertson, later Secretary of State for Defence and Nato's Secretary-General, and Giles Radice, Labour MP for Durham North and a veteran of Labour's internal battles, kept an eye on the way things were going. My team was further strengthened by the support of Frank Dobson, later Secretary of State for Health and the unfortunate casualty of Labour's muddle in the London mayoralty elections, and Norman Godman, Labour MP for Greenock and Port Glasgow.

Whatever happened, I resolved not to back down to suit the Tory grandees. The rules of the House – Standing Order No. 1 – provide for the election of the Speaker and nobody could dispute them. Sir Edward Heath, the Father of the House and former Prime Minister, would preside over the election and guarantee fair play.

Not for the last time during that tempestuous Parliament, the Tory whips were all at sea. They could have beaten me by the ordinary rules of parliamentary warfare, but were outmanoeuvred from the start. Even Northern Ireland's MPs, who seldom agree on anything, joined forces across the sectarian divide to support me. Willie Ross, Ulster Unionist MP for Londonderry East, and Eddie McGrady, SDLP Member for Down South on the anti-Unionist side, were supportive. Ian Paisley, the outspoken Protestant leader of the Democratic Unionist Party, said publicly that he dared not go home to his wife and three daughters unless he voted for me.

The Tory whips found lobbying difficult. Many MPs stayed in their constituencies until the new Parliament met and 160 of them were newcomers who found the election of a Speaker a mysterious event. That made an early decision about the Tory nominee all the more important. Mysteriously, it did not materialise. Nobody knew whom Tory MPs were supposed to work for, because it had not been decided. It seemed as if the vacant Speakership had not registered with the Tory leadership until it was too late to do much about it. It was 1983 all over again. If Thatcher had still been active in the Commons, Biffen's open support for me might have spurred her to rally the Tories against me more effectively than the whips did. Mrs Thatcher and I barely knew each other personally. We differed over Europe and I opposed her South African policy in the 1980s. But without her and Tebbit the Tory right were temporarily leaderless, which suited me – and, I suspect, John Major.

So I was strongly placed on my return from a short Easter break. Everything depended on finding enough Tories who would ignore their whips. I could not believe my luck at their disarray. They were the party with the reputation for fixing everything behind the scenes, in contrast to Labour's preference for public mayhem. Yet they were at sixes and sevens, agonising over who would be what the press obligingly dubbed the 'stop Betty' candidate.

I declared on 16 April, earning another spate of press coverage, which was overwhelmingly favourable. Major, it was said, had decided to leave the issue for others to sort out. That could only mean the executive of the 1922 Committee of Conservative backbenchers, the officers' mess of the parliamentary Tory Party. There was no shortage of hopefuls. All that was needed was somebody decisive enough to choose one.

While the Government whips burned up the telephone wires assessing backbench opinion, I discovered a surprising number of covert supporters in the Tory camp. William Powell, who represented Corby, lived in the next village to mine in Cambridgeshire and he and his wife Elizabeth were good friends. She rang to say that she had found a list of a dozen Tory MPs whom he was supposed to canvass for Peter Brooke, but had torn it up. Virginia Bottomley, the Secretary of State for Health, who had sent out the list to Elizabeth's husband, never knew. Other Tories followed their own judgement. A new Tory Member said that Sir

Bernard Braine, who retired as Father of the House
in 1992, had almost instructed him to vote for me
regardless of what the whips wanted. He duly did
so.

As my support grew, so did the media's interest.
The prospect of the first woman Speaker tickled
their fancy and made for lively copy. Edward Heath
was rumoured to be privately supportive, although
he said nothing. His role was critical to the way the
vote was taken and he was above anyone's
machinations. He had just been made a Knight of
the Order of the Garter, Europe's oldest order of
chivalry in the Queen's personal gift. He fulfilled his
duties impeccably.

Most newspapers, disregarding their usual party
loyalties, came down on my side. 'Four Tory wins
do not make this a one-party state,' wrote the
Sunday Times, reflecting a general feeling that it
was time for a change. Even so, I took nothing for
granted. The Tories had stopped the pendulum of
politics in four consecutive elections and Tory
bigwigs – whatever John Major thought about it –
were in no mood to concede to me.

The headline in the *Daily Telegraph* on the day of
my declaration reflected their determination: 'New
Speaker likely to come from Conservative ranks.'
Four grandees were put in the frame – Peter
Brooke, Paul Channon, Sir Terence Higgins and Sir
Giles Shaw, all ex-ministers with good credentials.
But which of them had the best chance of beating
me? The invincible Tory machine appeared not to
know.

Major recognised the impending change in character of the Tory parliamentary party before the new influx arrived at Westminster. He and Ryder anticipated a different kind of backbencher, less loyal to the leadership and dogmatically opposed to Europe. Their arrival created an unresolved problem for the next five years, one that he analysed well in his memoirs:

> The older county and aldermanic guard, steady under fire and largely without ministerial ambitions, were replaced by a breed of professional politicians who, as ideologues, did not seem to realise that the Tory Party's survival and success had always depended upon institutional self-discipline.

His fears were soon confirmed, but the new Tory Members were not to blame for their party's mishandling of the Speaker's election. When Peter Brooke's name finally emerged it was far too late for him to mount an effective campaign. He needed time to work on Tory MPs whose support was unsure and I reckoned I had twenty of them, which was enough.

Winning narrowly, however, would have been dangerous. I needed a convincing majority to stand up to the inevitable pressures of working with ministers who did not want me and with Government whips who had tried to stop me. My position would be constantly at risk, especially in the first year while I was finding my feet. The bigger my majority, the safer I would be, not only in dealing with the Government but in controlling the Opposition. The officers of the House, who run its departments, were particularly anxious on that score. They wanted somebody with the authority to keep a frustrated Opposition in order and the seemingly eternal Tory Government on its toes.

Outwardly, as the day of the election approached, I exuded confidence and optimism. Inwardly I reflected on my weaknesses. I was especially conscious of my lack of an academic education. I was not, and had no pretensions to be, an intellectual. I had not passed my eleven-plus, let alone gone to university. I was not, in Oxbridge terms, educated at all. On that score, Brooke (Marlborough College, Balliol College, Oxford, and Harvard Business School) versus Boothroyd (Dewsbury College of Commerce and Art) was a walkover.

I had to show I could be just as good a Speaker without the laurels of Academe. The growing coalition of Members from all parties and all kinds of backgrounds reassured me. If John Redwood, a Tory minister and a former fellow of All Souls, Oxford, thought I was up to the job, then perhaps I was. If I was not, then dipping into a barrel of well-turned Latin phrases would not help me.

To the world outside, the Speaker may appear to have all the advantages when he or she barks at a truculent House to come to order and it grudgingly does so, but that is an illusion. The chair's authority rests on the constant support and respect of MPs:

without it the Speaker is powerless. Were they to refuse their support on a motion to discipline a Member for ignoring a Speaker's ruling, the Speaker would have to resign.

My strength lay in knowing the mood, the temper and the procedures of the House of Commons. I knew how the place worked, by coming up through the ranks in a way no previous Speaker had ever done. I loved the House of Commons more than anything or anybody else in the world. The fact that I had never been a minister was immaterial. I was not running for President, but for the top insider's job in the Mother of Parliaments.

I had another advantage that Peter Brooke did not. I knew very well many of the leading political correspondents covering Westminster. While Peter and other ministers were building their reputations in Whitehall, I spent almost every working day in the Commons for nearly the whole of my parliamentary career. I knew how political correspondents think and operate and how important their role is in shaping public opinion, despite the brickbats thrown at them (sometimes deservedly).

Nobody loses four parliamentary elections in different parts of the country, as I did, without appreciating the influence of the press. Working in Washington in the early 1960s had given me a new perspective on how politics and the media interrelate. I also learned a lot by watching the way ministers, MPs and journalists create news over a corridor chat or a drink in the watering holes of Westminster. As my own network of media contacts grew, it became easier for me to reach their readers, both as I moved towards the Speakership and afterwards.

I probably gave more interviews as deputy Speaker than any of my predecessors – or former Speakers, for that matter. It was a practice I continued, not out of vanity but because I recognised the importance of building understanding and support for the role entrusted to me. While the Tories fumbled over their choice of Peter Brooke, newspaper columns about me generated interest and aroused awareness that the first woman Speaker was waiting in the wings. I did not want the job because I was a woman, but it was an irresistible angle for the newshounds and it would have been folly to ignore it.

Terry Lancaster and I worked on my speech accepting nomination. We rehearsed it, timed it and pondered every nuance for days. For me, this was the ultimate speech and every word had to count. I had to appeal to all sides of the House, particularly the waverers on the Tory benches. Like me, most of them had never held ministerial office and never would. Others, like John Biffen, had held high office but never would again. I liked and admired Peter Brooke and his emergence suited me admirably. He and I came from different tribes, but I always regarded him as a paid-up member of the human race. The roll of past Speakers is full of such figures of natural authority. Peter's misfortune was to try to join them in the wrong year.

The tone of the weekend press before the big day

– Monday, 27 April – could not have been more
encouraging. Peter Dobbie's commendation in the
Mail on Sunday took the prize for unrestrained
enthusiasm. He believed I had 'the philosophical
background' as well as 'the courage and the flair to
carry through such a momentous task'. The *Sunday
Express* reported disarray in the Conservative
ranks. Pressure was said to be growing on Cranley
Onslow, chairman of the 1922 Committee, to
persuade three of the four Tory front-runners to
stand down. A Government whip told the paper
that the voting procedure for the Speakership was
so archaic that 138 newly elected MPs might vote in
the wrong division lobbies by mistake. By 'wrong',
he meant that they might vote for me. But he was
right about the antiquated process of voting, which
inhibited other Tories from being nominated and
caused widespread criticism when Michael Martin
followed me in the chair.

The *Sunday Times* endorsed me on the grounds of
my gender and ability. 'Britain's political culture
remains lodged in a macho time-warp. The election
of a woman to the position of authority in the
House would go a little way towards redressing the
balance.' That was undoubtedly true, but it was not
a card I dared play to an electorate in which men
still outnumbered women by 5:1. As 27 April
dawned, the *Daily Telegraph* reported that Peter
Brooke would most likely be the Tory nominee and
declared itself unimpressed – not with him
personally, but with the whole notion of the Tories
opposing me at all! This was Tory topsy-turvy land

indeed. I had gone into the contest determined not to stand down, whatever the Government thought about it. Now the bible of Tory traditionalism was objecting to the 'specious' claim that the ruling party was entitled to the Speakership as of right.

I heartily agreed, but the next five years proved the *Telegraph* wrong in its final verdict on the quandary facing Tory MPs. The paper looked forward to my election ensuring that the new Parliament would be 'a harmonious one'. How wrong it was.

As usual, I walked to the Commons from my flat. Photographers waiting outside shouted, 'Good luck, Betty. You're going to make it today, gal.' I replied that I hoped so and would do my best.

I wore a red China-silk dress made of fabric bought for me on a visit to Beijing by Renée Short, a contemporary of mine on the NEC. A staunch left-winger, Renée and I usually voted on opposite sides, but I admired her great style and taste, and the silk she brought me became my No. 1 dress. One of its attractions that day was its pocket. It was just the right size for the note I had prepared if, by some chance, I needed to thank the House for electing me.

I had nowhere particularly in mind to sit when I entered the chamber, but thought a place on the fourth row back, near the gangway, would be as good as any. Everybody could see and hear me from there. Because the Commons chamber was deliberately built to cater for less than a full house – it has just 465 places for 651 Members – the benches were crammed, the standing area where Members enter the chamber was packed and the Speaker's chair was almost surrounded. Such close physical contact is a vital part of our tradition. Ministers and backbenchers look each other in the eye. Bad speeches are heckled or, worse, heard in grim silence, while good speeches and the occasional great parliamentary performance are savoured by one of the most demanding audiences in the world.

No other place of legislature was built to ensure there are not enough seats for its members. Winston Churchill defended this tradition when the Commons chamber was rebuilt after its destruction in 1941. 'We shape our buildings and afterwards our buildings shape us,' he said, arguing that good parliamentary debates required a confined space and 'on great occasions a sense of crowd and urgency'. I think he would have enjoyed watching his words come true for my election, whatever reservations he might have had about the gender of the winning candidate.

The sight of Members squashed together with minimum deference to rank or seniority adds drama to great events. So it was on the day of my election. Sir Edward Heath, frock-coated and enjoying enormously his prerogative as Father of the House, sat at the Clerks' Table and announced the procedure to be followed. He said that the proposal that Peter Brooke be the new Speaker would be the motion before the House and the substitution of his name by mine would be the amendment. That meant that I would speak last, which suited me fine.

Suddenly everybody seemed to be popping up, telling us which of us they wanted, and my palms began to sweat. I knew what I intended to say, but I was in turmoil. Peter appeared to have all the advantages – experience of government at the highest levels, an illustrious family, a patrician wit and the gravitas that goes with the wig, in which he would have looked splendid. I belonged to the underdog party, came from the underdog class and was inviting them to break with tradition by electing a woman. Peter, however, stood little chance after John Biffen's speech nominating me. He said later that he had been put on the spot when I asked him to propose me, but I knew the impact he would make on his own party and he could hardly refuse me after urging me to stand.

We did not plan it, but his speech prepared the ground for mine perfectly in its defence of the 'awkward squad' who speak their minds without fear or favour:

The task of the Speaker is to require balance and, above all, to see that dissent is not the prerogative of the lilac establishment of the Reform Club or of those who try to essay what are a permissible range of opinions. Dissent is very often the individual attitude, the pioneering deter-mination, of Members of this House . . . dissent, like truth, is many-sided, and in my view, is often many-splendoured.

Gwyneth's rallying call followed on beautifully. Terry was worried she would sound partisan, but he admitted to being wrong about that. She spoke of my long and hard apprenticeship and did not shirk the issue of my being a woman:

> Only one group have found it very difficult to be fully represented here in the numbers in which they should be represented. That group is, of course, women. It is time we had in the Chair someone for whom we shall vote not just because she is a woman, but because she is a woman parliamentarian whose intelligence and ability have proved themselves time and again in the protection of all Members of Parliament of all parties.

I began to think my turn would never come. When it did, my nervousness fell away. I have strong views about speeches. The best have no more than three points and last no longer than ten minutes. The aim is to leave people wanting more and never to bore them. I knew I had to do my very best or I would be letting myself down, so I did – and it worked. I confronted the gender issue by raising the larger question that lay behind it:

> This House must know that, although having a competent woman Speaker may be a good thing, having a bad woman Speaker would be disastrous. It would be a tragedy for this House, it would be bad for the country, and it would be

bad for the cause of women everywhere.

I know, Sir Edward, that on occasions such as this the House can be somewhat sentimental and there is nothing wrong with sentiment in some circumstances, but when it comes down to basics, the House is essentially hard-headed. So I do not urge this House today to make its decision only on the grounds of the qualities which have been revealed by my conduct in the Chair and by my membership of this House. I say to you, elect me for what I am and not for what I was born . . .

I have been a Member for nearly twenty years. For me, the Commons has never been just a career; it is my life. I have known it in all its moods – sometimes very dull, although even at its drowsiest it is always capable of erupting at the most unexpected moment. I have known it, unfortunately, docile, too, before the Executive. I have known it sometimes mutinous, and I have witnessed moments which are the very stuff that our history is made of . . . I have been a deputy Speaker, but always at heart I have been a backbencher and, except for a period sixteen years ago when I was in the Whips' Office, that has been my position. I have never sought, and I have never expected to occupy, one of the great offices of government.

It is true that I have seen Administrations grow enormously in size in the past twenty years. I have always been aware, though, that it is the backbenches which provide the overwhelming majority of the House, when all is said and done.

Whoever takes the Chair will have one overriding responsibility – to safeguard the rights of all Members.

Peter voted for himself in the division, which was his right, but I wanted the House to make up its mind without my taking part and sat in my seat as the House emptied into the division lobbies on either side of the chamber and filled up again.

Edwina Currie, who later wrote some steamy novels, told me during the division that there were more of her fellow Tories in my lobby than I could have imagined. Writing about me less charitably later on, she said that I had promised her my jewelled House of Commons brooch if she was elected to the European Parliament, as she hoped. I may have done so, but it was a safe offer; I knew she did not stand a chance.

But she was right about my majority. I won by a landslide of 372 votes to 238, a majority of 134. Seventy-three Tories had voted for me, including eleven ministers, and I had the support of every Opposition party, leaving the Tory whips crushed and isolated. My victory took me instantly above party politics, but brought my old party great satisfaction after its failed general election campaign. Labour had won a decisive parliamentary victory after thirteen years in the wilderness. The Commons had charted a new course after 700 years.

It did so with wit and humour. Peter Brooke's reputation was undamaged and his speech congratulating me was a model of its kind. He returned to the Cabinet as Secretary of State for the National Heritage six months later, and I was his personal guest at a City dinner to mark his retirement in 2001.

Startled perhaps by the scale of its boldness, the House watched me being 'dragged' to the chair, in accordance with age-old custom, with mounting excitement. The televised record shows me spurning John Biffen and Gwyneth Dunwoody as they take hold of me in the ancient ritual to remind us that Speakers once feared the axe if they fell foul of the sovereign. MPs around me – Hilary Armstrong, Tony Clarke, Bob Sheldon and Tam Dalyell among them – laugh, cheer and begin to stand. On the Opposition front bench, which is still sitting, Neil Kinnock grins, Gerald Kaufman shouts his delight, John Smith slaps his knees and Roy Hattersley and Margaret Beckett clap.

But my route to the chair does not pass them. Still held by John and Gwyneth, I cross the floor towards the government front bench and walk past John Major, Douglas Hurd and other ministers towards the chair. As I do so, the Labour benches and some on the Tory backbenches stand as the applause mounts. Graciously, Major and his Cabinet rise to their feet and join in the clapping.

The clerk stands, a posse of Tories – including Virginia Bottomley, Peter Lilley and William Waldegrave – make way and I pause on the bottom step of the chair to look at the note I had prepared for this moment. Tristan Garel-Jones, a friend of the Prime Minister's, looks bemused. Sir George Young, another supporter of Peter Brooke, watches with interest, betraying no emotion.

The noise has now reached a crescendo and I rest my hand on the arm of the Speaker's chair, take the second step and turn to face the House. I have never seen such a sea of excited faces and I smile appreciatively at both sides. The spring sun shines through the upper windows. It is the greatest sight in my life, but it is time to calm things down. 'Order, order,' I shout and am answered with a roar of laughter, which I acknowledge with a nod of the head.

I then read the words I have carried in my pocket all day in the hope that they will be needed. 'Before I take the chair, I wish to thank the House for the very great honour that it has bestowed on me. I pray I shall justify its confidence, and I pledge that I shall do all in my power to preserve and cherish its traditions.' That said, I sit in the Speaker's chair to hear congratulatory speeches from Major, Kinnock, Paddy Ashdown for the Liberal Democrats, and the Northern Ireland leaders.

The *House Magazine*, a weekly publication supervised by an all-party panel, described the ovation as 'spontaneous, moving and wholly appropriate'. For me, it was both moving and amazing. The accepted way to register approval is for Members to wave their order papers, stand if they are moved to do so and shout 'Hear, hear.' But there were no order papers that day because there was no order of business, just one item to consider:

the election of a Speaker. That left them empty-handed and, once the Labour MPs around me began clapping, everybody joined in, including those in the public gallery.

My theatrical training served me well that afternoon. From being a member of a crushed Opposition in Act One, I was transformed into the starring role of Speaker-elect in Act Two. Act Three, the royal confirmation in the golden robe of state, was still to come.

I returned in a daze to the small office I had occupied for the previous five years. Friends and supporters crammed in to congratulate me, but I had no idea what was supposed to happen next until Peter Kitcatt, Jack Weatherill's former secretary and now the head of my private office, made his way through the crush. 'Let's go to Speaker's House and have a glass of champagne,' he said. It was a perfect welcome from an officer of the House on whom I came to rely greatly.

The conventions that bind every Speaker were immediately apparent. His invitation did not extend to MPs who had rushed to my room to celebrate. An unspoken gulf had arisen. I was no longer the 'Betty' they had always known. I was the Speaker, who could show them no favours. So I went with Peter Kitcatt and a small group of non-parliamentary friends to meet my staff in the Speaker's state apartment. Terry Lancaster, soon to be inundated with media calls, came along. So did Helen de Freitas, whose family had meant so much to me over the years, along with John Rettie, a former *Guardian* correspondent who had flown in from Moscow that morning, and John Guinery, a long-standing friend, formerly a lobby correspondent and PR manager in industry and broadcasting.

That night I dined with John Guinery in the Albert, a cosy pub-restaurant in Victoria Street. We chose it because we thought it would be quiet, but I had reckoned without the eagle eye of the head-master of Ampleforth College, whom I had never met, who came across to congratulate me. Next morning I presented myself for another little-known ceremony before I was officially confirmed in my position.

The British constitution moves at a more stately pace than MPs may sometimes wish, but I believe in tradition and enjoyed it. Just as a new Prime Minister has to go to Buckingham Palace to receive the Queen's commission to form a Government, so a new Speaker has to walk in procession to the upper house to be confirmed.

It may seem so, but this is no flummery. The Speaker's position pre-dates the Prime Minister's by some 400 years and the Queen's approval of me affirmed the hard-won rights of the Commons as the chief forum of the nation and acknowledged my special position. For the Speaker is also the official representative of the Commons at state occasions.

My attitude to all this was straightforward. Such traditions survive because they serve us well. We have no written constitution, unlike the Americans, the Germans and the French, so we need to remind ourselves from time to time who and what we are. Besides, we enjoy pageantry and know how to put on a good show. My last words as Speaker-elect were to tell Lord Mackay of Clashfern, the Tory Lord Chancellor, that I had been chosen as Speaker.

A strict Presbyterian, who won Mrs Thatcher's dispensation never to work on Sundays as a condition of his taking the job, Lord Mackay replied: 'Miss Boothroyd, we are commanded to assure you that Her Majesty is so fully sensible of your zeal in the public service, and of your ample sufficiency to execute the arduous duties which her faithful Commons have selected you to discharge, that Her Majesty does most readily approve and confirm you as their Speaker.'

With those words, I became the 155th Speaker of the House of Commons. It was my cue to ask the Queen to endorse the undoubted rights and privileges of the Commons, 'especially to freedom of speech in debate, to freedom from arrest, and to free access to Her Majesty whenever occasion shall require'. I also asked the Queen to hold me responsible for any errors I might inadvertently make and not to blame my fellow MPs.

I was finally in business. Preceded by the Mace, symbolising my authority, I returned to the Commons.

Terry had arranged a photo-call in the ornate Moses Room of the House of Lords, but we switched it to the Commons terrace, which gave the photographers better light and more lively pictures.

Calls flooded in for instant interviews and exclusive picture shoots, which I had to turn down. There was enormous foreign interest: *Paris-Match* magazine telephoned to announce they were sending a chartered plane with their top photographers; an American radio station asked to be put straight through to Speaker Boothroyd for a show already on the air. They all received the same regretful response.

Terry and Joan did not even have a functioning office. The room they inherited from Jack Weatherill's secretary had been stripped of furniture and telephones, and Terry did not even have a Commons pass. While they struggled to cope with a stream of bouquets, magnums of champagne, congratulatory messages and media requests and enquiries from Boothroyds around the world who wondered if they were related, Peter Kitcatt took me outside to hear the bells of Westminster Abbey salute me with a traditional Yorkshire peal. I had been close to tears while I stood on the steps of the Speaker's chair as both sides of the House cheered. Now I could no longer hold them back. I thought of my mother, and how wonderful it would have been if she had been there. Her struggles would have been rewarded beyond her imagination. Win, lose or draw, I was still her daughter.

CHAPTER NINE

Isolated Splendour

When the Right Hon. Member for Chesterfield [Tony Benn] and I first came to the House, the Speaker was like a High Court judge. One did not speak to him or see him socially. No one was ever invited to Speaker's House, and his role had no social aspect.

Sir Peter Emery, Conservative Member
(1959–2001).

I LOVED LIVING IN Speaker's House, but the early weeks were traumatic. Protocol had prevented my officials from talking to Peter Brooke or me beforehand about the practicalities of the job. My housekeeping needs were hardly their concern, anyway.

I had been happy in my cosy flat in Buckingham Gate, within easy walking distance of the Commons, but it never occurred to me to work a full day in Speaker's House and then go back to my flat at night. Speakers are expected to live on the premises for the same reason that Prime Ministers live in Downing Street. That was why Speaker Addington moved into the original Speaker's House in 1795 with his family and retinue of servants – he needed to be on hand to deal with the growth of parliamentary business. He was also the first to receive an official salary for his services: £6,000 a year, a princely sum worth more than £300,000 in today's money, nearly three times the present rate for the job.

I, however, had neither family nor live-in staff. By training and temperament I was better prepared for the challenge of presiding over the Commons than I was for living alone in the stately accommodation that went with the job. I came to terms with it, but the enormous constraints on my personal freedom meant that I had to adjust to a totally new lifestyle.

I found this all the more irksome at first because I had no intention of retiring my social skills or neglecting new opportunities to use them in the service of Parliament. I had the position, the place and the means to fulfil my ambition. I wanted Speaker's House to play a more positive role in the life of Parliament and to open its doors wider to the nation and the world, especially to visitors from former communist countries eager to experience our system at first hand and breathe the air of freedom.

Sir Charles Barry, the Victorian architect of the present Houses of Parliament, would doubtless have blinked at my arrival on the doorstep of Speaker's House carrying two suitcases with sufficient clothes to last me a week. The rest of my wardrobe followed when I knew where to put it. My immediate thoughts were for the State Opening, only eight days away.

Jack Weatherill described my new quarters as 'the

best tied cottage in England', in the sense that they were tied to the job. But it was I who felt tied during those early days. When Peter Kitcatt handed me the keys to my private apartment, after a day of great excitement, I felt utterly alone. I locked the door behind me and looked down the corridor to my new sitting room. The walls were bare, apart from sketches of the personalities who had attended the India Round Table Conference in the twilight years of the Raj. Until that day I had never seen beyond the Speaker's private study on the right and knew nothing of the warren of lofty rooms that lay beyond.

I was bewildered and disorientated. I was unsure where I would sleep or where the bathroom and kitchen were. There was nothing of me in this place, so how was I going to make it a home? More urgently, how was I going to manage, cut off from the shops and the ordinary life of the Commons, from which I was now excluded. I had always enjoyed the camaraderie of the restaurants, canteens and bars that cater for MPs, officials, press and visitors. These were now denied me, because Speakers are expected to keep their distance from other MPs in order to prevent suspicions of favouritism and cronyism.

By custom, the Commons tells the Speaker: 'We have provided a home for you – go and live there. If we want to gossip about you or criticise you, we want to be free to do so without reprisal.' The Speaker likewise benefits by not being buttonholed by Members who want to speak in a particular debate or be called at Prime Minister's Questions. So the arrangement suits both sides.

I had no quarrel with that, although others appear to disagree. Tony Benn's farewell speech as a Member approved of my successor, Michael Martin, having 'moved the Speaker's Chair into the [Member's] tearoom', thus breaking a long-established and wise custom.

All this posed an immediate problem: how was I to eat? Until I sorted out my domestic arrangements I would have to rely on food being brought in by others. Through the sitting-room windows, the riverside lights and traffic on Westminster Bridge seemed a world away. I am not a nervous person, but this was different and I did not know how to cope with it.

I soon became the happy slave to a demanding schedule – and there was much to learn. Being a deputy Speaker is nothing like the real thing. I had become chief executive of the Commons, as well as its presiding officer. That made me responsible for a large budget and 2,000 staff. I was also the constitutional link between the Commons, the monarch and the outside world. I enjoyed learning about all these duties and being briefed by officials. I have never been daunted by responsibility. My household arrangements – or rather my lack of them – were my only problem.

I inherited a daytime domestic help and a batman-chauffeur, who made me a cup of tea at 4.30 p.m. They were willing people, but I needed a housekeeper if I was to get on top of the job. The security cordon around Westminster heightened my sense of isolation. Three police boxes stood between my front door and Parliament Square. By the time my car reached the gates, a policeman was standing in the road stopping traffic to give me right of way. Privileged though I undoubtedly was, I badly needed a few home comforts.

Terry and Joan reported for duty and sandwiches and fast food became our staple diet. It was not until Moira Thomson, a thoughtful member of Peter Kitcatt's staff, hit on the idea of getting the catering department to deliver a hot meal every evening – a sort of Speaker's take-away – that I began to eat properly again. I paid for whatever I ordered and eagerly awaited the arrival of the nice waitress who brought my hot tray down the Commons corridors under the gaze of our national heroes.

My independence was fully restored only when Roseanne O'Reilly was persuaded to come out of retirement to be my housekeeper. Roseanne watched over me with great style for the next eight years. She had served in the Women's Royal Naval Service during the Second World War and worked in the Commons Library until she reached retirement age. On that occasion on the floor of the House, Neil Kinnock praised her services and Jack Weatherill and the clerks signed the relevant page of the Hansard report and presented it to her.

She accompanied me on official visits to India, Russia and Central Europe and finally retired a few weeks after my own departure. She chose to return nightly to her flat in Pimlico, rather than live in

Speaker's House. Less sensibly, I sold my flat; I had to find another one in London eight years later.

With Roseanne's arrival, a routine quickly asserted itself and I turned my attention to the decor of my new home. I started by replacing the peeling wallpaper in the sitting room, choosing an innocuous cream colour to show off the paintings I wanted to display. Derry Irvine had a look around when he became Lord Chancellor in 1997, but had his own ideas for his apartment in the House of Lords.

Acquiring the sort of paintings I wanted was more difficult than I expected. Lady Anne Cavendish-Bentinck had loaned the Weatherills paintings from her collection at Welbeck Woodhouse in Notting-hamshire and these had now been returned under the terms of the loan. Jack and Lyn had needed to do far more than I when they moved in to Speaker's House. A visitor described the apartment in former years as 'grubby and forbidding', but they successfully made it into a comfortable home.

I consulted widely about works of art that reflected my taste and at first things went well. Malcolm Hay, the resourceful curator of the Houses of Parliament, persuaded the London Borough of Islington to loan three etchings by Walter Sickert, which I hung in my bedroom. One, called *Cheerio*, was of three dancing girls doing their routine; another, *That Old Fashioned Mother of Mine*, I liked a lot. I was also indebted to the council for the loan of Thérèse Lessore's 1923 oil painting of Kensington Gardens.

Wendy Baron, then the director of the

Government Art Collection, which displays 15,000 paintings in the great offices of state, official residences and British missions abroad, turned down my request for pictures. Her reason was that I was neither a minister of the Crown nor an ambassador and the House of Commons was not a Government building, which made me ineligible. Baffled and somewhat disappointed, I did not make a fuss. The Guildhall Art Collection in the City of London offered to help but had nothing really suitable. So I went next to Christie's, the great auction house, where I saw four oil paintings of Parisian street scenes in their waiting room. I wished they had been London scenes but they were lovely and I was thrilled when Christie's loaned them to me for the principal corridor.

Next I turned to the Earl of Airlie, the Queen's Lord Chamberlain, whom I had met with his wife at state functions and liked enormously. Perhaps the Royal Collection might have a picture or two to spare? A charming courtier, he promised to do what he could and was as good as his word. Christopher Lloyd, Surveyor of the Queen's Pictures, wrote saying that 'in principle, and subject to the Queen's approval, the Royal Collection would of course be very pleased to help'. Could he come and check the dimensions of the rooms and see the spaces that might be filled by paintings? He could indeed, and the loan of four very fine pictures followed. The apartment was thus magnificently decorated, by the Queen's gracious permission. My response to being thwarted in life by bureaucracy has invariably been to knock on better doors. In the world of art, they come no better than the Royal Collection.

After the 1997 general election a number of paintings with a strong parliamentary interest came on the market and I bought some with the Speaker's Art Fund, which raises income from the sale of Commons Christmas cards. One, a splendid family portrait of the great seventeenth-century Speaker William Lenthall, who defied Charles I, now hangs above the grand staircase of Speaker's House. I also acquired a painting by Edward Matthew Ward depicting the Great Fire of London in 1666, showing the view from Highgate Hill, with St Paul's Cathedral and the House of Commons in the distance enveloped in flames.

The threat of terrorism was a constant concern. Between 1979 and 1990 three MPs were murdered by Irish republicans. Airey Neave, the Conservative spokesman on Northern Ireland, was killed by a car bomb in the Commons car park in 1979; Tony Berry, MP for Enfield, was killed in the Brighton bombing in 1984; and Ian Gow, Margaret Thatcher's former PPS, was blown up in 1990. Terrorists made another attempt to destroy the Cabinet in a mortar attack on John Major and his ministers in Downing Street in 1991.

I held regular meetings about parliamentary security and had excellent relations with the police. Arrangements were made for me to take refuge in Downing Street if the Commons was ever attacked while I was taking my morning walk in St James's Park. The police did not like me walking out alone without notice, but visiting the hairdresser with a personal protection officer alongside seemed to me an extravagant use of manpower. So my hairdresser came to Speaker's House instead.

My first formal engagement was the rehearsal for the State Opening, which begins the Commons year with a mixture of pomp, good humour and raw party politics. Trained from childhood to practise my lines and steps to perfection, I approached this event as I would an opening night. It was my first command performance and I did not want to let the Commons down.

The rehearsal went well and meetings with Sir Clifford Boulton, Clerk of the Commons, and Tony Newton, Leader of the House, followed. Clifford and Peter Kitcatt both gave me gold-plated service. Horrified to learn that Peter was due to retire in December 1992, I asked him if he could stay on a little longer. 'I'll ask Audrey [his wife],' he said, and to my great relief they agreed to postpone his departure until the following Easter.

At our first meeting I told Clifford that I would value his judgement on matters beyond his official duties, although I might not always accept it. He said nothing, but smiled and never let me down. He had been in the clerks' department ever since I became a Commons secretary. He was appointed assistant Clerk of the House in the year that I became an MP, and I became deputy Speaker when he was appointed Clerk of the House, the oldest parliamentary position under the Crown, pre-dating even the Speaker.

We had reached our destinations by different routes, but we were both committed to defending the rights of the Commons and making my Speakership a success. His advice about the stress of the State Opening was typical of his measured approach. All he said was, 'Calm your mind and your body. Relax. This is going to take a long time.'

Peter, Clifford and I knew my authority would soon be tested on the floor of the House and we had no doubts about the consequences if I buckled. A strong start was imperative after my defeat of the Government's candidate. To some of those waiting to ambush me I probably looked like a forceful but untutored Speaker, buttressed by two cautious professionals. The three of us prepared to give them a shock.

I recognised my weaknesses. I never pretended to know more than I did, and Clifford and Peter appreciated that. They found me a willing listener, prepared to argue and unafraid to make decisions. We knew it was bound to be a difficult Parliament because of the narrow majority and the unstable state of the Tory Party. But if I failed to keep order and ensure fair play, it would become an impossible one – and preventing that meant more than knowing the rules according to Erskine May, their original author. My reputation in the country also counted. If I was thought to be doing a good job, then my critics would have to be careful in taking me on. If I was not, I was sunk. A weak Speaker cannot survive.

Fortunately, Tony Newton and I got on well from the start and our opposing political backgrounds made no difference. I liked and respected him and found him a straight dealer. My relationship with him weathered all the difficulties I had had with the Tory whips in the early years.

One commentator said that I broke the tradition of Speakers who appeared to be the 'stuffy bewigged defenders of a distant Westminster club'. That was unfair to my predecessors. I merely wanted to open a few windows, not to bring the walls tumbling down.

Before I decided not to wear the Speaker's traditional full-bottomed wig, I took Clifford's advice and sought the agreement of both front benches. 'Never forget that you are a servant of the House,' he advised. I would have been uneasy in a full-bottomed wig. Besides, I had sufficient thatch of my own.

By tradition, I attended John Major's reception for his ministers at 10 Downing Street on the eve of the State Opening. The doors to the room were ceremonially locked and Sir Robin Butler, the Cabinet Secretary, read aloud the Queen's speech. Major spoke encouragingly to his frontbenchers and I responded, feeling a little like Ruth amid the alien corn, having fought the general election on the opposing side: 'Prime Minister. I am honoured to have been invited on this occasion. It is a privilege to be here for the first time in No. 10. You and I will remember tonight and tomorrow for the rest of our lives. I shall be Speaker and, for the first time, you will be the Prime Minister elected by the whole of the country and not only by your party. I wish you health and strength to carry out your commitments.'

Major's programme had sixteen bills, including measures to privatise the coal industry, offer rail franchises to private operators and encourage schools to opt out of the control of local authorities. Neil Kinnock, in his last big Commons speech as Labour leader, focused on the country's economic problems and rejected the Tory commitment to a classless society. But the battle between the two main parties lacked fire and Labour MPs were more concerned with their own party's future than with the Government's plans.

John Smith succeeded Neil Kinnock and Margaret Beckett replaced Roy Hattersley as deputy leader that summer. Gordon Brown became shadow Chancellor and Tony Blair shadow Home Secretary. The next generation of Labour's leadership was in place.

My appointment to the Privy Council followed the State Opening and I was awarded my own coat of arms. I chose as my motto: I Speak to Serve. Some of my predecessors had Latin mottoes, while George Thomas opted for Welsh. I chose those few simple words in English, which I thought summed up my role. For my arms I chose the Mace, Yorkshire's white rose, Dewsbury's heraldic owl and the mill-rinds of West Bromwich, with a background of Labour red. I was given a woman's lozenge-shaped coat of arms because the College of Arms ruled that shields were for men only. They indicated my status as a single woman with a 'forget-me-not' bow on top of the lozenge. I had my own shield – my determination to preserve the rights of the Commons against all-comers.

John Major had been surprised that I was not already a Privy Councillor and had quickly corrected the omission. The oath sworn by Privy Councillors binds the newcomer to serve the Queen 'to your uttermost' and to defend her rights 'against all foreign princes, persons, prelates, states or potentates'. Some may regard it as fuddy-duddy. I do not.

My first reception in the state apartment at Speaker's House enabled me to return John Major's hospitality and greet Opposition leaders, elder statesmen and personal guests. I tried hard to put people at their ease at these gatherings. Speakers have held formal dinners and levees for centuries, and guests were expected to attend in court dress. The dinners continued (without court dress) and I added buffet suppers and musical evenings to the social diary, as well as carol concerts and scores of engagements to which MPs and their partners were invited, along with other guests. I discovered that many long-serving Commons staff – such as cleaners, canteen and post-office workers and police officers – had never seen inside the house and did my best to remedy that.

Thanks to a wartime economy by Speaker Clifton-Brown, no modern Speaker has lived in the state apartment on the second floor and I cannot imagine anyone wanting to. The only room used daily when the House is sitting is the library, where the Speaker presides over the noon conference to review the day's business, receives distinguished visitors and meets MPs and officials.

A. W. N. Pugin, Charles Barry's partner, designed the wallpaper, as he did for other large rooms in the Commons. He died before Speaker's House was finished, but his woodcarvings and panelling, metalwork, furniture, stained glass, tiles, textiles and wallpaper are everywhere. The *World of Interiors* magazine said that I lived in 'a Pugin exhibition':

> She finds the date on a Pugin calendar, fills her pen from a Pugin inkstand, warms her hands at a Pugin fireplace. She keeps Pugin's own china in her cabinets, lights her way with Pugin candelabra, and when she looks up from her Pugin settee, rests her eye on Pugin friezes.

That might sound oppressive, but his style and craftsmanship never palled for me. Some visitors believed I actually lived in the state rooms and slept in the state bed, which was built for sovereigns to sleep in on the night before their coronation. Thanking me for showing them round, one Russian delegation wrote to say that 'to have photographs taken around the Speaker's bed made a lasting impression'. I did not disabuse them. George IV (better known as the Prince Regent) was the last monarch to observe the old tradition in 1820, but the bed remains in its restored glory, with hangings of geranium and gold-silk brocatelle and an embroidered pelmet bearing the emblems of England, Scotland and Ireland. Small children who visited me with friends loved to climb on the bed and have their photographs taken. Visiting West Indian fast bowlers tried it out for size and strength, but Jack and Lyn Weatherill were the only ones I know who actually spent a night in it. They found it a hard resting-place.

I was privileged and delighted to represent the House of Commons on the international scene and to witness the esteem in which it is held overseas. Many ambassadors taking up their post in London paid courtesy calls and this custom increased as more countries became democratic. A delegation from Latvia, only just emerging from Soviet control, was among my first visitors. Some organisations that invited me to attend their events outside Westminster appeared to think that I confined my appearances in the chamber to a few major events for prime-time television and had the rest of the day to myself. The reality was that apart from two daily spells in the chair, I was constantly on call, holding meetings and planning ahead. I was also patron, president or trustee of seventy-four organisations and, I was surprised to discover, an ex-officio Commissioner of the Church of England. That was one institution in which I did not interfere.

Most MPs, past and present, have a special feeling for the House, regardless of their party or how high they rise in the pecking order. Sometimes they turn to the Speaker to express this. One young Conservative Member who lost his seat in the 1997 general election brought his wife and two-year-old twins to be photographed with me in Speaker's House. Sir Robin Maxwell-Hyslop donated his father's George Cross to the Commons collection of medals for gallantry.

My first summer as Speaker brought invitations to join the Queen and the Duke of Edinburgh for lunch at Buckingham Palace, where my friend Patricia Hodge was among the guests. Had we been sitting, I could not have gone. When the Government held its celebratory lunch for the fiftieth wedding anniversary of the Queen and the Duke of Edinburgh, I needed special dispensation to slip away in order to be on time for the 2.30 p.m. Speaker's procession.

An invitation to sit in the Royal Box at the All England Lawn Tennis finals at Wimbledon was another summer delight during my first year, and other treats followed. The Worshipful Company of Glovers presented me with a pair of hand-stitched, gauntlet-length, black suede gloves. Late August found me in a village church in Gloucestershire, unveiling a family memorial to Speaker Morrison, who had a much harder time controlling the House during the Suez crisis than I ever did.

My social year ended with the annual banquet in Guildhall given by the Lord Mayor Elect and the Sheriffs of London. A glittering occasion. The invitation states that guests should wear evening dress or uniform and decorations. I decided to wear evening dress and a tiara, which I wore at every state dinner after that.

At first I hired one, but it was such an expensive business that I used a heritage fund that I controlled to buy a neoclassical diamond tiara, made by Garrard's in 1900, for use during my Speakership. It

had six brilliant diamond pinnacles and what the
jewellers call a graduated form of anthemions
(honeysuckle), each encircled with a trail of forget-
me-nots. When I retired it was sent to Wartski's, the
Queen's jeweller, to sell at a handsome profit and
repay the cost of purchase. My mother might have
wondered at me wearing it, but she would have
approved of my saving the rental and getting a good
return for the taxpayer.

My department not only lived within its means
during my time; it underspent the £5.7 million it was
voted by £1.1 million, a handsome saving. I vetoed a
suggestion that my private apartment needed a new
kitchen; the old one suited my needs.

My tiara may have been nice (although Geoffrey
Munn at Wartski's thought it a little small), but my
eyes boggled when I saw the gems worn by the wife
of the Sultan of Brunei during his state visit in
December 1992. They were as big as hen's eggs. She
wore them to the state dinner at Buckingham Palace,
where I sat between the Duke of Gloucester – a
sensitive and interesting man – and Prince Michael of
Kent, who seemed to be greatly involved in business.

Princess Anne, the Princess Royal, was always
friendly on these occasions and I admired her
greatly. Noticing me looking for a cigarette in the
retiring room at the Brunei dinner, she said that
Aunt Margaret was bound to have one – and she was
right. It was a Marlboro, and most welcome.

Five days later I represented the Commons at my
first Cenotaph service. As we lined up, I thought Sir
Edward Heath looked somewhat isolated standing

next to Baroness Thatcher. Chatting to him later, I told him that I needed a benefactor to loan a piano to Speaker's House. I wanted to give buffet suppers with some light piano music in the background to encourage guests to mix more freely than they could at formal dinners. 'Leave it to me,' he said and was as good as his word. I lunched afterwards with David Hope, the Bishop of London (now Archbishop of York), whom I liked a lot. His appeal to Tony Blair not to call a spring general election in 2001 while foot-and-mouth disease raged attracted wide publicity.

For Boris Yeltsin's state visit I wore a new Speaker's gold robe. The old one was more than 200 years old and falling apart. I had been proud to wear it at that year's State Opening of Parliament, but I was afraid of the damage that further wear would cause to such a valuable part of our heritage, so we retired it. It was subsequently put on show at the Jewel Room exhibition opposite the Commons. I had hoped the new robe would be lighter, but there was not much difference.

I moved the vote of thanks to President Yeltsin in the Prince's Chamber in the House of Lords and ended with a Russian greeting that Douglas Hurd, the Foreign Secretary, thought 'a splendid touch'. It went down well with our guest too, for he beamed and kissed my hand, confessing that he had been nervous about speaking. 'That makes two of us,' I assured him.

I said how much I had admired him for standing on top of a T-72 tank to defy the communist coup a year before – it was 'a picture of genuine heroism, and one which we shall not forget'. There was no parallel in modern times with what he was attempting in Russia, and I told him that we wished him and the Russian people nothing but success.

When it came, the collapse of the old Soviet empire ignited a spontaneous turning to the West. Only the week before Yeltsin's visit, I welcomed three Speakers from regional parliaments in the former East Germany. I decided it was time to change the traditional French menus at Speaker's House to English ones. 'The language of our Parliament is English,' I explained. 'It seems only right that the hospitality I give should be in English too.' We drank an award-winning English wine from Kent: Chiddingstone 1989.

I returned to Dewsbury to be made an honorary freeman of Kirklees Metropolitan Council, the town's local authority, and was similarly honoured (along with Peter Archer, the former Solicitor-General) by Sandwell Borough Council, which covers West Bromwich. In the *Spectator*'s view, I was Parliamentarian of the Year, 'the right man for the job' who 'despite appearances, really does wear the trousers.'

That was their judgement in November 1992. Three weeks later the House was plunged into disorder by a challenge to my authority that forced me to suspend the sitting and then adjourn it. The honeymoon was over. I was about to be put to the test.

CHAPTER TEN

Storm Clouds

*The Palace of Westminster is a theatre of the emotions;
in the glare of its footlights, loyalties and hatreds,
friendships and jealousies loom larger than life, waxing
and waning with bewildering speed.*

David Marquand,
The Progressive Dilemma

EVERY NEW SPEAKER has a learning curve, no matter how long he or she understudies the role. There is no beginner's *A–Z* to thumb through when problems arise. Successive clerks gave me excellent procedural advice and my own private secretaries provided a Rolls-Royce service, but I alone was responsible for my decisions.

My attitude towards the question of maintaining discipline was simple. I welcomed vigorous debate, pertinent exchanges and productive Question Times. I had no time for bores, oafs and incompetents, but I had more patience than I was given credit for with conscientious Members who were not always as incisive as I would have wished. Those who chanced their luck by indulging in unparliamentary behaviour, however, were pulled up and those who persisted paid the price.

Some misbehaved for reasons of their own, and Ian Paisley was one. He knew he was out of order when he accused Sir Patrick Mayhew, the Northern Ireland Secretary, of falsely denying that the Government had been engaged in secret contact with the IRA. He declared that Sir Patrick's offence was worse than a falsehood: 'It was a lie.' In saying that, he broke the rule that requires all Members to treat each other as honourable people. I appealed to him to withdraw, he refused and I was forced to 'name' him – to ban him from the House by mentioning him formally by name as being guilty of disorderly conduct – whereupon the House voted to suspend him for five days.

But he held no grudge. On his return he asked to see me and, full of foreboding, I met him in the Speaker's library at midnight after a long stint in the chair. Never leave a day's problems to fester overnight has always been my policy. Full of beans, Paisley offered his hand. 'I want to thank you for the gracious way you threw me out the other day,' he said. 'I got the front page of the *Belfast Telegraph* and you got page three.' We then had a friendly chat, and he supported me on numerous occasions afterwards. When I retired, he and his family gave me two engravings of Westminster Hall, which hang in my small flat in London.

Members are expected to speak their minds freely, but there are rules that the Speaker must enforce.

Dennis Skinner tested them from time to time. One of his offences was to call John Gummer, the agriculture minister, 'a little squirt'. When he refused to withdraw his jibe I banned him from the House for the rest of the day, whereupon he took refuge in the Members' tearoom and refused to budge until he was shown a transcript of my ruling.

Skinner's abuse of Gummer came as no surprise, given his visceral dislike of Conservatives, but I could make no allowances for that. I reprimanded him again for his buffoonery when he thought it would be a good prank to sit in my chair while I was in the House of Lords for the State Opening of Parliament. I rebuked him on my return, but did not hold it against him. 'I wipe the slate clean on each occasion,' I told him a little later. 'That is why you and I are such good friends.'

He had his own code of conduct. He was the only MP I know to refuse an invitation to a social occasion at Speaker's House. He turned down an invitation from Jack Weatherill, which other Members would have coveted, with a terse note stating that he did not 'get mixed up in these sorts of events' and had set his face against 'junketing' when he became an MP. He could make no exception, he said. Anyway, he had a strikers' rally to attend that night.

Some Labour colleagues found him hard to take. Even Geoffrey de Freitas, a mild-mannered man with friends in all parties, took exception when Skinner once berated Labour moderates at a chance encounter. I had a more robust Yorkshire attitude and acknowledged Dennis's assiduous attendance in the chamber by calling him frequently. He was also a great sedentary commentator, although he could misfire. One of his asides helped make Margaret Thatcher's farewell speech as Prime Minister a great success, when she turned it to her own advantage.

Some backbenchers tested my tolerance in more guileful ways. Barry Porter, Tory MP for Wirral South, asked me to adjudicate on the use of the word 'pillock'. He said that a Labour Member had used it during Prime Minister's Questions and was it in order? 'As I was brought up in a fairly genteel society, I am not sure what the word means,' he claimed. I had my doubts about that, but replied: 'I do not know what the word means, I do not wish to know what the word means, but I find it rather ugly and I prefer it not to be used.'

I was more concerned at the failure of ministers and Members to make their points quickly and allow others to contribute to a debate. I called in Tony Newton and Margaret Beckett and both tried to speed things up, without lasting success. When John Major defended himself at inordinate length during Question Time, as unemployment rose above three million, I was besieged with complaints about his long answers, which prevented backbenchers from questioning him. I sent for Graham Bright, Major's PPS, to ask for the Prime Minister's co-operation. I also appealed for brisker statements and answers from Kenneth Clarke and Michael Heseltine.

Some issues could not be dealt with swiftly,

especially those that affected people's livelihoods. For that reason I allowed two hours for questions on Heseltine's statement about the shrinking coal industry. The clerks were not happy, but it kept the House in a reasonable mood and was the right thing to do.

Sometimes I could expedite matters without saying anything. Tony Newton and I got to know each other's minds and he gave me valiant support. Between us, we stopped Neil Hamilton, the voluble consumer affairs minister whose career ended spectacularly, in full flow. I gave a stage yawn and Tony immediately scribbled Hamilton a note telling him to wrap it up. I meant it when I praised Tony at a No. 10 reception as 'a jewel of a man'. He wore his party hat when he had to, but was devoted to the House of Commons, and we talked freely. I told Major I would miss him greatly if he was moved in a Cabinet reshuffle and Tony soldiered on until the end.

John Major had need of loyal people like Newton around him. Within months of the 1992 general election he faced a widening split in his party over Europe and an economic crisis. Norman Lamont's imposition of VAT on domestic fuel caused a great row and Major's hopes of winning quick parliamentary approval for the Maastricht Treaty ran into the sands. At first, most Tories accepted the compromise deal that he had negotiated at the inter-governmental conference in Maastricht. It provided for more majority voting in the European Council, thus reducing the scope of Britain's veto, but Major had secured a British opt-out from its social-chapter provisions giving employees more rights.

He had every reason to be satisfied, but the Euro-sceptics on the Government benches thought differently, and in May 1992 twenty-two voted against the Maastricht Bill. Three weeks later, boosted by the Danish referendum vote against the treaty, eighty-two Tory sceptics called for a 'fresh start' – on their terms. It was clear that the Tories were moving towards a bloodletting that nothing could prevent. When Major took over the presidency of the European Council in July, the conflict inside his party worsened.

The sceptics began to do everything they could to wreck his bill ratifying the treaty, regardless of the effect on the Government or their party – or the problems it raised for me. It is the chair's responsibility to select the amendments to be debated during a bill's passage. Normally the choice is straightforward. However, the Maastricht debate was anything but that. Its intensity on both sides of the House meant that, if I chose an amendment that happened to unite the Tory rebels and the Opposition, the Government could be outvoted.

With these thoughts at the back of my mind, I went on holiday with John Guinery to Sicily and returned, quite by chance, on a day that was to haunt John Major for the rest of his time in office – 16 September, 'Black Wednesday' for the pound sterling and pro-Europeans. I knew nothing of the drama in the exchange markets that caused this until we picked the newspapers up on our return to Gatwick airport.

The telephone was ringing as we arrived in Thriplow and I was tempted to ignore it. It was Peter Kitcatt. He had been trying to call me on the car phone to tell me that the Prime Minister wanted me to recall the Commons for two days on 24 and 25 September for an emergency debate on the economic crisis. Sterling had been taken out of the European Exchange Rate Mechanism (ERM) after losing billions on the markets – and the Government was in crisis.

A notice was issued on my authority next day in the *Official Gazette* summoning MPs for an emergency two-day sitting. MPs crammed into the chamber to hear Major's explanation of the catastrophe, which some estimates said had cost the reserves £11 billion on 16 September alone. My concern was to allow all sides of the House – and differing opinions within parties – to be heard.

After calling the three main party leaders and Sir Edward Heath, the Father of the House, I called a Euro-sceptic from each side: John Biffen and Peter Shore. The Tories were far more divided over Europe than Labour, but Labour's benches were not unanimous and its Euro-sceptic minority had a right to be heard.

Major tried to quell the Tory revolt, which was backed by Margaret Thatcher and Norman Tebbit in the Lords, by promising to take 'a profound look' at the future of the European Community. But the parliamentary situation was clear. The Government lacked a big enough majority – or the will – to ratify the Maastricht Treaty quickly and the rebels had ample time to fight a war of attrition.

They were not the only pressure group with a disruptive agenda and I awaited a challenge from a determined group of Opposition Scottish MPs who were intent on harassing what they regarded as an alien Tory administration. In late 1992 I showed the limits of my tolerance. I believed that all minorities should have a voice, but they were not entitled to a free run. As the *Guardian* later noted, the last thing I was likely to say was: 'Do as you please. It's Liberty Hall around here.'

Welsh Labour MPs discovered that, when I told three of them in succession that their questions to Welsh ministers were irrelevant to the subject under discussion – a reputed record. When a Tory backbencher then sought to involve me in something he had heard on the radio, I dismissed him with 'I've been much too occupied over the weekend to listen to the radio' and told him to sit down.

John Major asked if he could see me on 9 December about a matter that had nothing to do with the political agenda, but which tugged at the nation's emotions in the following years to an unforeseen degree. He told me he wished to inform the House that afternoon that the Prince and Princess of Wales had decided to separate.

I was sad, but not surprised. It was obvious that two young people who we had thought had a great future before them were parting for ever. When they married, everybody believed they would become King and Queen one day, but they were human beings like the rest of us and things had gone wrong. Many couples start out happily, only to separate or become divorced; theirs was another such casualty.

Major told me nothing in advance, beyond the statement he read to the House, and I did not enquire. I found it strange, however, when he said that the decision to separate had no constitutional implications and there was no reason why Princess Diana should not be crowned Queen in due course. I deduced that this was a step towards divorce, as events proved.

Normal hostilities resumed with a vengeance seven days later when Maria Fyfe, Labour MP for Glasgow Maryhill, accused the Government of being 'gutless' and adopting 'hole-in-the-corner' tactics to announce its transfer of Scottish hospitals to NHS Trust status, a move the Opposition deplored. Ministers at the Scottish Office had decided to bypass Labour's fury at this important change by announcing it in the form of a written answer to a planted question, a 'trick of the trade' to which most governments resort in difficult times.

A running battle followed on the floor of the House that quickly wrecked the day's business and placed me in an impossible position. There was nothing I could do about the way the Government announced its policies, provided they did so in the House first and not on the *Today* programme.

MPs could have raised the issue directly with ministers after the recess, but they refused to wait that long because they knew the heat would have gone out of it by then and they were furious at being outmanoeuvred. So they decided to vent their anger on the floor of the House, whether or not the issue was on the order paper – which it was not. They demanded the presence of a Scottish minister for an immediate confrontation, which the Government had no intention of allowing and I had no powers to facilitate. The debates for the final day before the recess had been arranged long before and were allocated to backbench Members who wished to raise their own subjects. Scottish hospitals were not among these.

The Scots rebels, operating independently of their front bench, who made no efforts to stop them, were incandescent. What should have been a low-key, reflective day gave them a golden opportunity to create mayhem and bring Parliament to its knees. Clifford Boulton and I noted how they competed to raise the temperature with repeated points of order.

Michael Morris, my deputy, was in the chair when a group of them rushed from their places to stand in front of the Mace – a flagrant breach of the rules. Michael had no option but to suspend the sitting, but he did so for just five minutes, which gave me no time to summon the Chief Whips and instruct them to control the situation.

The rebels were still facing the chair when I entered but reluctantly returned to their places when I refused to listen to them until they did. Members may not speak in the well of the chamber, and to demonstrate in front of the Mace is a parliamentary sacrilege.

My appeals for order were just as fruitless as

Michael's, so I suspended the sitting again, this time for forty minutes. It was clear that the Scots intended to sabotage the day's remaining business, so I decided to bring the proceedings to a swift halt and send everybody off for their holidays. It was either that or a demeaning, dragged-out row with a group of backbench hotheads – and I had no intention of indulging them.

I returned to the chamber, briskly reported the Queen's approval of three acts we had recently passed and adjourned the House until 11 January. With that, I got up and left, leaving the rebels gawping. Maria Fyfe was on her feet, trying to raise yet another point of order, but the House was up and I was off.

Richard Ryder, the Government Chief Whip, was livid and complained that I should have 'named' the rebels for disorderly conduct, a move that requires a vote to suspend them from the House. No Speaker has ever lost such a vote, but there is always a first time. Had I lost on this occasion I would have resigned. Could his whips have mustered enough MPs on the last day of the year, in a thinly attended House, to support me on a motion to discipline them?

I did not think so. Whitehall was awash with Christmas parties and Ryder's claim that there were enough ministers around to support me in the division lobbies was nonsense. Defeat would have meant a rebel victory over the chair and the rules of the House, making my position untenable. I could not have survived. I did not want to rely on the

Government's payroll anyway. Many ministers had not voted for me to become Speaker and I was not going to put myself in their hands now.

Stopping the rebels in their tracks pleased nobody. Derek Foster, the Opposition Chief Whip, was as aggrieved as Ryder. He complained that I had abandoned a Labour-sponsored debate that was billed to round off the day's business. But he had done nothing to contain the rebels and I was unrepentant.

Clifford Boulton sent me a full report four days later, setting out the facts of what had happened and making recommendations. The clerks had learned during Michael Morris's suspension of the sitting that the rebels were 'already deeply committed to creating disorder' unless the Government made a statement. In addition, neither the Government nor the Opposition had any idea how to resolve the problem. Clifford also believed there were unlikely to be sufficient MPs present in the House on its last day to support a move to suspend the rebels. Irvine Patnick, the duty Government whip, had agreed with this assessment (although later he changed his tune). Clifford's conclusion was that if I had allowed the sitting to continue, there would have been even more disorder and that any attempt to 'name' the rebels would simply have made matters worse.

'Such was the mood,' he reported, 'that there would have been obstruction in the [Division] Lobbies and on the Floor of a worse kind than we saw.' By failing to make a statement about its policy on Scottish hospitals at the start of business, the

Government had shut the door. The shambles that followed was a classic example of how a government's attempt to escape criticism can cause chaos and push the Speaker into the eye of the storm.

I endorsed Clifford's assessment and handed copies to both sides. He concluded: first, that suspensions for disorder should never be for a period of less than fifteen minutes and that both Chief Whips should report to the Speaker immediately that happened; second, the Speaker's 'naming' of Members was only likely to work when an individual or a small group was involved and, when a determined group disrupted proceedings, the dignity of the House was best protected by suspension or adjournment; finally, responsibility for preventing disorder of the sort staged on 16 December should rest primarily with the colleagues of the disorderly Members – in other words, peer pressure.

I had a fretful Christmas worrying about it all and noted in my diary: 'Protest is fine. That is what the Commons is about, but the Scots went too far.' I left for Namibia for the Commonwealth Speakers' Conference and returned determined to prevent more disorder by the Scots or anybody else. This depended on the Labour leadership getting a grip on its Scottish troublemakers. But would they?

When the House resumed, I called in John Smith, Margaret Beckett and Derek Foster and asked John if he was going to take his rebels on. He said he could not. He could talk with Labour moderates but could do nothing with John McAllion (Dundee

East), George Galloway (Glasgow Hillhead) and those MPs he called 'Scotland United'.

In that case, I said, I would deal with them myself, but I demanded his full support and that of the Parliamentary Labour Party if it came to a showdown. John said I would get it, but I doubted that if the issue involved the Government's plans for the Rosyth Shipyard. Foster claimed that he was not alerted to backbench demonstrations, but he looked uneasy and, when I demanded to be kept informed about forthcoming demonstrations, John instructed him to do so. John also said he would talk to Ian Lang, the Scottish Secretary, about being so provocative.

I raised the separate problem of Ann Clwyd, Labour's shadow National Heritage Secretary, who insisted on parking her car in Speaker's Court, against the rules. John laughed and said it was easier to deal with Scotland United than with Ann Clwyd, so that was another matter for me. I noted in my diary: 'John Smith is not interested or can't control members of the PLP or his own Shadow Cabinet.'

On 12 January 1993 I called in Tony Newton and Richard Ryder to talk over the Scots revolt. I made it clear to Ryder that ministers would not have been able to support me in a Christmas division, and Newton backed me up, saying that many ministers had been at parties and one group had been at the Palace. Both men had been aware of impending trouble, but had not informed my office or me. As I had done with Labour, I insisted on being informed in future.

Afterwards I met John Home Robertson, MP for East Lothian – who sent me a feeble apology for his role in the demonstration – and two Scottish frontbenchers: Alistair Darling and Donald Dewar. Donald confirmed my suspicion that I could not rely on Scots moderates if Rosyth's future was the issue. Fortunately it never came to that.

On Members' first day back I condemned the rebels, deploring their 'extreme selfishness' in preventing important issues from being discussed, and added: 'I trust that I shall have the active support of honourable Members in all quarters of the House in my determination that such an outrage – which is what I consider it to be – against the long tradition of freedom of speech in the House shall never be repeated.'

I also dealt with Ann Clwyd by warning her that, if she parked in Speaker's Court again, she would not be able to move her car. She listened in silence to my admonition and never gave any further trouble. George Thomas wrote encouragingly from Cape Town:

Never forget, Betty, the Speaker cannot afford to be defeated behind the scenes, any more than in the public eye. I was thrilled to see that you leave no one in doubt about who is in charge.

Nicolas Bevan joined me after Easter as my private secretary and head of the Speaker's Office. We worked closely for seven years and my confidence in him was amply rewarded. All the candidates for the job were first-class and three of them would have done it superbly. I chose Nicolas because he was cautious and not impetuous and thus balanced my own temperament. I judged that he was also as tough as nails, which meant we could work well together. His professionalism and background were impeccable and his references and CV faultless.

He confessed later to having doubted his ability to do the job when he was working with Peter Kitcatt and to having been tempted to quit. The throng of Members in the chamber overwhelmed him at first and he feared he would let me down by not knowing the names of those who stood, hoping I would call them. Identifying those who try to 'catch the Speaker's eye' is a vital part of the private secretary's duty, as he stands by the Speaker's chair, watching closely as Members jump up and down.

Nicolas's memory for names proved much better than mine and he soon overcame his apprehension of a full and noisy chamber. He proved a brilliant success, as I knew he would. When a few Labour frontbenchers had the temerity to question my choice, on the spurious grounds that Nicolas had worked closely with Conservative ministers as a civil servant at the Ministry of Defence, I sent them packing. I told one, who went on to hold high office, that I could not believe he could be so stupid.

The House was in jovial form for my first anniversary on 27 April 1993. George Foulkes called 'Order', which is of course my prerogative, and I retorted: 'There is no vacancy here. The House will recall I was elected just a year ago today.'

Writing in *The Times*, Matthew Parris rather humorously summed up my first year's performance thus:

> All at once, Betty Boothroyd appeals to affection for Mum, deference to Miss, fear of Madam, and a male eye for Mademoiselle. A woman can be cross and men will take it. They do not see it as a challenge. When Miss Boothroyd barks her reprimand, the working-class machismo of a score of Labour MPs from northern coalfields, and the pride of a dozen Glaswegian Jimmies, is not threatened – as it would be by a Tory brigadier or a Labour sergeant major. They grumble, but they take it. They remember the doughty schoolmistresses of their childhood. When she appeals for order, the chivalrous instinct of a hundred public school boys on the Tory benches leaps to her support . . . If MPs do not actually queue before the Speaker's Chair with apples for the teacher, it is only because the rules forbid the bringing of food into the chamber.

John Biffen assessed my first year from a different perspective. 'She has a strong reverence for the traditions and institutions of Parliament. She enjoys the job and knows it is to provide the authority and framework essential for its smooth running.'

That smooth running was soon threatened by renewed hostilities over Europe. Opposition leaders signed an amendment to remove the British opt-out to the social chapter and the Conservative Party began to buckle under the strain. Tensions had risen when Michael Morris allowed a debate in the committee stage of the Maastricht Bill on the social provisions of the treaty, but then refused a vote. He was much respected and had gone to great trouble to accommodate both sides of the argument. His ruling against a vote, however, was too much for Tony Benn, who tabled a motion regretting it and inviting Morris to reconsider. It was the first time the chair had been criticised in this way for twenty years.

Tony refused my appeal to withdraw his motion and its defeat by 450 votes to eighty-one was scant comfort. Four members of my Chairmen's Panel failed to support Michael in the division lobby – Ann Winterton, Gwyneth Dunwoody, Roy Hughes and Frank Cook. I wrote to each of them expressing my disappointment and Gwyneth resigned. Frank, who explained that he had been unwell, did the same and so did Roy, who said that he had abstained on grounds of conscience. But I refused their resignations, which I had not sought. It was time to close ranks again.

Michael Morris's ruling was not binding, but it placed me in an awkward position. For obvious reasons the Government did not want a vote on the provisions in the social chapter of the treaty: it would unite the Opposition parties and incite its own rebels to make fresh mischief. But I could not be swayed by party considerations. I was not above politics, but I had removed myself from party strife. All that concerned me were the rights of Parliament.

Even so, I was aware there were sufficient Tory rebels to defeat the Government if I allowed a vote. The timing – 5 May – was doubly embarrassing, because it came on the eve of the county council elections and a critical parliamentary by-election at Newbury the next day, which the Tories badly needed to win. Setting all such considerations aside, I decided to allow a vote on three grounds.

First: the issue had not been properly and fully debated in the bill's committee stage and the Government's critics were entitled to a proper debate. Second: the Government had only itself to blame if it could not win a majority on such a critical issue. Third: there was no harm in having a proper debate because the government had said that a vote to include the social chapter in the treaty was meaningless, since the treaty had been negotiated on a special basis for Britain and gave us an opt-out.

Exceptionally, I allowed myself to be lobbied before reaching my decision. Clifford Boulton advised me that there were no clear guidelines on this, but I thought it was right to listen to the various arguments in the privacy of my office. The historical reason for my exclusion from the animated social scene on the terrace below my sitting room was never clearer than it was during the Maastricht crisis.

Two sceptics – Michael Spicer and Christopher Gill – argued for the rebel amendment to be heard, while Jack Cunningham, George Robertson and Derek Foster lobbied for the Opposition amendment. I listened but said nothing. That encouraged the press to deduce that I was agonising over my decision.

I was doing no such thing. I retired to my private study and took comfort from the flow of the Thames, which seemed to me at that moment to symbolise the continuity of our long history. Britain's place in a more integrated Europe was, and remains, a sharply divisive question. I had to ask myself: was it my role to stifle a vote just because the Government did not want it? Or was my role to allow free speech and let MPs weigh up the arguments, as they have for seven centuries?

My decision was unequivocal. I would allow a full debate and a vote. I had intended to make the announcement on the Friday before the debate, but in the event postponed it until the day before, which was a mistake. When the whips heard of the delay they assumed that I was having second thoughts and the Opposition added more names to their amendment, to increase the pressure on me, which was irritating. As Speaker, I was unconcerned by the motives of individuals or groups, however strong. I had read the committee proceedings and was convinced that the House should come to its own decision.

Clifford Boulton was the first to hear of my decision and agreed with it. I explained it to Michael Morris and he understood. I had not the slightest doubt I was right. I felt it in the mood of the House and the country. There was certainly no doubting the popularity of my decision. It united even the *Guardian* and the *Sun*, at the opposite ends of the European debate.

The former said I had shown 'earthy common sense' and that to do otherwise would have made Parliament an ass. The latter declared I had been brave and had thrown 'cynical calculations' into disarray. Asked for his opinion, Jack Weatherill said that he had prayed for me. I was grateful for all the help I could get.

When Ryder came for his weekly meeting, I asked him what the Government would do. 'As Willie Whitelaw would say, we shall have to see,' he replied. 'But, Richard, you are no Willie Whitelaw,' I said. Whitelaw acquired his leadership skills by dealing with people as Heath's Chief Whip and Thatcher's Deputy Prime Minister. Like Bob Mellish, he was regarded as an old bruiser, but he knew the rules of the game. Ryder was like a young terrier out of control, the product of a freak situation that allowed him to occupy one of the most sensitive positions in Government without ever having sat on the Opposition benches.

Major also rose from backbencher to Prime Minister without knowing the frustrations of opposition, but he and I enjoyed a civilised relationship. Ryder's single-minded views made a rapport between us impossible. He behaved as if his job were to stand 'no nonsense' from the House. I was not alone in my opinion; others whose judgement I valued despaired of his tunnel vision.

Faced with certain defeat, the Government ran for cover and accepted Labour's amendment in favour of the social chapter on the grounds that it made no legal difference to the treaty. Politically, of

resigned as a Northern Ireland minister, from breaching our *sub judice* rule by delving into the tangled legal background to his departure from the Government.

MPs may say anything in the chamber under the protection of parliamentary privilege, so we have a self-denying ordinance to say nothing that might interfere with the course of justice. It is an important constitutional rule that we impose on ourselves. We make the laws and leave it to the courts to apply them. Outside the Commons, of course, no one may say anything that prejudices an accused person from receiving a fair trial, without breaking the law.

My problem was that Mates's resignation was unlike others because of its legal undertones. He quit after the disclosure of his friendship with Asil Nadir, a businessman who fled to Turkish-occupied north Cyprus charged with serious fraud offences connected with his Polly Peck group. I was anxious that nothing said should prejudice Nadir's standing trial at some future date.

On the day of his statement, I had difficulty tracking Mates down to reassure myself on this point. I reached him by telephone less than an hour before we began. He assured me he would say nothing that was legally prejudicial, and read me an extract which emphasised that it was for the courts to decide whether Nadir was innocent or guilty. Hearing that, I was content.

I had little choice: ministers' resignation speeches are not vetted in advance. They are usually political statements – unlike the personal statements by

Members on matters affecting their reputation. So I was taken aback when Mates began to give a crowded House his views on the way Nadir's case had been handled, accusing the Serious Fraud Office of exerting improper pressure on a judge and alleging conspiracy and collusion.

Such speeches are normally heard in silence, but I called him to order as soon as I suspected he was straying into dangerous territory. When I urged him 'not to follow in detail the line on which he now appears to be embarking', Mates replied that a senior lawyer had looked at his speech.

Had he told me during our telephone conversation that his comments were so sensitive that they required legal approval, I would have insisted on seeing his speech and showing it to my own counsel. I warned Mates a third time that the *sub judice* rule must be observed, but he said he was 'simply reporting to the House some aspects of the handling of the case' and that this had 'nothing to do with what is going on in the court'. That struck me as nonsense. I told him that his comments might well be used in the courts and that he should re-examine his notes.

But Mates was unstoppable. 'I hear what you are saying. Please trust me,' he implored – and on he went. I appealed to him yet again, but he had convinced himself that he was a better judge of the rules than I was. I disabused him of that but asked the House to hear 'a little more'. When he alleged that improper pressure had been brought to bear on Mr Justice Tucker, I told him to resume his seat. But

Mates stood up again and I called for silence so that I could hear him. On a later occasion I was hailed in the press for having 'a velvet fist concealed in an iron glove'. I must have left the glove behind that afternoon.

Mates said that his allegations had already been reported in the newspapers. I replied that I wanted to hear his statement, not what appeared in the press. This gave him the chance to plead that if an MP could not tell the House what was wrong with the system, 'What is the point, Madam Speaker, of being here?' The House murmured its agreement and so I felt powerless to stop him. He continued without interruption, leaving Sir Nicholas Lyell, the Attorney-General, shaking his head in dismay and me reeling from a serious blow to my authority. It was my worst experience as Speaker, made all the more painful because I had accepted his assurances that I had nothing to worry about.

Gyles Brandreth, the writer and Tory MP for Chester, had been speaking before Mates rose. His account is the best independent report of what he rightly calls 'a truly bizarre, uncomfortable half-hour'. He described in his diaries how Mates began predictably about how he had loved his time in Northern Ireland.

> . . . then, suddenly, the genial ramble took a more sinister turn as Mates launched himself on what appeared to be a detailed, highly damaging full-scale attack on the Serious Fraud Office . . . The clerk kept swivelling round in his seat urging the

Speaker to get Mates to stop. She was angry, he was flustered, she was confused. I don't think she was listening to what he had to say. She was just determined to stop him. But he wouldn't be stopped. On he went. It was agony.

Agony was exactly the right word for it and others thought so too. Sir Peter Emery, chairman of the Procedure Committee, wrote to me after the debate to say that action was needed to avoid a repetition of such a situation and that 'the Speaker should never be put in this position ever again.'

Terry Lancaster, who stayed with me for five years as my public affairs officer, thought I had been badly damaged. Publicly he defended me robustly, informing one of my local papers that I feared that Mates's comments could force a trial of Nadir to be abandoned. Mates's allegations did no lasting damage. I recovered, and Nadir is still, at the time of writing, a fugitive from British justice.

On reflection, I was not wrong in trying to prevent Mates from breaching an important rule; my error was in fluffing it. Andrew Marr wrote in the *Independent* that because of the Mates affair I suffered 'some of the worst press coverage a modern Speaker has endured' and that disgruntled ministers were saying they did not like my 'wigless informality'. But there was little they could do about it, he noted. The Government's majority had fallen to eighteen and I had been elected by a margin of 134 votes. 'So don't mess with Betty' was his cheering advice.

The historical balance between Parliament and the courts was raised again a week later. This time I was on unassailable ground. 'Don't mess with Parliament' was the burden of my message to the High Court when Lord Rees-Mogg, a former editor of *The Times*, sought a judicial review of the way we had dealt with the Maastricht Treaty. Tony Benn wanted Rees-Mogg referred to the Commons Privileges Committee, but I saw no need for that. I invoked the 1689 Bill of Rights, which prohibits judges – or anybody else – from interfering with the rights of Parliament. The bill, I said, declares that 'the freedom of speech and debates in Parliament ought not to be impeached or questioned in any court or place out of Parliament'. The bill might be three centuries old, but it is still on the statute book.

Benn welcomed my statement in ebullient terms. 'You have told the courts today, in language that I am sure they will understand, that we do not interfere with their jurisdiction and they do not interfere with our jurisdiction.' He compared my reassertion of primacy over the courts with Speaker Lenthall's famous refusal to Charles I to disclose the whereabouts of five Members whom he wanted to arrest. Benn may have exaggerated, but the principle is an important one and worth defending.

Maastricht, however, was not over yet, and we eventually gave it 163 hours of debate in the bill's committee stage. The crisis reached its climax on 22–23 July, in an electric atmosphere reminiscent of the night James Callaghan lost the vote of confidence that caused the 1979 general election. I took the chair with a prepared statement in my pocket, in case of a tied vote. When that happened – with 317 votes for Labour's amendment in favour of the social chapter being included in the bill and 317 against – I read it out:

> The numbers being equal, it is my duty to cast my vote. It is not the function of the Chair to create a majority on a policy issue when no majority exists amongst the rest of the House. In accordance with precedence, therefore, I cast my vote with the Noes. The Noes have it.

So the Government survived. We learned later that my vote was unnecessary, because the tellers had undercounted the Government's vote by one. But there was no mistake in the second division on the Government's motion. Twenty-three Tory rebels voted with Labour and the Government lost by 324 votes to 316. It was Labour's first Commons victory on a policy issue for fourteen years and the resulting noise was painful. Major did what he could to retrieve his position next day by calling his rebels to heel in a vote of confidence, but he had suffered a cruel blow.

The opinion polls suggested that if an election had been held the next day, Labour would have won with a majority of 163 seats (this was four years before Tony Blair won by 176). Major could do little about it. He struggled on against the odds, but they were too great.

In September 1993 Gallup asked the public how

they thought I was doing. The result was: a very good job – 36 per cent, fairly good – 43 per cent, fairly bad – 5 per cent, very bad – 1 per cent, don't know – 14 per cent. Maastricht and the Mates affair were behind me. My position, despite the sniping, was now secure.

As we prepared for the summer recess, the bickering inside the Tory Party reminded me of Labour's own trauma ten years earlier. On 28 July Major came for a drink, arranged months previously. I wrote in my diary:

He's a nice chap. Isolated and despondent as he must feel at this time, he turned up smiling and relaxed. He is suffering a terrible beating from the press and his own party. I felt I couldn't unburden myself on him as he had problems enough and any I had were minuscule in comparison. So I listened to what he had to say.

He complained about the media, their total lack of integrity and inaccuracy. He picked up a newspaper – a big story about Fergie [the Duchess of York] becoming a UN Ambassador-at-Large, a controversial story. He said there was absolutely nothing in it, all media imagination.

He told me: 'If you think Ted Heath put the knife into Thatcher when she was PM, it's nothing in comparison with what she is doing to me.' The night before the Maastricht vote, she had Euro-sceptics with her until two in the morning, telling them how important they were and they must save the Tory Party and the country. She has never let up on Major in private meetings since she went to the Lords. He obviously expected her public and private support and is deeply hurt by her antics.

He talked about the charade of Prime Minister's Question Time and how he and John Smith disliked the performance. He said: 'I would far rather answer serious questions about serious issues than the number of Sanilavs at St Thomas's Hospital.' He thought it would be worthwhile introducing new procedures to bring changes. I agreed that PMQs were more like the John-and-John Show and a mixed blessing, and had to admit that John Major got the better of it. But to make such changes would be enormously radical and an upheaval. I'm not sure the House or the country would approve. The problem lies in daft and localised questions from backbenchers from all sides. I was optimistic that we would get back to good-quality debates and exchanges, but the PM did not share my optimism.

We both agreed that the new intake of Members was confident and had found their feet earlier than we had done as newcomers. JM added that they were not only confident, but far too many on his benches were arrogant into the bargain.

He was depressed by the constant attacks on Tory Party funding and called it a dirty game by the Labour Party leadership. I suggested the Tories publish their donations, but there was no response.

He sympathised with me over my difficulties with Michael Mates and said he was not surprised.

He said I would not be opposed by a Tory candidate at the next election, but looked wistful at this, as he did not know where he might be at the next election. On leaving, we ran into Andrew Marr of the *Independent* and it looked as if I was about to give Marr an interview. In fact, he had come on the wrong night for a party at Speaker's House. Nicolas rang No. 10 next day to explain.

I spent the next few days clearing up and dealing with outstanding correspondence. The lovely Joan Booth retired as my personal secretary and Yvonne Carson took over. They both served me faithfully, and Yvonne stayed with me until I retired. I wound down at Thriplow for the first few days of the recess and returned to Westminster for an interview with C-Span, the American public affairs channel, which wanted to broadcast a curtain-raiser to my official visit to Washington in late September.

Winding down may be good for the body, but I find it does not have many benefits. I have withdrawal symptoms and the adrenalin does not flow. The American interviewer was nice enough, but he pulled faces at some of my answers and that disturbed me. Terry Lancaster told me it went all right and that I should not worry. 'Comforting but not convincing,' I wrote in my diary.

By November 1993 I was in Richard Ryder's bad books again. At our weekly meetings he was even less talkative than usual and complained about my ending Prime Minister's Questions with the instruction 'Time's up'. He resented the expression, because he believed it implied that John Major's time as Prime Minister was up. I had never heard such nonsense.

Nor was the phrase derived from the language of bar ladies, as some commentators supposed. Instead it sprang from Peter Kitcatt alerting me that 'time's up' as he stood by the chair during Question Time watching the digital clock reach 3.30 p.m. The House had a good laugh when they first heard me say it, and only Ryder complained. I sent him away with a flea in his ear, telling him that I would use the phrase constantly from then on and there was no need for him to fret.

He had enough trouble on his plate without concocting fantasies. Labour's morale was recovering and in November I had to remonstrate with both sides for 'bawling and shouting'. George Thomas still regretted my not wearing the powdered wig, telling me: 'It was the wig that saved me when the House was disruptive; it gave me authority.' But I preferred to rely on my own resources rather than a stage prop, however venerable. Besides, every Speaker needs a facial joyride from time to time and I suspect that a full-bottomed wig would have inhibited my laughter. Not that there was much gaiety on offer as Major struggled to keep his party and the Government together.

The Opposition renewed its attack on the Maastricht Bill that month. The outcome was so uncertain, and Ryder so agitated, that he enquired which way I would use my casting vote in the event of a tie. That was no problem for me because the precedent was clear, as I had shown earlier that year. By voting against whatever the proposal is to change legislation, the Speaker enables the House to keep the issue open and thus to continue the debate. Why Ryder did not know that was a mystery.

No casting vote was needed anyway, because Labour's amendment was narrowly defeated and the Government escaped. A very sick Jo Richardson left St Bartholomew's Hospital to be counted through the Opposition lobby. David Lightbown, a senior Government whip, was so busy arm-twisting that he actually failed to vote himself. I was relieved by the outcome, but aware that we faced four more years of cliffhangers like this.

The 1992–3 session was the longest and one of the stormiest in my twenty years as an MP and there was little prospect of the new session being any better. Eighteen months of bitter debate on Maastricht were drawing to an end, but the rancour that had been generated involved me in an extraordinary test of will-power. This arose from an outrageous display of disruptive behaviour that marred the final votes on the Railways Bill.

A number of Opposition Members physically obstructed one of the division lobbies on 3 November and I immediately sent the Serjeant at Arms to restore order. The division lobbies run parallel to the chamber on either side: the 'Aye' lobby on the right of the chair and the 'No' lobby on the left. Members walk through, give their names to clerks who sit at desks at the far end and are counted by tellers (usually whips from both sides), who then agree the final total. The Speaker stays in the chair while the vote takes place and the process usually lasts about twenty minutes.

Other assemblies have their own ways of voting, some by electronic switches and screens, others by roll call. The British system is rooted in tradition and has its own merits. It puts each Member on an equal footing – literally. Prime Ministers must walk through the lobby in the same way as the humblest backbencher. Members wanting a word with a minister can stalk their prey during divisions. The atmosphere in the division lobbies is usually good-humoured and orderly, but the votes on railway privatisation – like Maastricht – were an exception.

Some miscreant jammed the entrance to the 'No' lobby by putting a bound copy of Hansard across its door handles. Two of the lobby's lavatory cubicles were also locked from the inside, making it appear that they were occupied. This further hindered the Serjeant's inspection.

As a result, the Government's victory was delayed by half an hour and Tony Newton complained to me that a 'constitutional outrage' had taken place. Next day I cut short an inquest on the floor of the House, which would have led to further disorder, and condemned the 'disgraceful behaviour' that occurred. I said I would make my own inquiries and that the matter was 'best left there'.

Richard Ryder thought differently. He sent me a detailed account of what he believed had happened – as he was entitled to do – but added a warning note. Senior Conservative Members, he wrote, assumed that I would take the matter up 'at the highest level with the Opposition parties': a reasonable assumption, but one on which I needed no prodding.

He laid another charge against the Opposition. He said that Eric Illsley, a Labour whip, had crossed the floor of the House and forcibly tried to prevent Tony Newton from complaining to me about the disruption by seizing the Hat – the top hat that Members had to wear if they wanted to raise something with the Speaker during a division.

This was not so silly as it sounds. Wearing the Hat was a useful tradition (since abolished) that enabled the Speaker to see a complainant above the hubbub of Members coming and going during a vote. Anyone wearing it could not be missed, which is why it was always on hand. But as I did not witness Illsley's attempted Hat-grab, and as Newton did not complain about it, I could do nothing.

Ryder had a valid case, but he went about it the wrong way. He asserted that my strictures were 'aimed at the House, and not at the perpetrators in the Labour Party'. What, he asked, could he tell Conservative MPs about the way I had dealt with what happened?

I replied briefly the next day:

I have, as you know, already made my views known to the House about the events of Wednesday night and I have told the House that I shall make my own inquiries. I shall, of course, take your points into account. I shall take whatever action I think is necessary to protect the reputation of the House.

Ryder's answer on 9 November stepped up the pressure. He looked forward to the outcome of my inquiries and asked how I would announce the results. He also wanted confirmation that any statement I made would be clear about 'the nature of the delaying tactics' and would identify the Members involved. He warned that unless I did so 'in detail', I could expect Conservative Privy Councillors – he instanced Sir Giles Shaw – to raise further points of order.

This was too much. I was being harried on a disciplinary matter of which I, and not he, was the judge. The implication was clear: if I refused to do as he asked, the Tories would make life difficult for me and Ryder would say I had only myself to blame. I was appalled by the presumption, as were my advisers, and all the more determined not to yield. From the start Ryder seemed to me totally out of sympathy with my approach to the House and interested only in exploiting advantages. He had ignored good advice on the Maastricht Bill; he had misread my motives in an unnecessary way; he had got the vapours concerning my treatment of the Scots rebels; he had behaved throughout as if my Labour background made me an irreconcilable enemy. I concluded that he had finally decided to bring me under control, which I was not prepared to tolerate.

I wrote to him again in measured terms, which I hoped would resolve the problem:

18 November 1993

Dear Richard,

Thank you for your letter of 9 November about the disorder of Wednesday 3 November. I have had certain conversations, which I trust will prevent a recurrence of the type of behaviour we saw on that occasion and which I publicly condemned on the following day.

I do not propose to re-open the matter on the floor of the House in the new Session, but to keep a close watch on conduct during Divisions following the warnings I have given.

I am convinced that it would not enhance the reputation of the House for the embers of last Session's disputes to be fanned into flame again, and I shall not entertain points of order on the events of that evening.

Yours,

Betty.

Anybody with an ounce of savvy would have known that I would not be budged. Then Ryder raised the stakes by quoting Erskine May, the bible of parliamentary procedure. He wrote on 22 November informing me that his letter of 4 November had been written at the suggestion of Cabinet colleagues, and that in his view, my reply of 18 November was unsatisfactory. Specifically, he wanted to know what action I had taken or proposed to take. Ministers, he said, wanted to know why the names of the accused Labour MPs had not been taken. 'How many prolonged divisions have to occur before the Chair instructs the Serjeant at Arms to collect names?' he wanted to know.

Nor, he told me, did the problem stem from a breakdown in the day-to-day business relations between the Government and Opposition. Quite the contrary, it had 'everything to do with the delay of business and the undermining of good order in the House for which the Chair is responsible'. In other words, me.

I had no doubt where I stood with Ryder before, and my judgement was vindicated. Not satisfied with saying that the Government wanted the perpetrators of the disruption brought to book, he asked: 'Is it not the case that the Government has as much right to be protected by the Chair as backbenchers or the Opposition?'

Ryder's insistence that names be taken whenever trouble broke out clouded his judgement. He also erred in thinking I would be swayed by references to the Cabinet, the Prime Minister and senior ministers, or by his hectoring tone. I made that clear next day:

23 November 1993
Dear Richard,

Thank you for your further letter of 22 November about the events of 3 November. As I have already explained in detail to Tony Newton, I have taken the action I consider appropriate. The activities of some Opposition members constituted disgraceful behaviour and I have described it as such both in the House of 4 November and subsequently in private conversations with senior Opposition figures ... I have made clear that I do not expect a recurrence and I have sought and received assurances that I regard as satisfactory. I have also made clear that if there is any recurrence I shall take action to ensure that it does not succeed in disrupting the Business of the House.

You may be assured that I shall continue to be even-handed in exercising my responsibilities; it goes without saying that I shall protect the Government where it is appropriate and necessary to do so. I must, however, ask you to respect my judgement as to what I should say publicly.

Yours,
Betty

What Ryder did not know was that I had warned the Opposition Chief Whip during the night of 3 November that I would 'name' those responsible if the Serjeant at Arms reported further obstruction in the division lobbies. There were five lengthy divisions that night and I sent the Serjeant to the lobbies each time, after that first disruption. There was no further trouble and the Government got its controversial bill.

Had I named the disrupters after the first division, there would have been uproar and the Government's business would have been lost that night, after a total of 200 hours of debate on privatising the railways and 1,400 Government amendments to make sense of its own legislation. Ryder should have been grateful.

As with the Scottish revolt, there were lessons to be learned. The Opposition told me that relations with the Government's business managers were not working well (contrary to Ryder's assertion) and that there was no direct contact between the two Chief Whips. Better liaison was essential and I asked to be kept informed. I ended by appealing to both sides to make a fresh start, but Ryder was determined to have the last word. He fired his final salvo on 25 November, when he said that he and his colleagues (he mentioned John Major and Sir Marcus Fox, Chairman of the 1922 Committee) remained disappointed by what he called my 'reluctance to share with the House' the results of my inquiries or what I intended to do to prevent a repetition. He ended with a further warning making it clear that if Labour's assurances turned out to be shallow, senior Tories would re-open the controversy by referring publicly to our correspondence.

It was time for me to take my own soundings from the Tory knights of the shires with whom Ryder was threatening me. I invited Sir Marcus Fox and Sir Giles Shaw to Speaker's House. I knew Marcus from our Dewsbury days, of course, and Giles was a parliamentarian of the old school who respected the Speaker's independence. They seemed somewhat embarrassed by the whole affair, we had a pleasant chat over drinks and I heard no more about Privy Councillors preparing to take me to task. Nor were there any further disturbances in the division lobbies.

Ryder's strictures were an affront, but I dealt with him in the way I managed other challenges that are best resolved in private. I refused to be intimidated, but called in senior ministers and Opposition leaders and held them responsible for keeping the rules and upholding the reputation of the House. Calling Members to order by berating them in the chamber made good television viewing, but my struggles off-camera were just as important – often more so.

Ryder's award as the *Spectator*'s Whip of the Year referred to his reputation as 'ruthless and unprincipled'. I put his behaviour down to his being over-tired and over-sensitive. I was in no great shape myself. Heavy with cold, I stayed away from the diplomatic reception at Buckingham Palace. As the *Christian Science Monitor* had commented when I became Speaker: 'The job is no sinecure.' I could testify to that.

CHAPTER TWELVE

Labour Changes Gear

We have to change the rules of government and we will.
Tony Blair

JO RICHARDSON'S DEATH in February 1994 deprived me of my closest woman friend and comrade. Comrade is a term I seldom use. It has no Soviet connotations for me, but instead conveys the finest greeting that one human being can offer another. Jo and I had the same hopes, the same ambitions and the same basic beliefs. The Labour Party had allowed us to express them, each in our own way.

Neil Kinnock would have made Jo Minister for Women, with Cabinet rank, if he had become Prime Minister. However, she was not concerned with women high-fliers, even though she was one herself. Margaret Thatcher presented her with the *Good Housekeeping* Magazine Award for her contribution to women's lives. Jo said: 'I'm concerned about all the women with expertise and wisdom who never get to first base. They're poor, they've got kids and they're struggling to hold on to a low-paid, part-time job. Their lives are drudgery.' Her father was a Methodist, her mother a Congregationalist. She exemplified the nonconformist tradition in the Labour Party.

In her last two years, when I thought her health was improving after numerous operations and spells in hospital, I invited her to recuperate at Speaker's House, where she could see all her friends and be fussed over. She wanted to come, but never did. 'I just can't cope with myself and I don't want to impose,' she would say when I tried to make the arrangements; or 'I just can't manage it this week, but it won't be long and I'm looking forward to it.'

Jo had a severe arthritic condition and for years had taken twenty or thirty painkillers daily on medical advice. Even when she led a reasonably active life there were times when her body seized up and she was immobile for a few days, although she seldom complained and carried on working and travelling. Two operations on her spine failed and she sat on the Opposition front bench with her head bent forward. Her curved posture made it impossible for her to see people as she walked. She recognised those who spoke to her in the corridors only by their voices.

She eventually became housebound and I understood then why she did not want to take a break at Speaker's House. She could not feed herself and became totally dependent on others for her daily care, relying entirely on her sister-in-law, Pam, and her nieces. Tragically Jo's desperation increased as her condition worsened and she returned to hospital. At the end, she was paralysed and lay flat on a high, hard bed snatching glimpses of television and visitors by means of an overhead mirror. 'I hope you've brought a shotgun' was her wry greeting on my final visit. Her parting words were, 'You are my best friend. Don't forget me.' Nor shall I, ever.

I came under renewed fire after the Easter recess, this time for allegedly showing bias in favour of the Conservatives. The *Observer* reported that 'a senior [Labour] party source' had told it that I had become 'a prisoner of the establishment' and was applying 'an iron fist' to former Labour colleagues, while treating errant Tories 'with kid gloves'. The anonymous source cited my rebuke to Hilary Armstrong, John Smith's PPS, for making a din during Prime Minister's Question Time, and my reaction when John Major said that Margaret Beckett had 'peddled an untruth' about the lack of NHS treatment for elderly people.

These incidents were supposed to prove my 'pro-Tory tilt'. According to my critic, they showed that I had become 'over-protective towards an already powerful government'. The facts were somewhat different.

I had rebuked Hilary Armstrong for barracking and had asked her to contain herself. Smith later remonstrated with me, saying that I had upset her and that he was upset, too. But Hilary's father, Ernest Armstrong, agreed with me. Ernie, a

Robed in the State Apartments of Speaker's House

In the Chair with Sir Nicolas Bevan alongside

In my Pugin study in Speaker's House

Testing the mattress on the Royal bed in Speaker's House

Speakers' Reunion. With Lord Weatherill (left) and Viscount Tonypandy (right).

The staff of Speaker's House, January 1997

Wearing my tiara for a State occasion

Dinner with the Queen
and Prince Philip,
Speaker's House 1996

With Margaret Thatcher at the reception to mark the anniversary
of the Marshall Plan at Speaker's House

Steamrolling the Opposition. Campaigning in West Bromwich in the 1997 General Election.

'Madam Speaker' rose

'Which twin has the Toni?'
Madame Tussaud's waxwork.

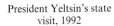

President Yeltsin's state
visit, 1992

President
Chirac's
state visit, 1996

In the
White
House rose
garden
with
President
Clinton,
1993

'I was cold on the outside and frozen on the inside by what I had witnessed.'
Auschwitz, 1996.

Durham MP for twenty-three years, knew the problems involved in keeping order only too well, because he had been a deputy Speaker for six of them. I ticked Members off all the time when the House was becoming rowdy, and my long-standing friendship with Hilary's family and her position as Smith's PPS did not exempt her from my strictures.

Pulling up a Prime Minister, however, involves different considerations. The weekly joust with the leader of the Opposition draws a packed House and a full press gallery and provides material for television and radio news. It was not always so gladiatorial and, in my opinion, that aspect is much overdone. But I had to take account of the high expectations that surround the event and react accordingly.

On 14 April 1994 I called for brisk questions and answers. The May local elections were only a few weeks away and both sides were eager to score vote-winning points. I wanted to deter them from wasting time in doing so. Margaret Beckett, standing in for John Smith, accused the Government of mismanaging the health service. Major replied that she was either 'ill-informed or scare-mongering', and she retorted by alleging that there was a two-tier health system. There was no such policy, said Major, and she had 'peddled an untruth'.

'Withdraw,' shouted the Labour benches.

'Order,' I called. 'I am sure that the Prime Minister will reflect, and I hope he will withdraw that last remark.' Major rose to speak, but the noise

was too great. 'Order. I will have order in this
House,' I declared. He tried again, this time
accusing Beckett of being inaccurate – a lesser
charge.

I again invited Major to withdraw his accusation
that Beckett was guilty of an untruth, but he
ploughed on, accusing her of misleading the House.
What was I to do? Beckett resolved the matter by
resuming the exchange on the issue of health. Had I
persisted in requiring an explicit withdrawal by the
Prime Minister, I would have wrecked the fifteen
minutes set aside for him to answer questions. I
reckoned I had done my imperfect best.

But I was no more a Tory stooge than a Labour
one. I told a Tory backbencher to apologise for
calling Labour's Peter Hain a liar, and I told Hain
to apologise for naming Tory MPs who were
members of Lloyd's underwriters, without giving
them notice. If I erred it was in being too
sympathetic to the pressures that ministers and
Members were under. I preferred short, sharp
action to full-blown disciplinary inquiries by the
Privileges Committee.

When Nicholas Scott, Minister for the Disabled,
apologised unreservedly for misleading the House
about his department's involvement in a move to
block the progress of a non-Government bill, I let
the matter rest. His error made him Labour's top
target for a few days, but he had owned up to a
common practice and the storm soon passed. Olga
Maitland, a Tory associate in the subterfuge,
should have followed Scott's example. By persisting

in her denial, she exasperated the House – and me –
by denying any involvement and I rebuked her for
it, extracting a belated apology.

I also warned Bill Cash and Tony Marlow,
leading Tory Euro-sceptics, not to use points of
order for political ends. And I took John Patten, the
Education Secretary, to task when he tried to make
capital out of the choice of a selective school for her
son by Harriet Harman, a Labour frontbencher.

Labour's turn to be ticked off came a few days
later, when Peter Mandelson informed us that he
had discussed the cost of maintaining the Royal
Yacht with the Queen. I reminded him that such
disclosures are not usually made in the chamber,
but instead of taking the hint, he replied: 'Her
Majesty's private secretary has graciously given me
permission to disclose this information.' That was
too much.

'It's actually the chair of this House, not Her
Majesty's private secretary, who rules here,' I
roared.

Whoever the snipers were, I was in nobody's
pocket and was becoming used to petty criticism.
One scurrilous rumour was that I had become a
quasi-regal figure who invited only VIPs to
Speaker's House. That was quickly disproved. The
records showed that nearly half the House of
Commons and their spouses had been invited to
dine at Speaker's House before the end of my
second year – some 290 out of 651 Members.

Not everyone was able to accept. Bill
Etherington, Labour MP for Sunderland North,

wrote a charming letter, so typical of him,
explaining why he and his wife could not come on
16 March:

> We have several animals living with us, including
> dogs, a horse and a hamster, and they cannot be
> left unless my youngest daughter can be there to
> attend to their feeding and welfare. Because my
> wife would very much like to meet you, I would
> respectfully request that you invite another
> couple to replace us and be so kind as to consider
> us for another occasion when hopefully my wife
> could be present.

Bill was one of a diminishing band of Labour MPs
who had earned his living in heavy industry as a
younger man. He was apprenticed at Austin &
Pickersill shipyard (now closed), worked as a fitter
at Dawdon Colliery (also shut down), and became
an official of the National Union of Mineworkers
before entering Parliament in 1992. He and I were a
dying breed. With each election, more professional,
graduate MPs from middle-class backgrounds sat
on Labour benches and people like John Prescott,
who made his name in the old seamen's union,
became rare.

Trade-union traditions were still strong when I
first entered the House, and I was glad of them.
New Members had to compete for desk space and
many worked in overcrowded corridors and the
division lobbies, balancing papers on their knees.
Finding an empty chair in the library was like

winning the lottery and we kept our files in
numbered lockers in the corridors.

One day I strolled into a small room in the library
corridor and found half a dozen Labour Members
cracking jokes. Bill Blyton, an old Durham coal
miner, asked me if I was a trade unionist.

'Yes,' I replied. 'A fully paid-up member of the
General and Municipal Workers.'

'In that case, bonny lass, you're welcome in here
with us.'

I had stumbled on the trade-union room,
occupied by union veterans. Listening to them
talking about the Commons and how to get things
done was better than a seminar. London's
cosmopolitan ways washed over them. They had
their dinner together at 6 p.m., after which they
adjourned to the Strangers' Bar. They were the salt
of the earth and their contributions on industrial
and labour-relations legislation were unrivalled.
Ulster Unionists occupy their room these days.

I did not know John Smith as well as I knew Neil
Kinnock. We had worked our way up the Labour
Party by different routes, but I admired his abilities.
His sudden death on 12 May robbed the country of
a future Prime Minister. Hilary Armstrong
telephoned me at 7.30 a.m. on the morning of his
death to say that something terrible had happened
and it was not known whether John was alive or
dead.

I told her to come and see me straight away. She
sat in my bedroom, sobbing and barely able to

speak. She had gone to meet him early that morning at the Barbican, where he and Elizabeth, his wife, lived when in London. He had been hale and hearty at a public function the night before, but suddenly collapsed that morning. She was told that an ambulance had been called as she waited in the lobby. Hilary told me that from what she had witnessed John could not survive.

Within an hour John Major telephoned to confirm that John Smith had died. He was very shaken and told me: 'None of us has the heart to go ahead with today's business. Let's cancel it.' I readily agreed.

The House met at 2.30 p.m., when I made the formal announcement and suspended the sitting. We reassembled an hour later, with the House at its reflective and non-partisan best. The Prime Minister set the tone by describing the difficult role that leaders of the Opposition play in our national life, in words that stand the test of time.

'Under our constitution, the role of the leader of the Opposition is unique. It is a vital role – not in government, but vital to the determination of the way in which we conduct our affairs and to the protection of people who oppose the Government on a range of issues. The leader of the Opposition is in the anteroom of power, yet not in the seat of power itself. In that position – perhaps for a short time, perhaps for a long time – he must maintain his party's hunger for government and never let that appetite diminish. He must remain confident and never let the years of waiting sour or embitter him or the nature of public life. He must keep alive hope and ambition and must keep sharp the cutting edge of his own party's beliefs.

'If I may judge him from this side of the House, it seemed to me that John Smith trod that path for his party and its supporters in the country with skill and assurance that few have matched. Political differences are not the be-all and end-all of relationships for Members of the House. When I think of John Smith, I think of an opponent, not an enemy; and when I remember him, I shall do so with respect and affection. When I think of his premature death, I shall think of the waste that it has brought to our public life – the waste of a remarkable political talent; the waste of a high and honourable ambition to lead our country; the waste of a man in public life who, in all his actions, retained a human touch; and, in some ways above all, the waste of the tranquillity and happiness that his past endeavours would have so richly deserved in the years to come.'

Margaret Beckett then spoke for the Labour Party as its acting leader in charge of the official Opposition. She responded with a natural dignity and warmth that captured the mood of the House and made me proud of her. We had been on opposite sides of party rows in the past, but nobody could have surpassed the fondness of her tribute to her fallen leader. She told us that she had been with John at a gala dinner the night before and heard him make an unscripted speech, which he closed with his last words in public life. They were, said

Margaret, '"The opportunity to serve our country –
that is all we ask." Let that stand as his epitaph.'

Margaret was exemplary as acting leader and her
handling of the transitional period between John
Smith's death and Tony Blair's succession did her
party, and the country, great service. I attended the
funeral in my official capacity and flew to
Edinburgh in Major's aircraft along with Norma, a
few Cabinet ministers and others. Major's
invitation to me to accompany them was a typically
kind gesture, which I appreciated. We joined
hundreds of people from all walks of life, including
overseas leaders from the Socialist International, in
paying tribute to John Smith.

The election of Tony Blair as Labour's youngest-
ever leader, at forty-one years of age, invigorated
the Opposition at a time of continuing Government
misfortunes. Here was a man with a good chance of
becoming Prime Minister after only eleven years in
the House. Major had actually beaten that by
becoming Prime Minister within that time-span,
and had held two of the glittering offices of state:
Foreign Secretary and Chancellor of the
Exchequer. Blair had held only shadow portfolios.

I first met Tony Blair with Elinor Goodman,
political editor of *Channel 4 News*, during the
Darlington by-election that returned Ossie O'Brien
for Labour in March 1983. Tony became MP for
Sedgefield, a neighbouring constituency, a few
months later and could not wait to get to
Westminster. 'The general election can't come soon

enough,' he told me over a pint and a sandwich during a lunchtime break from canvassing. He struck me as a nice, clean-cut chap, the sort of man any mother would like her daughter to marry, and I wished him well. His determination – and unforeseen events – showed that almost anything is possible in British politics.

Labour's generational shift in leaders exacerbated the Government's problems. Tory losses in May's local elections were followed by the triple blow of dire by-election results in June, a near-catastrophe in the European Parliament elections and a Labour revival in the south of England. The folly of two Conservative MPs who succumbed to a newspaper 'sting' operation brought accusations of sleaze, which further tarnished the Government's reputation. Blair seized his opportunities and never let go.

Sunday Times undercover reporters asked a number of Labour and Tory MPs if they would table parliamentary questions for ministers to answer, for a £1,000 fee. The reporters posed as businessmen wanting Government information about a company in which they planned to invest. Two Tories rose to the bait and were exposed by the newspaper on 10 July. Labour's targeted Members declined, giving the Opposition a clean sheet. Complaints were made to me that the two Tories had breached the privileges of the House, and I made a statement two days later.

I recalled Speaker Weatherill's advice to the Select Committee on Members' Interests that 'a

Member must be vigilant that his actions do not tend to bring the House into disrepute' and, in particular, that Members who hold financial consultancies must not use their position improperly. Following the *Sunday Times* article, I believed there was 'an urgent need to clarify the law of Parliament in that area' and stated that I would give precedence to a motion on the complaint, without judging the conduct of the two Members referred to by the newspaper. I also wanted the paper's actions investigated under the rule forbidding the offering of a bribe, fee or reward to influence a Member's conduct. I added that the paper's secret tape-recording of conversations with the two MPs – Graham Riddick (Colne Valley) and David Tredinnick (Bosworth) – also needed examining.

The scandal caused by the wider issue of 'cash for questions' arose from the uncertainties that had crept in concerning the sort of outside interests MPs undertook. The convention that Members were in order if they declared a general interest had been abused. Some allowed themselves to be used by people who would go to any lengths to put temptation in their way. The complaints against Riddick and Tredinnick raised serious and difficult issues that needed urgent investigation and I allowed an emergency debate on 13 July. Riddick and Tredinnick were suspended as parliamentary aides to two ministers, the traditional stepping-stone for promotion. Riddick apologised, but Tredinnick did not attempt to be called to speak, although he had written to me agreeing to an inquiry.

The House agreed to set up a committee of senior MPs to consider the *Sunday Times*' allegations and the clandestine way in which the paper had tempted the two Members. I quoted Speaker Weatherill's warning that a financial inducement may constitute a bribe and an offence against the law of Parliament.

Tredinnick was suspended for twenty sitting days and Riddick for ten – his lesser penalty recognising his second thoughts about the £1,000 payment and his decision to return it before he realised he had been entrapped. Worse followed. Before 1994 was over, media allegations of parliamentary sleaze involved amounts far greater than £1,000 and figures more prominent than Riddick and Tredinnick.

In September 1994 I went on a trip to the Indian subcontinent. Anyone planning an itinerary taking in Sri Lanka, India and Nepal would normally start at one end of the subcontinent and end up at the other, visiting India en route. That was not how my visit worked out, and my health paid the price.

My hosts had their own plans for my tour, which did not dovetail as smoothly as they might. Instead of visiting the three countries in order, my itinerary began in Sri Lanka, involved a flight across the whole length of India to Nepal (via Bangkok!) and then backtracking to New Delhi for a full Indian tour.

I first visited Sir Lanka in the mid-1970s and it

became one of my favourite islands, along with St Lucia and Cyprus. I used to go there twice a year to see friends and explore. I went to places now closed to tourists by the conflict in the north and east, and I became active in the all-party British-Sri Lanka group at Westminster. I knew the country's Presidents and leading parliamentarians and loved the cultural triangle in the centre: the old Kingdom of Kandy, the bustling port of Colombo and the golden beaches.

When I became Speaker, ethnic violence restricted my visits, but I continued to go there and the Sri Lankan Speaker was the first to send me an official invitation. I developed a deep affection for all the people of that beautiful country and worked hard to promote reconciliation. Tragically, some of my friends were assassinated when the violence was at its height and I mourn the loss of Lalith Athuladhmudali, Gamini Dissanayake, both ministers who were still young when they were killed, and many others in the nation's public life.

My visit to Nepal, a fledgling democracy and old ally of Britain, proved to be the most dramatic part of the journey. At first, all went as planned. I was met at Tribhuvan International Airport by the Speaker of the House of Representatives and taken to the Hotel Yak & Yeti, from where I went to Parliament House.

Britain had presented the Nepalese Parliament with Speakers' chairs for the upper and lower houses, at a ceremony I attended at the Foreign Office in 1992. The chairs were made by the firm of

Robert Thompson's Craftsmen Ltd in Kilburn,
Yorkshire, and were handed over to Major-General
Bharat Simha on his retirement as Nepalese
Ambassador in London.

As the country's Parliament was modelled on
Westminster, my visit was a special expression of
Britain's interest in the progress of Nepal. After
meeting Girija Prasad Koirala, the Prime Minister,
I flew next day to Pokhara to visit the British
Gurkha camp. A meeting followed with Man
Mohan Adhikara, the Nepalese communist leader,
who briefly became Prime Minister shortly
afterwards. I was then taken on an unscheduled
visit to meet King Birendra, which was a great
honour.

Timothy George, the British Ambassador, and I
saw the King alone in his study. He had dissolved
Parliament two months earlier and had announced
the holding of elections in November. Political
parties had been banned for thirty years until
1990, when King Birendra proclaimed a new
constitution establishing a multi-party democracy.
His assassination in June 2001 was an appalling
tragedy.

Our meeting took place on a dark, rainy night
and everything went well. I am a good listener and
the King told me what he hoped to achieve for his
country and his people's progress. On the way back
to the hotel, however, the ambassador realised that
something was wrong when I asked him, 'Who am I
with here? Am I with a delegation?'

A doctor was sent for from the American hospital

in Kathmandu. The ambassador told Nicolas Bevan, 'She seems disorientated. She was very quiet in the car. She didn't know what she was doing there.'

I regained my bearings when I saw Roseanne O'Reilly, who was accompanying me, but the doctor said I had extremely high blood pressure and was suffering from exhaustion and dehydration. The British Embassy dinner in my honour went ahead without me and the following day's programme was abandoned. The medical advice was to rest for twenty-four hours, cancel my two-week tour of India and return to England from New Delhi.

That night Roseanne slept in my room, and the British High Commissioner in New Delhi made arrangements for me to fly back to London for further medical examination. It was thought I might have suffered a slight stroke. I doubted that and decided that if I could get my blood pressure down I would go on with the Indian visit, tiring though it was bound to be.

Aspirins and exercise in the swimming pool at Delhi's Oberoi Hotel did the trick – my blood pressure came down and my energy levels were restored. I suffered no recurrence of my Nepalese 'turn'. The highlight of my Indian tour was my address in the Central Hall of Parliament House, New Delhi, where British sovereignty was transferred to India in 1947, in honour of Pandit Pant, a hero of the fight for Indian independence.

It says much for the special relationship between

Britain and India that my hosts asked me to speak
in his memory, on the theme of 'Britain and India:
democratic giants'. My audience represented the
legislature, the judiciary, the diplomatic corps, the
city of Delhi and the universities. It was as if our
two countries had never had any relationship other
than that of old friends who shared common values.
My political upbringing may also have helped. 'I
can tell you one thing,' I said. 'There were not many
imperialists in my working-class family.' However,
I claimed better relations with Buckingham Palace
than many of my predecessors, nine of whom
forfeited their lives after falling out with the
monarch. We also worked a lot harder in Parliament than our forebears. In 1993, I told my
audience, we sat for 1,993 hours and forty-eight
minutes over 240 days.

As for myself, I disclaimed any notion of being a
different sort of Speaker because of my gender:
'Indira Gandhi became your Prime Minister in
1966. We had to wait until Mrs Margaret Thatcher
in 1979 before we had a woman as head of
government.'

What mattered more were the great changes that
had taken place in our lifetimes since the end of the
Second World War – the independence of India,
the ending of apartheid in South Africa and the
collapse of communism after the tearing down of
the Berlin Wall. I recalled the service we had held in
Westminster Abbey only four months before to
celebrate South Africa's return to the Commonwealth – an occasion of great emotion – and

welcomed the election in South Africa (where Gandhi's campaign of non-violent protest began) of a Speaker of Indian origin.

In one sense Britain, the old imperial power, had shown the way to equal rights for all. Not long before, I had unveiled a statue at the Indian High Commission in London to mark the centenary of the election of the first Indian Member of the House of Commons in 1892, Dadabhai Naoroji.

What he or the new South African Speaker would have thought of the scene that greeted me on my arrival at the Rajasthan assembly in Jaipur is another matter. It was the first day of the monsoon session and I was given a place of honour in the old Governor's box. The Speaker explained that members were demonstrating against a new item of legislation; they were taking their revenge on the chair and he believed the assembly would settle down on my arrival. My presence, however, produced the very opposite effect. Instead of encouraging the assembly to reflect on our common roots, my appearance resulted in scenes of total disorder, the like of which I had never previously witnessed.

The entire Congress Party jumped into the well of the chamber to thump the Speaker's table and shout slogans against the state government. As their fury grew, they snatched papers from the Speaker's hands, tore them up and threw them away. Files were scattered and microphones up-rooted. Unable to suspend the sitting, the Speaker abandoned the chair.

I left before the fisticuffs began and consoled my

host in his room, but the pandemonium was still raging when I returned half an hour later and I duly departed. I told the unfortunate Speaker that the House of Commons had witnessed many scenes of high passion, but nothing like that. It was a salutary experience. Compared with his troubles, I had the easiest job in the world.

There was no denying, however, that the reputation of the Commons had suffered as a result of the various sleaze accusations, which triggered deep doubts about our performance and practices. *The Economist* contrasted my international status with 'the grey men, the placemen and the hired men' who sat on the benches before me, but questioned whether I was exerting myself sufficiently to improve matters:

> She senses the mood of the House, but brooks no nonsense from the Commons' barrack-room lawyers. Now that she has found her footing, she rarely wobbles. Ms Boothroyd, then, is monarch of all she surveys. The real question is not whether she is doing a good job. It is whether she is doing the right job.

But what was the right job? The *Economist* acknowledged my promotion of better working hours, crisper questions and answers, and more modern offices for MPs, but dismissed these as 'marginalia, compared with the crisis of legitimacy into which the Commons is sinking':

In these circumstances, the Speaker, who truly loves parliamentary democracy, cannot afford to back reform by nudge and by wink. She must instead place her authority and her popularity behind the forces of change to give Britain a Parliament that is fit for the 21st century instead of one stuck in the 19th.

If I was less impressed than others by calls to modernise the House, it was because I wanted real reform, not superficial changes to make life easier for MPs. I wanted the Commons to be the centre of democratic debate in our country, not an adjunct to the *Today* programme or an echo chamber for party spin-doctors.

I was conscious throughout that we could only do our duty to the nation if we maintained high standards in our debates and the highest possible standards in our personal conduct. The tragedy was that though few Members were actually involved, sleaze inflicted disproportionate damage on the reputation of us all.

Labour made the most of the Government's embarrassment and the Tories tried desperately hard to retaliate – sometimes too hard. A leaked memorandum from Conservative Central Office suggested that Major had authorised 'a few yobbos, of our own' to make life difficult for Blair. I deprecated the suggestion; infantile ideas like that were not Major's style anyway. In my experience yobbos, on whichever side they sit, do not need any encouragement.

To renew our spirits as 1994 ended, I ordered brilliantly lit Christmas trees to be erected for the first time, one in New Palace Yard, where passers-by could see it through the iron railings, and the other in Westminster Hall, where the Salvation Army brass band traditionally led us in carols. For the second year running I invited Commons staff to a wine-and-mince-pies party, with carol-singing around the tree, in Speaker's House.

It was decorated with golden baubles, sparkling lights and red velvet bows to match the cassocks of the choristers from Westminster Under-School. 'I know I'll never have as good a Christmas as I did all those years ago in Yorkshire,' I wrote in the Commons *House Magazine*. 'But I'll have a good try.'

CHAPTER THIRTEEN

Good Temper and Moderation

Democracy means government by discussion, but it is only
effective if you can stop people talking.

Clement Attlee

TRY AS HE MIGHT to reunite his party, John
Major was accused of pandering to one side or
the other. He pledged to defend British sovereignty
on key issues, but was berated for keeping his
options open on joining the single currency at some
point in the future. When he attacked Labour's
plans for Scottish devolution as 'one of the most
dangerous propositions ever put before the British
people', Tory MPs agreed, but preferred to argue
about issues that divided them.

Blair's mastery of the Labour Party put the Prime
Minister at a double disadvantage. Sixteen years in
opposition had made Labour thirsty for power and
tired of fighting over matters that absorbed a few
thousand activists but had no relevance to people's

daily lives. From the start Blair showed what sort of party he wanted by ending decades of argument about its core principles.

Under Clause 4 of its constitution, Labour was still committed – in words, if not in deeds – to strive for 'the common ownership of the means of production, distribution and exchange'. The Tories used this pledge to allege that Labour wanted the total nationalisation of everything that moved. I cut my electioneering teeth on that false argument and saw Hugh Gaitskell's efforts to end it fail. Blair succeeded because the old left was by now much weaker and the grass roots were tired of Toryism and ready for change. And the Conservatives behaved as if they too wanted a rest from office, which made Blair's task easier.

Nine Tory Euro-sceptics lost the Government whip and seven voted with Labour on 16 January 1995 on an issue concerning Spanish fishing rights in British waters. There were said to be a hundred on the Tory backbenches who shared their views but preferred to stay inside the fold. I did not have to wait long for the inevitable explosion.

In February the Ulster Unionists ended their informal alliance with the Government in protest at its overtures to the nationalist community in Northern Ireland. I had learned during the Maastricht ordeal that there was only one way to handle an unstable situation that threatened to become uncontrollable. That was to assert my authority, ensure that all sides were heard (including the minorities within parties) and enforce the rules of debate, in the hope that Members would support me.

On 7 February Blair challenged Major three times to declare whether or not he supported Britain joining the single currency. I understood Major's dilemma, but Blair was entitled to exploit it. Major, however, had been taunted enough and snapped: 'Anyone who would commit his party to a common currency before all the facts are known is a dimwit.'

The word had the impact of a verbal hand grenade. Members bellowed, I called for order and Question Time was soon up, but the danger signals were clear. 'Dimwit' is a borderline word in the lexicon of banned expressions. It does not impugn a Member's honour – which is forbidden – but it is abusive and calculated to cause offence. The next day Labour Members returned fire by calling ministers 'nitwits' and using an Anglo-Saxon word I did not wish to hear in the chamber.

I acted before Members dug deeper into the barrel of insults and told the House: 'Good temper and moderation are the characteristics of parliamentary language. I hope that Honourable Members will bear that in mind in future interventions and make use of the richness of the English language and select elegant phrases that express their meaning without causing offence to others.'

An American commentator, probably an enthusiast who watched our proceedings on the C-Span channel, reflected on my alarm at the use of 'dimwit' and on the coarseness of American political dialogue. He noted that President Clinton had been called 'a traitor' on the floor of the House of Representatives. By American standards, he considered Major's choice of words quaint.

To me, however, robust debate does not depend on personal insults and the House of Commons – at its best – is unrivalled as a forum for debate because of this. My disciplinary powers and political neutrality allowed me to chastise the House in a way that other legislatures would not have accepted.

As 1995 unfolded, I was reminded of the unique role that the Speaker plays in our constitution. In May I said what I thought about our country and its values in the presence of the Queen at a ceremony in Westminster Hall commemorating the fiftieth anniversary of the end of the Second World War.

Presenting a loyal address, I recalled the night in 1941 that the Commons chamber was destroyed by enemy bombs and how Churchill, on the day of victory, had rejoiced at Parliament's strength in preserving 'all the title-deeds of democracy, while waging war in the most stern and protracted form'. I went on, 'What were our thoughts as he spoke those words? You and I, Your Majesty, are almost of the same generation. We knew the hopes and fears of a people at war. We heard the bombs, we saw the results. And I suggest, with respect, that we must both have been suffused with the same feeling of exhilaration on that day in 1945 . . . It was a war worth fighting. It was a war worth winning. The price was high. But the consequences of defeat would have been incalculable. One thing we know. Our democratic institutions would have been destroyed; Parliament as we know it would not have survived . . . Truly victory was a national achievement.'

I paid special tribute to those who contributed to the war effort on the home front in the police and fire services, to the air-raid wardens, doctors and nurses, the Women's Voluntary Service, the Land Girls, the Bevin Boys and many more, not least our civilian population, whose resolution never wavered.

Prince Charles wrote appreciatively and I also had numerous letters from people thanking me for mentioning the civilian services, especially the Bevin Boys. They were so called because Ernest Bevin, the Transport and General Workers' leader and wartime Minister of Labour, drafted them into the coal mines by their thousands, young men aged between eighteen and twenty-five who had no mining background at all and were given no medals (and scant recognition) for their essential work. Many were not released until several years after the war ended.

Six days later we were brought back to earth. Lord Nolan, appointed by the Prime Minister to examine standards in public life, proposed an independent scrutiny of the conduct of MPs and the prohibition of Members undertaking paid work for lobbyists. He called for the swift implementation of his recommendations, but reported that he had found no evidence of 'systematic corruption' in public life. I welcomed this because I knew it to be true. We had been subjected to a string of sensational 'sleaze' stories because of the folly of a few Members and the inexcusable greed of one or two individuals. Their behaviour had led Nolan to propose the appointment of an independent Parliamentary Commissioner for Standards to oversee tough rules on the declaration of MPs' outside interests. Nolan warned: 'unless corrective measures are promptly taken, there is a danger that anxiety and suspicion will give way to disillusion and growing cynicism'.

His report ranged wider than Parliament, to include the need for ex-ministers to seek clearance for jobs they took on within two years of leaving office, and new measures to ensure the highest standards of propriety in the appointments to quangos. Not surprisingly, his proposal for an independent watchdog, with powers to investigate complaints about the probity of Members, attracted most comment.

Some Members resented Nolan's remedy, but serious damage had already been done and we had no choice. The public regarded the folly of the few who were caught out as being typical of a wider slackening of standards. John Biffen was among the first to voice the unpalatable truth when he said: 'The conduct and investigation of these matters is too serious to be left merely to Parliamentarians, however distinguished. They are not matters which can be sensibly resolved within the arcane practices of this Chamber.'

The ink was hardly dry on Nolan's report when Sir Jerry Wiggin, the Tory Member for Weston-super-Mare, was exposed for breaking the rules in a way that confirmed public suspicions. He had used another Member's name to sponsor an amendment to a bill in which he himself had a financial interest. The innocent Member had objected and the subterfuge had been revealed.

I said it was 'about time that Members realised what was expected of them' and trusted that this was the last distasteful occasion on which I would have to enquire into a Member's conduct. Wiggin's personal apology to the House was jeered. I confined myself to observing: 'Whatever structures and procedures we have in this House, we cannot legislate for integrity, and Members should act in such a manner whereby their integrity is not called into question.'

That, so I hoped, was that, but I was wrong. I was roundly attacked for being too lenient and got almost as bad a press as Wiggin himself. 'So he has got away with it then?' Dennis Skinner called out at the end of my stricture. This was how it seemed to Labour Members who wanted Wiggin's head and I was pilloried for not giving it to them. The *Daily Mirror* rebuked me in a full-page outburst of anger and sorrow, stating that there was no doubting my integrity, toughness and even-handedness, but that I had 'sent out the wrong message to other MPs who abused the system'. It went on:

> More important, she sent out the wrong message to the British people, most of whom think MPs are on the make. They aren't, of course. But when

one who abuses Parliament is let off like this, it does nothing to reassure us. When even the most respected person in the Commons lets us down, it's a black day for the Mother of Parliaments.

The *Guardian* took a similar line:

At a time when Parliament is in low repute, and MPs are widely thought to be on the fiddle, Speaker Boothroyd's decision is either very brave or very stupid, and possibly both . . . it makes it look as though the political class is wriggling to avoid legitimate investigation.

That was palpably wrong, because there was nothing more to investigate: it was an open-and-shut case. But my critics wanted Wiggin punished for his misdemeanour, and the fifty-four Labour MPs who signed a Commons motion calling for a Privileges Committee inquiry reckoned that the errant knight was fair game. I responded to a letter from Peter Hain, explaining my reasons for not doing what they wanted. 'In the first place, there is no dispute about the facts. Secondly, it is the practice of the House to accept without further demur the bona fides and candour of a Member who makes a personal statement. That being so, it is hard to see what task the Privileges Committee would be asked to do.'

It was a case of being damned if I did and damned if I didn't. My overriding concern was to put the Nolan reforms into effect and end the sort of criticism that Peter Riddell, a shrewd observer of parliamentary practices, voiced in *The Times*. He saw the 'unwieldy' Privileges Committee and its party divisions as part of the problem, not the answer. 'Self-regulation is close to breakdown,' he reported; the swift implementation of Nolan's reforms was urgent. I agreed.

Sleaze had now become a strong campaigning issue for the Opposition. Paddy Ashdown, the Liberal Democrat leader, said his party would not support the 'sleazy, rotten' Tories if Major lost his majority. I loathed the impression that corruption was rampant and hated the damage it did to our reputation.

Whatever new rules were introduced, the health of Parliament depended on Members behaving honourably. What had gone wrong? Sir Terence Higgins, Tory MP for Worthing and a much-respected elder of the House, wrote to me later in the year, after announcing his retirement at the next election: 'I share your concern about the membership of the House. We have a serious recruitment problem in terms of motivation and talent.'

Obsessed as we were with pre-election manoeuvring, an event occurred that drew us together. On the day I was being slated, Harold Wilson died and we paused to pay tribute. Wilson's death had a curious repercussion in my own inner circle. Terry Lancaster, who knew Wilson well, was so upset by the *Mirror*'s attack on me that he refused to allow it to publish a tribute to Wilson that he had written after retiring as the paper's political editor. The *Mirror* had commissioned him to write it, for use whenever Wilson died, but had forgotten to pay him for it. Terry held the copyright and withheld the article.

Such was Terry's loyalty to me, but I was sorry because the *Mirror*'s readers were deprived of a superb analysis of Wilson's strengths and weaknesses. Terry noted that Wilson and Stanley Baldwin were the only Prime Ministers to have left office voluntarily that century. Wilson, he wrote, 'regarded Labour as the only desirable agent of change and even of government and he believed his main task was to keep the Labour Party together . . . His party owes him so much more than it acknowledges today.'

For the second time in twelve months John Major paid handsome tribute to a dead Labour leader. He hailed Wilson as a Yorkshire man 'whose roots mattered to him', whose 'background motivated his politics' and whose 'family's experience during the Depression, when his father was unemployed, shaped his politics, his thinking and his future policies'.

Tony Blair's admission that he was barely eleven years old when Wilson became Prime Minister for the first time brought some of us up sharply. It showed how quickly Labour's leadership had passed to the younger generation.

Back in the bear pit, some silly-billies thought I ought not to recognise Major's right to remain as

Prime Minister when he resigned as Conservative leader in July, to seek a renewed vote of confidence from his party. I closed my ears to such nonsense. How parties managed their internal affairs was no concern of mine and Major had not informed me of any change in his status. The Queen had appointed him Prime Minister and he remained head of the Government. That was enough for me.

It was a curious event, all the same, and I was glad to get back to business as usual. Happily, Major's acceptance of Nolan's main points made sleaze a less corrosive issue. I was also cheered by the arrival of Alastair Goodlad as Government Chief Whip, in place of Richard Ryder. Major's mid-term reshuffle also made Michael Heseltine the Deputy Prime Minister and took Malcolm Rifkind to the Foreign Office, but Tony Newton was still Leader of the House.

From the outset, Alastair and I established a good rapport, although that did not inhibit him from expressing himself forcefully. He wrote to me on 18 July of his 'extreme concern' at the way an incident had been handled during a debate on parliamentary pensions. He supported his complaint by referring to a videotape recording of the proceedings – probably the first time evidence was offered in this way.

His concern arose from an all-party move to improve the way that Members' pensions were computed, regardless of length of service. Long-serving Members had been made comparatively worse off by later improvements and the trustees wanted to put matters right.

Alf Morris, speaking for the trustees, was opposed by Tony Newton on behalf of the Government. When Alf's proposal was put at the end of the debate, Goodlad claimed that Janet Fookes, my deputy, had declared it carried without calling a vote. He further claimed that the tape recording showed that he, Newton and a Government whip had all made their objections to the move 'perfectly audible'.

The inference was that Janet had turned a deaf ear to the Government's protests and that Alf's highly popular measure had been improperly approved. I had full confidence in my deputies. Janet had done as she saw fit, amid considerable noise. Three hundred and fifty-four Members had signed a motion supporting equitable pensions, and I backed my deputy and refused to reopen the matter.

The Government entered the summer recess with a new Cabinet but no improvement in the opinion polls. Reshuffles, in my experience, serve little purpose when a government is in real trouble. Those dismissed from office or passed over for promotion tend to view the world with a jaundiced eye.

Peter Butler, a Tory MP from Milton Keynes, encapsulated the way MPs feel about reshuffles in a ditty written for one of my musical evenings. Peter never held office, but never lost his sense of humour, either, and was a wonderful raconteur. To the tune of the 'Teddy Bear's Picnic', we sang:

> *If you go down to the House today*
> *You're sure of a big surprise*

If you go down to the House today
You'd better go in disguise
For all MPs that ever there was
Will gather there for certain because
Today's the day the Government does
Reshuffle!

Every Member who's been good
Expects promotion today
There's lots of marvellous jobs to take
And all give us lots more pay
Behind the scenes where nobody sees
We'll hide and seek as long as we please
'Cause that's the way the Government does
Reshuffle!

During the summer recess I escaped Westminster as a guest of fellow Speakers overseas. I began with a tour of South Africa at the invitation of its Madam Speaker, Dr Frene Ginwala. She had visited me the year before but was no stranger to Britain. She holds two British degrees and was the African National Congress spokesperson in London during the struggle against apartheid.

The system over which she presided was quite different from our own. The order of speeches was pre-arranged by the whips, according to their party strengths. They found it odd that I had to choose between thirty Members all trying to catch my eye at the same time. I said that if the whips approached me to suggest who should speak, I would send them away with a flea in their ear.

Each unto their own, was my message: 'Look at what we've got, which has its blemishes and warts and may not suit you, and take anything that suits you and adapt it to your needs.' Like us, South Africa's Parliament was considering a tougher code of conduct. I said I was confident that the Nolan reforms would work on a voluntary basis, which the South Africans also thought odd, but 'very British'.

I met Cyril Ramaphosa, chairman of the constitutional committee working on the way forward for South Africa's new democracy, and Thabo Mbeki, the Vice-President and later President.

Mbeki told me of the Commission on Truth and Reconciliation to be chaired by Archbishop Tutu, which he believed would go some way to healing the open wound left by apartheid. My meeting with Nelson Mandela had to wait for another year, when he made his historic trip to London in 1996.

I also visited Japan during the summer recess at the invitation of another woman Speaker, Takako Doi. Women were making headway everywhere in Japan, in areas that were formerly male preserves, but I doubted whether the introduction of quota systems guaranteeing women's candidature was the right way to hasten the change.

On my return home, I found Major relaxed and cheerful at the Downing Street reception to usher in the last full parliamentary session before the election. He told ministers to prepare for a challenging and exciting time ahead and I wished them health and strength to carry out their duties, adding a personal tribute to Tony Newton as 'a golden man'. Before battle resumed the next day, two backbenchers moved and seconded the Loyal Address to the Queen, a ritual that precedes the resumption of hostilities between party leaders and gives the chosen two the chance to impress and amuse a packed House.

It is a very in-House occasion, low on partisan content and high on local pride and good humour. Success depends on style as much as content. The two Members have to select the right ingredients, mix the appropriate measures and serve them at the correct temperature. It can be a gruelling test, even for long-serving Members, and I did what I could to help them, keeping my eyes on them throughout their delivery and willing them to succeed. Gyles Brandreth, who has earned thousands of pounds and a reputation for wit making after-dinner speeches, appreciated my support when he seconded the Loyal Address on 15 November. He gave a graphic account in his memoirs:

Madam Speaker, bless her, was sitting forward on the edge of her seat looking directly at me. I looked directly at her, concentrated entirely on her, she was willing me to keep my nerve – the rumbling opposite was subsiding, they were beginning to listen and then, about three minutes in, I began my passage extolling the virtues of the matchless city of Chester. 'It has two thousand years of history,' I said, and from the far end of the second row of the Labour benches, Joe

Ashton cried, 'And a one thousand majority!' The House roared. I rallied, and suddenly they were on my side.

President Clinton visited Britain in November and told us that he often watched the Commons on cable television and marvelled at the rough-and-tumble debates in which Major and Blair 'sliced each other up' with such wit and skill. Unbeknown to me, Clinton had visited the House privately six years earlier, during a trip to London with Hilary and Chelsea.

They were shown round on that occasion by a policeman, Laurie Mullin, whom the President remembered and subsequently invited to a reception at the American Ambassador's residence. I've always found the easy picking up of old contacts like that is a special American quality.

By December I was under attack again, this time from undeclared right-wing Tories who were said to be compiling a record of my decisions, with the aim of proving that I was biased. I was becoming used to this pre-Christmas ritual and paid little heed. Alan Duncan, MP for Rutland and an unpaid aide to Brian Mawhinney, the Conservative Party chairman, was named as my secret accuser. A few weeks later he sent me a copy of a cartoon, as 'a gi'normous olive branch', accompanied by a greetings card that promised: 'I will be a good boy in '96.'

He may have been feeling the heat. The *Evening Standard*, which MPs devour from midday onwards, wrote a splendid leader rebuking 'a small and rather unpleasant set of Conservative MPs' for their 'worrying lack of confidence and maturity' in their attitude to me. They picked up on Duncan's sedentary retort – to my quip about whips who used a double-nelson in my time: 'It's not funny. It's not funny.'

> The petulant Mr Duncan might like to consider where this campaign might lead. Would he wish, say, to institute a Speaker Monitoring Unit . . . this anti-Betty Boothroyd campaign is silly and unbecoming.

My response, when a Labour backbencher objected to the sniping by unnamed ministers and others, was to make it clear that if there was any criticism of the chair, there had to be a motion on the order paper and it would be debated immediately. 'I don't believe everything I read in the newspapers,' I added, 'and a good thing, too.' But that did not mean I disbelieved everything, either.

The *Daily Telegraph* reported that feelings about me among Tory MPs were running high in the Commons tearoom. One of its informants alleged that I had protected Tony Blair from attack, 'while some of our people have had a rough time'. Apparently my accusers intended to raise the matter at the weekly meeting of the 1922 Committee of Tory backbenchers.

I waited, with unbated breath, while the press had a field day. The papers reported every groan and gripe about me, lambasting my critics at the same time. The tougher I was, the more they lapped it up. 'Long may she show womanly common sense at Westminster and wield her rolling pin at Ministerial moaners and backbench bullies,' wrote Geoffrey Wheatcroft in the *Sunday Express*.

Labour complainants trying their luck got the same short shrift, as Gerry Bermingham, MP for St Helens South, found out. He tried to get Ann Widdecombe, a Home Office minister, pulled up for using a biblical quotation against the Liberal Democrat David Alton. Bermingham complained that Widdecombe had effectively called Alton a liar by referring him to the Commandment 'Thou shalt not bear false witness against thy neighbour'.

Janet Fookes was in the chair and disagreed. When Bermingham appealed to me the next day, I did too. But Bermingham persisted, something I rarely allowed on a point of order. He asked me: 'Am I now to understand that I can use any quotation – from the Bible or from Shakespeare, for example – to call anybody anything?'

'Not at all,' I replied. It depended on how the quotation was used and interpreted at the time. My judgement from reading the debate was that Widdecombe meant that Alton had made a poor or a false point. I added, 'We do not go in for inquests', at which Dennis Skinner piped up, 'The quality of mercy is not strained.' That too, I believed, depended on the circumstances.

The real parliamentary problem, as Michael White of the *Guardian* pointed out, was 'the virtual collapse of substantial government business' and the 'ghostly atmosphere around Westminster' outside the three core days of the week, Tuesdays, Wednesdays and Thursdays.

The renewed outbreak of sniping against me was an unintended compliment. It showed that I was still an independent force to be reckoned with, despite the House being put on short time. Moved to break his silence on my conduct of business, Jack Weatherill said that I was tough, robust and unbiased, but – like all Speakers – vulnerable to criticism. 'Why?' he asked. 'Because the Speaker alone decides who speaks' and it was 'a hideously difficult job'.

My alleged offence was compounded by my allowing fuller licence than was usual to critics of a Government decision to cut the benefits payable to asylum-seekers. Social-security orders reducing their entitlement were tabled only three days before the House rose for its Christmas recess and were due to come into force one day before it returned. Normal practice was to allow at least eighteen days between orders being laid before Parliament and their implementation. David Alton wrote to me complaining of 'a blatant abuse of Parliament' and a few Labour MPs protested.

I allowed them to vent their anger on the floor of the House and added that I hoped the Government had taken note of it. 'Another black mark' against Boothroyd was how one reporter wrote the story up, but after three years in the chair, I intended to continue as I had begun.

I was more concerned to warn Members that they did not impress the public when they made personal attacks on each other. 'I attend many public functions daily,' I said. 'Many people tell me they are disappointed in our legislators. They are looking for exchanges on policy and the governance of this country and not personal attacks – they are sick and tired of personal attacks.'

Charles Powell, Margaret Thatcher's foreign-affairs adviser for six years, commented that the Speaker alone could not change the way the Commons behaved, although 'a strong Speaker can give a strong lead'. He hoped I might still 'save it from the creeping irrelevance and disrepute which may otherwise be its fate'.

CHAPTER FOURTEEN

Bouquets and Brickbats

> *Efficiency is no less essential in a Senate*
> *than in a factory.*
> Thomas Erskine May, Clerk of the
> House of Commons 1871–86

I VISITED MOROCCO at Easter 1995 and stayed on after the official programme for a day with friends. The plan was to drive by Land-Rover to a private house in the High Atlas Mountains, leaving in plenty of time before my return flight from Casablanca. We had not, however, bargained on the weather. The drive out was a sightseer's delight and we had an enjoyable lunch. Then the heavens opened and torrential rains made our route back impassable.

I telephoned the British Ambassador, who offered to send a helicopter to rescue us – if he could get one. I had to be in the House when it reassembled the next day and could not risk being marooned in Morocco. There was nothing for it but to try our luck and go across country.

A sea of mud and water cascading off the slopes

stopped us in our tracks. Turning a corner, we saw what seemed to be an entire mountain crumbling in front of us. Our vehicle was swamped and immovable and it was getting dark. Absolutely soaked, we crawled out through the sunroof, because the doors were stuck, and went for help.

We found a tiny hamlet, where the villagers were astonished to see us but very polite. The nearest Berber village was an hour's trek away across a swollen river and our hosts sent men on mules, which swam across the torrent, to raise the alarm, serving us mint tea while we waited.

When the police at Marrakesh heard I was stranded, they sent a bulldozer to escort me back. They knew who I was because, they said, they watched the Commons exchanges on satellite television. Thankful for Berber hospitality and telecommunications, I took a quick bath and a long drink before heading for the airport. I was back on parade next day as if nothing had happened. That was more than could be said for some MPs with questions on the order paper, who were absent when I called them.

Without my intervention, questions to the Prime Minister would have become questions to Tony Blair long before the general election. I had to call Tory backbenchers to order twice as they sought answers from Blair during the first clash between the two leaders in 1996.

Blair was questioning Major on his Cabinet's discussion of the single currency that morning when David Evans, a voluble supporter of the Prime

Minister, shouted at Blair, 'What's your policy?'

But I was ready for him. 'Order. This is not a time when the Opposition answer questions; it is a time when the Opposition asks questions.' Minutes later Henry Bellingham invited Major to consider the 'gaping hole at the heart of Labour's spending plans'. I cut him off in mid-sentence. 'Order. The honourable gentleman must ask a question about the Government's policies. If he can do that, I will hear him, but if he cannot, he must resume his seat.'

Andrew Rawnsley noted in the *Observer* that the Tories wanted to behave 'as though they were already the Opposition by turning every session into an attack on Labour policies and personalities. What irritates them about Madam Speaker is that she asks them to behave like a Government.'

Keeping the proper balance was made infinitely harder by further accusations of sleaze and the controversy surrounding Sir Richard Scott's inquiry into arms sales to Iraq during the 1980s, which exploded in February 1996. After an investigation lasting three years and 200,000 pages of documentation, Sir Richard submitted his findings to Downing Street and the Opposition awaited sight of it.

Ministers, however, were in no rush to let Labour have it ahead of their response to the Scott findings. They proposed sitting on it for seven days to allow Whitehall time to 'coordinate' its reply. When the Opposition appealed to me to give them the same chance as ministers to digest Scott's 1,800-page report, I told the House that I was powerless to do so.

But I added: 'In my experience the questioning on any statement is much better focused when some steps have been taken to enable Opposition spokesmen and minority-party spokesmen to have access some time in advance to the text of complicated reports, provided steps are taken to maintain confidentiality.'

The press seized on this common-sense statement as a move to put pressure on No. 10, but it had little effect. Robin Cook was given only three hours to study the report on behalf of the Opposition. Yet he delivered one of the best speeches I ever heard in the Commons, flaying the Government and using his hastily assembled notes to fire a battery of pertinent questions. It was a masterly performance of forensic skill, with no quarter given.

The Government's embarrassment led to my being accused, in the usual unattributable way, of being unfair. Julie Kirkbride, a lobby reporter who subsequently became a Tory MP, wrote in the *Sunday Telegraph* that 'senior Tories' were thinking about breaking the convention that the Speaker was returned unopposed at the general election. To further frighten me, they said that unless I mended my ways 'they could not guarantee that any freshly elected Conservative government would be able to reinstate her'.

An unnamed friend, someone unknown to me, told *The Times*: 'If some pipsqueak in the Tory Central Office thinks he can put his frighteners on Betty, he must be in dreamland.' Senior ministers were reported to have assured me that these snide attacks had nothing to do with them. I had already chosen my election colour: House of Commons green.

A Valentine's Day poem from Alan Simpson, Labour MP for Nottingham South, cheered me up. He wanted to be called in a debate about his city's local-government status and thought he stood a better chance if he asked in verse. It ended:

So I'll take my place quite quietly,
And wait coyly for the chance,
To see if Cupid's arrow
Helps to direct Madam's glance.

It did not. Sir Geoffrey Lofthouse was in the chair for that debate and Alan felt obliged to own up to the Valentine when he was called, adding: 'It might be helpful if I clarify that the terms of my *billet-doux* were addressed to her rather than to you, Mr Deputy Speaker.'

Once again, the latest Tory agitation fizzled out. Peter Snape called it a 'disgraceful and wholly unfounded smear campaign' and Marcus Fox denied that any criticism of me had been aired at the executive of the 1922 Committee. I ended up smelling of roses – literally. A hybrid tea rose, named 'Madam Speaker', was presented to me on the Commons terrace by its grower, J. B. Turner of Wisbech.

Sprinkling its roots with champagne, I said: 'I hope it will embody the characteristics every Speaker should have: hardy by nature, disease-free, flourishing in all conditions and a pleasure to have around.' *Cosmopolitan* magazine paid me the less formal compliment of naming me one of its favourite 'babes', along with Cindy Crawford, Madonna, Whitney Houston and Zsa Zsa Gabor. It said I was proof that 'a great babe is like fine wine – she just gets better with age'. In my job, I needed to.

During the last summer before Major was obliged to seek another mandate our minds focused on the coming election. His opinion-poll ratings ruled out any possibility of dissolving Parliament before his five-year term ran out. Nor was the Conservative Party in any shape to face the electorate. In June, seventy-four Tory backbenchers voted for an early referendum to rule out further losses of British sovereignty to the EU, and the Prime Minister was reported to be 'incandescent with rage' at Lady Thatcher's support for the Euro-sceptic critics.

Attacking the Government became as easy as shooting fish in a barrel. No opportunity was lost to portray the Tories as extreme right-wingers who had lost the plot. Peter Hain ingeniously raised a point of order with me about the use of a Commons room by an allegedly extreme group. I replied that I did not mind, provided the room was properly booked, and I added: 'I have to tell the House that at the next election I shall be fighting the Militant Tendency and the National Front. I call them both extremist groups and I am very happy to take them on.'

I also gave short shrift to ministers who used the dispatch box as an electioneering platform, but it was a thankless task. Commons tempers are invariably shorter during the summer months. Even John Major, criticised by the press and scorned within his own party, said that he had had 'a bellyful'.

In July party warfare was suspended by the most remarkable visit of any overseas visitor to Britain in the whole of my parliamentary career. As Speaker, I welcomed three Presidents to Westminster during my first four years in the chair – Boris Yeltsin, Bill Clinton and Jacques Chirac. Each was a memorable occasion, but none matched the emotional intensity of Nelson Mandela's arrival among us as South Africa's first democratic leader.

We met at the state banquet at Buckingham Palace on the eve of his speech to the joint Houses of Parliament in Westminster Hall. Mandela wore a patterned silk shirt and made a refreshing sight amid the pomp and circumstance around him. He was looking forward to the next day's ceremony: it would be the first time that a foreign head of state had been honoured in Westminster Hall since General de Gaulle spoke there in 1960. South Africa's new constitution was only two months old and I could hardly believe that the man who had done more than anyone else to take his country from apartheid to democracy was with us, after decades of imprisonment and struggle.

There was one logistical problem. His entrance to Westminster Hall involved negotiating a wide flight of steps that he would have to descend in front of several thousand dignitaries watching his every move. The steps had no handrail and I was worried that, remarkably fit though he was for a man of seventy-eight, he would find them difficult. I mentioned my concern when we talked briefly after dinner at the palace before he circulated among other guests who were keen to meet him.

But Mandela showed no anxiety when he arrived at St Stephen's entrance to the Commons the next morning. He said how pleased he was by his enthusiastic reception by the large crowds that gathered wherever he went. There had never been a state visit quite like it. Here he was in the Parliament where our predecessors gave power to a white minority, to do what they liked to his people for eighty-five years. It was the fulfilment of the struggle to which he had given his life and which Jo Richardson and I had supported as young women.

But there were those steps. I cautioned him again about them as we waited for the signal to enter the hall. 'But don't hurry,' I said, 'I will take them at your pace.'

'Don't worry,' he replied. 'I came to look at them at six o'clock this morning.' Unknown to me, he had already reconnoitred the route he was to take and had assessed the situation. It was a revealing example of how painstaking this extraordinary man was. His foresight matched his warmth and natural dignity. Reassured, I escorted him in as the state trumpeters blew a fanfare.

It was then that he took my hand as we walked down the hall's age-old narrow steps, framed by the memorial window to the units of the armed forces in which Members and staff of both Houses served in

the Second World War. The band of the Grenadier
Guards played South Africa's new national anthem,
'Nkosi Sikeleli Afrika'; Lord Mackay of Clashfern,
the Lord Chancellor, formally welcomed the
President; and then Mandela spoke to us.

He recalled Westminster's rejection of the pleas of
former black leaders that Britain, then an imperial
power, accord their people the same respect as white
settlers. But there was no resentment in what he
said. Without glossing over his people's suffering
under the oppressive system that Britain had
endorsed, he spoke of new beginnings and of
gratitude for what was best in our historical
relationship.

'Despite that rebuff and the terrible cost we had to
bear as a consequence, we return to this honoured
place neither with pikes, nor with a desire for
revenge, nor even a plea to your distinguished selves
to assuage our hunger for bread. We come to you as
friends.

'We have returned to the land of William
Wilberforce, who dared to stand up and demand
that the slaves in our country should be freed. We
come to the land of Fenner Brockway, who, through
his Movement for Colonial Freedom, was as
concerned about our liberty as he was about the
independence of India.

'We are here in the Houses in which Harold
Macmillan worked: he who spoke in our own
Houses of Parliament in Cape Town in 1960, shortly
before the infamous Sharpeville Massacre, and
warned a stubborn and race-blinded white oligarchy

in our country that "the wind of change is blowing through this continent".'

Mandela's speech ran to four pages in the official record (over 2,000 words in all), but it was his sheer presence that made the greatest impact. In thanking him, I tried to convey that, by saying what he could not say about himself – and what I felt everybody who had come to pay tribute to him wanted said.

'It is not too much to say that you represent an outstanding victory of the human spirit over evil . . . As a result of your determination to end apartheid you spent more than a third of your life in prison, though your spirit was freer there than that of your captors outside. And when you were released, it was remarkable to see you emerge with no feeling of personal bitterness towards those who had denied you your freedom. In the end you not only held the key to your own release but also the key to establishing a new and multicultural nation . . .

'Along with some others of my generation, I stood with Black Sash outside South Africa House in the hope of instilling some shame among government supporters inside. We were realistic. We had no great hopes of influencing their policy, but it was a matter of principle. And you were one of those in our minds throughout silent vigils . . .

'I never expected to stand here under the famous hammer beams of Westminster Hall, which have witnessed so many of the great events of British history, to see you honoured so rightly and full-heartedly by both Houses of Parliament.

'Tomorrow, Mr President, you will walk across Trafalgar Square to South Africa House, where you were once vilified and which now you will enter as Head of State. I have no doubt that some of my old Black Sash colleagues will be among the crowds paying their tribute. My thoughts will be with them and with you – one of the men of whom our twentieth century is justly proud.'

There were no party differences in Westminster Hall that morning. Tony Blair sat next to Sir Edward Heath, Michael Heseltine next to Cherie Blair. We were just happy to be there.

Mandela's letter of thanks to me reflected the unostentatious nature of the man. It bore no seal of office or national crest. His high office was denoted by just five words in small type at the top of the page: President (set left) and Republic of South Africa (set right). It read:

Dear Madam Speaker,

I am writing to thank you most sincerely for your considerable contribution towards making my recent visit to the United Kingdom so successful. I felt very honoured and privileged to address Parliament in Westminster Hall with its ancient history. The pomp and ceremony which accompanied the occasion was truly majestic and dignified.

I was also very touched by your address and appreciate your support and understanding of South Africa, both past and present. It is friends like yourself who have contributed to making our country the democratic rainbow nation we are today.

There are so many aspects of this State Visit which I will recall fondly, especially the graciousness of my host HM Queen Elizabeth II and the warmth of the people of the United Kingdom.

In September 1996 the Speakers of Slovakia, the Czech Republic and Poland invited me to see how they were faring as new democracies after nearly fifty years of totalitarian rule. I welcomed the opportunity to encourage them and share my views on the proper relationship between governments and parliaments.

My address to Slovakia's National Council in Bratislava was the first by a foreign visitor since that country ended its union with the Czech Republic in the so-called 'velvet divorce' of 1993, four years after the communists were overthrown. Vladimir Meciar, the Prime Minister, and the whole government were present.

Meciar was an authoritarian populist, whose mistreatment of the country's ethnic Hungarians and dubious commitment to democratic principles earned him a poor reputation and hindered Slovakia's chances of joining the European Union. So the theme of my speech was somewhat unpalatable. It was that the winning party in British elections did 'not take all' and that the Opposition had rights, too. Moreover, an effective Opposition was vitally important in ensuring the continuity of parliamentary institutions and the electorate's ability to hold the Government to account.

My remarks were strongly applauded by the opposition benches, while Meciar and his ministers sat with boot faces. I had been well briefed about the Slovak political situation and the Foreign Office was delighted. The state-controlled television relayed my call for a strong parliament live, with only a soft Slovak 'voice-over'.

Encouraged by my exhortation, the opposition tabled a motion of no confidence while I was still there. When Meciar refused to debate it, they tabled another motion stating that it was clear from what I had said that the government's tactics would never be allowed in the Mother of Parliaments. 'Objectives fully achieved,' said the British Ambassador's telegram. He added: 'It will, of course, take more than one visit by Madam Speaker to bring about sustained cultural change' in Slovakia.

Meciar assured me that he too found the speech 'very impressive', but he had a strange way of showing it. When we met afterwards, he sat me at a table with the light behind him and the sun shining directly in my eyes. My mascara ran into my Max Factor as he harangued me about Slovakia's fitness to be accepted by the West. He lost power two years later when the opposition won ninety-three of the Parliament's 150 seats, paving the way for the country's renewed application to join the EU.

Prague was less challenging than Bratislava, although the Czechs have their own curious ways of running things. My host, Milos Zeman, was both the chairman of Parliament and leader of the Social Democrat opposition. My message to them was that neutral Speakers are best, that parliamentary discipline is essential and parliamentary committees play a crucial role. Because my own political neutrality allowed me to express uncontentious British views without difficulty, I was able to reassure Josef Zieleniec, the Foreign Minister, that we fully supported Czech ambitions to join the EU and Nato.

My visit to the Charles University Medical Faculty in Prague was particularly moving. After an ebullient reception, the students told me how much the restoration of democracy meant after the Nazi and communist eras.

I ended my tour in Poland, visiting Warsaw and Krakow and talking to political leaders there. At my host's request, I was taken to the site of the Auschwitz concentration camp and to Birkenau railway depot, where four million Jews and other victims of Nazism were disembarked for extermination. I knew the horrific history of the place, of course, but I was unprepared for the exhibition of household equipment that the camp's internees had brought with them, believing they were going to be resettled. They came with their kitchen utensils, knives, colanders, chopping boards and pots and pans in the hope of finding a new life.

After laying wreaths at both the camp and the rail depot, I asked Nicolas Bevan to share my car, while the rest of our party drove in a people carrier behind. I was cold on the outside and frozen on the inside by what I had witnessed. On arrival at the Grand Hotel in Krakow I asked Nicolas and Roseanne to join me in my room. We said hardly a word and downed a bottle of Scotch before going to our restless beds.

After the start of the new session I gave a dinner at Speaker's House for the Queen and the Duke of Edinburgh. As a reminder of President Mandela's visit, the first wine to be served was Stormy Cape 1995, the year South Africa rejoined the Commonwealth, an event that meant a lot to the Queen. John Major, Tony Blair, Paddy Ashdown, David Trimble and other senior figures were among the guests and the House of Commons refreshment department surpassed itself with a menu of sea bass, roast Gressingham duck with forest mushrooms, baked plum galette and cinnamon ice.

The political fare in the Commons was less appetising. Sleaze was back at the top of the agenda and I was determined to deal with it as quickly as possible. On our first day back I called for a full inquiry into allegations made against MPs and ministers following the collapse of a libel action against the *Guardian* by Neil Hamilton, the former Trade and Industry Minister. The *Guardian* accused Hamilton of taking money from Mohamed Al Fayed, the owner of Harrods, for tabling Commons questions, Hamilton sued for libel and his case had collapsed in court.

In my view, the reputation of the whole House was threatened and the Hamilton affair needed clearing up, fast. I told MPs that Sir Gordon Downey, the new Commissioner for Standards, would have the resources he needed to investigate it. But the ultimate remedy lay in the hands of Members themselves. As the *Financial Times* stated the next day:

> The success of parliamentary democracy in being the least bad system, as Churchill said, must ultimately depend on its ability to be its own guardian against corruption and to demonstrate that wrongdoers will be properly disgraced or shamed into resigning.

Hamilton, however, was not easily shamed, and some of his former colleagues in Government were not overjoyed at the prospect of his being disgraced. I left it to the new Standards and Privileges Committee to decide how wide its review should be, in the light of Sir Gordon's report. While he and they got on with it, I turned my attention to another recurrent outbreak that invariably landed me in trouble – the never-ending European debate.

Again, my concern was not the rights and wrongs of the issue but the need to safeguard Parliament's good name. The latest spat began in a normally ill-attended committee that scrutinises draft European directives before they have the force of law. This occasion was different. The meeting was crowded and fractious. A division was called and a Tory Euro-sceptic swung the vote against the Government. Under debate was a wad of documents, 300 pages thick, setting out the terms of joining the single currency and the EU's powers to ensure that member states complied with them in the so-called Stability Pact.

It was clearly a matter of enormous potential importance for Britain, even though we had not yet decided to join the single currency. Instead of bowing to the majority who wanted a full Commons debate, ministers ignored the committee vote and declared that the matter was not urgent because it had not yet gone through all the EU stages. Uproar ensued and an appeal was made to me.

Once again the Government was in a bind. Europe was as poisonous a subject as ever in the Tory Party and raising it on the floor of the Commons threatened to make things worse. What mattered to me, however, was Parliament's right to debate difficult issues, whether or not the Government found it inconvenient. It was not within my power to dictate what should happen; I could only indicate what I thought. When furious MPs raised the matter with me I promised: 'I will make further enquiries. I am concerned about saving the integrity of the procedures of the House.'

The media interpreted this as a tilt at the Government, and when Tory backbenchers anxious for a debate joined in the clamour, the Government backed down. Had they accepted the committee's call for debate in the first place, they would have averted an unnecessary row and not lost face. As Churchill said: 'To jaw-jaw is always better than to war-war.'

December, a hazardous month for me in my first years as Speaker, turned out in 1996 to be more of a problem for the Government. David Willetts resigned as Paymaster General after being criticised by the Standards and Privileges Committee, and Sir John Gorst said that the Government could no longer rely on his support as a Tory backbencher, which left his party teetering on the brink of losing its overall majority. It was 1979 all over again, when Jim Callaghan clung to power before losing it to a more vigorous Opposition. Major held on until the last gasp of what Blair called the 'fag-end of a burnt-out Government'.

There was still time before the hustings for me to call the media to order. Tam Dalyell gave me the opportunity by protesting at unfair attacks against the House and saying that there should be 'some defence of the good name of us all'. Tam later became Father of the House. He had been affronted by a television programme which gave the impression that the Commons was a den of iniquity.

I too was sick of insinuations that every MP had a finger in the till and gave a considered response to Tam's complaint on 28 January. I noted that damaging, often sweeping, attacks against the good name of the House had become common in newspapers, television and radio programmes, books and even learned articles. I repeated my concern that accusations against individual Members already under investigation should be resolved as soon as possible. But such inquiries were enormously time-consuming and painstaking and could not be unduly hurried, and the new Commissioner and the Standards Committee were carrying out their quasi-judicial role under arrangements that were little more than a year old. I went on: 'It is deplorable that many sections of the media have drawn only scant attention to the fact that, following the original work of Lord Nolan's committee, the House has made many far-reaching changes to its rules and mechanisms. The House as a whole, and I as its Speaker, are determined that these new arrangements should work effectively.

'It should be noted that the first Nolan report stated: *"The great majority of men and women in British public life are honest and hard-working, and observe high ethical standards."*

'After a lifetime's experience in politics and nearly a quarter of a century as a Member of this House, I know that to be true. Members of this House have a responsibility to conduct themselves according to the high standards which the electorate rightly expect of them. The overwhelming majority of Members do so.

'There can be no complaint about the role of the media in identifying cases where it appears that Members have fallen short of those standards. Indeed, in so doing, the media perform a public service. But it is reasonable to expect that the media do not repeat and pursue allegations in a way that prejudges their validity pending the outcome of investigations by the Parliamentary Commissioner for Standards ... Above all, they should not use individual allegations as the occasion for making highly generalised and unsubstantiated comments against Members of this House as a whole and against our parliamentary system.

'The Nolan committee's first report also stated: *"We would prefer more acknowledgement from the media that the overwhelming majority of public servants work hard and have high standards. We would prefer more recognition of the value of our democratic mechanisms and the dangers of undermining them."*

'Again, I agree. It can hardly be a coincidence that it is to this House, above all others, that parliamentarians from all over the world come for consultations and advice.

'I am determined that the new procedures and rules that the House has established should work in such a way as to bolster our democratic system. The media can play their part with fairer and better-balanced coverage and comment. I also look to Hon. Members in all parts of the House for constructive support for this historic institution to which our constituents have sent us, and which all of us have the honour to serve.'

A predictable media flutter followed and some journalists who normally supported me were put out. Stewart Steven took me to task in the *Mail on Sunday*: 'It is not fairer or more balanced coverage she's after, but coverage of the kind which Parliament was once used to – grovelling and sycophantic.' Just when that period was, he did not say, but having MP after one's name has never entitled anyone I know to sycophantic treatment.

Newspapers were at their most craven during the pre-war years when they defended Neville Chamberlain's appeasement policies as Hitler unleashed his terror on Europe. It takes two to tango.

But it was true that many news desks had long ceased to regard the Commons as anything more than a fertile hunting ground for stories that had little to do with Parliament. Even when they did, they often reflected discredit on it. The more intrusive newspapers became about Members' personal affairs, the more defensive MPs grew. Journalists were excluded from the Members' terrace, unless they were invited, following complaints about their abuse of the privilege by writing offensive stories that breached all the lobby rules. These allowed journalists to have access to the Members' lobby and other restricted areas on the basis that they respected confidences, protected their sources and had due regard for the rules of the House.

Journalists accredited to the House asked me to intervene when a Commons committee voted to restrict their right to use the terrace, but I felt unable to do so. I regretted that, because I have known many political reporters and commentators over the years, have enjoyed their company and valued their opinions. I owe much to Terry Lancaster and Ted Castle and cherish the memory of other press pals no longer with us, such as Gordon Greig of the *Daily Mail* and Geoffrey Parkhouse of the *Glasgow Herald*. They rank alongside Ian Aitken of the *Guardian*, Alan

Watkins of the *Independent on Sunday*, Elinor Goodman of *Channel 4 News*, Peter Dobbie of the *Mail on Sunday* and Peter Riddell and Philip Webster of *The Times*, John Deans of the *Daily Mail* and Secretary of Lobby Journalists, and Chris Moncrieff of the PA as people whose integrity I respect.

Generations of brilliant sketch writers have contributed to the quality of our parliamentary life by describing our proceedings with wit and perception. Which other Parliament has had talents in its press galleries to match those of Bernard Levin, Matthew Parris and Simon Hoggart, let alone Charles Dickens? The regional media also has many fine journalists whose professionalism I admire and with whom I have worked closely in Westminster and the provinces.

I learned about freedom of speech and freedom of the press – or lack of it – at grass-roots level. When I was a child the local newspapers in Dewsbury were under Liberal control and Labour candidates rarely got a mention. Young Betty Boothroyd made more headlines by being a woman during her early contests than by fighting for the causes in which she believed. The more experienced I became in Westminster, the more I learned about the pressures on political correspondents to find exclusive stories. To many lobby correspondents, the Commons is the background – seldom the centrepiece – of their work. It is where journalists and governments fight over the next day's headlines while MPs look on and the public yawns.

The quality of political debate suffers when the media switches its attention from the issues that affect people's lives to the trivia, gossip and malice that make 'good stories'. Foolish politicians and professional 'spin-doctors' encourage this by fishing in the same polluted waters, while editors egg them on. I attended one memorial service for a popular tabloid journalist whose editor said from the pulpit that he had not raked up as much Commons scandal as he would have liked. That may help circulation, but it also creates a climate of low public expectation that undermines our trust in democracy.

After my statement urging a balanced media approach, one columnist who took a dim view of it all berated me for not doing more 'to keep the gutter clean'. I failed to see what more I could do. I had called for MPs to observe high standards, I fast-tracked inquiries into serious allegations, and I presided over the imposition of the tightest rules and procedures against improper conduct in Parliament's history.

Against the odds, Major kept his Government afloat until the very end. Everybody reckoned he would call the election on 1 May 1997 and I made my own preparations in West Bromwich on that basis. As we waited for the dissolution, our proceedings were interrupted by a startling intrusion of electioneering technology that I was not prepared to tolerate. Brian Wilson, a Labour frontbencher, was prompted by a pager message (from a party researcher who had been watching Prime Minister's Questions on television) to question the outside interests of a Tory whom I had called.

Others saw Wilson take the electronic message alerting him to his prey – and he freely admitted it. 'I strongly deprecate such practice,' I declared when the story came out. I ordered that Members should turn their pagers off when they entered the chamber. 'I can have no objection to instruments which merely vibrate to attract the attention of the bearer . . . I am not, however, prepared to accept the use of such instruments as an aide-mémoire by a member who is addressing this House.'

Tessa Jowell had been the last Member to transgress in this fashion by allowing her mobile phone to go off during a debate. 'The Speaker has very strong views about technology,' Janet Fookes told her. If allowed to go unchecked, we would end up with the situation I had encountered when I addressed the Latvian Saeima while one Member grunted into his mobile phone.

I gave a farewell party for Members who were retiring from the Commons, many of whom I had known for a quarter of a century – some longer. Roy Hattersley, Stan Orme, Harold Walker, Gordon Oakes, Greville Janner and Andrew Faulds, my constituency neighbour, were among the Labour group; Douglas Hurd, John Biffen, Cranley Onslow, Janet Fookes, Giles Shaw and James Spicer among the Tories. Two former party leaders were also there: David Steel from the Liberal Democrats and James Molyneaux from the Ulster Unionists.

I could have held a larger party for Tory Members

with little prospect of being re-elected, but that would have meant them admitting defeat, which would never do. As it was, 117 Members announced their retirement: seventy-two Tories, thirty-eight Labour, six Liberal Democrats and Jim Molyneaux. No fewer than 126 Tories went on to lose their seats. Some of them joined the retirees in the chamber on the last day when Parliament was prorogued for the election.

For ex-Cabinet ministers, and a few others, there was the prospect of life peerages. For others less fortunate, it was a last farewell. I sat in the lower chair with a lump in my throat as they passed by to shake my hand. I am a tough old bird but I was losing many friends and it was a sad occasion. Terence Higgins gave me a farewell kiss and John Biffen spoke for many when he commented, 'I will miss the discipline, the companionship.'

I left to fight my own campaign in West Bromwich, this time with the support of the three major parties. My early failures had taught me never to take re-election for granted and I had an enthusiastic group to get out the vote, called Friends of the Speaker, led by an old Labour and trade-union comrade, David Warburton, and by my agent, Doug Parish.

I stood as the Speaker Seeking Re-election and was opposed by somebody claiming to be the Official Labour Candidate – which he was not – and a right-wing extremist. My supporters delivered 35,000 leaflets to inform people that Labour supported me and I was returned with my biggest-ever majority of 15,423 votes.

All the same, as I went around my constituency I found people who were unhappy at being denied the chance to vote for the party they supported. They held no grudge against me, and I understood and sympathised with them. The fault lay with the convention that says the Speaker must be politically neutral and be given an unopposed return at elections. I explained that, but it was not an easy campaign for me.

The only remedy is to make the Speaker an ex-officio Member of the House without constituency responsibilities. Had I been in that position, I would have had more opportunity to undertake national engagements in my capacity as Speaker. Attending two weekend 'surgeries' every month and other constituency events, after being in the House all week, restricted my ability to do that.

All the same, it was a thrill to be re-elected, and my supporters turned out in strength throughout the constituency in Tividale, Oldbury, Tipton, Wednesbury and West Bromwich. It was a night to remember. I never went to bed, but experienced the biggest electoral sensation of my life. After all those years of domination by one party, the people had decided that it was time for a change. For me it was poignant, because old comrades in arms who had fought the battle for so long were not there to savour their victory. As we watched Labour's landslide that night, I became even more convinced that the new Parliament would be as difficult in its way to manage as the old one. I was soon proved right.

CHAPTER FIFTEEN

To Swear or Not to Swear

*By virtue of the oath, or affirmation of allegiance taken
by all Members when they are elected to the House,
Members have a duty to be faithful and bear true
allegiance to Her Majesty the Queen, her heirs and
successors, according to law.*

Article Two of the Code of Conduct
for Members of Parliament, 1995

UNEXPECTED NEWS AWAITED me on my return
from West Bromwich to Speaker's House
after the 1997 election campaign: there would be no
more twice-weekly Question Times to the Prime
Minister. Instead of submitting himself to MPs'
questions for fifteen minutes on Tuesday and
Thursday afternoons, Tony Blair would start his
term in office by appearing at the dispatch box for
thirty minutes on Wednesday afternoons only.

It was a major change in the way we managed
our affairs. The week had been built around two
Prime Minister's Question Times and Members did
not wind down until after the session on Thursday.

We risked losing momentum and public interest a day earlier by this change, although Ann Taylor, the new Leader of the Commons, told me the Government reckoned that a single extended session would allow more backbenchers' questions and would be better for the Prime Minister, who would now have more time for his other duties.

I was neither forewarned nor consulted about this – merely informed. But I understood the thinking behind it and did not object. Labour had been in the wilderness for eighteen years and had the right to re-arrange its parliamentary schedule. My powers were unaffected. They gave me plenty of scope to ensure fair play, no matter how large the ruling party's majority.

John Major, who stayed leader of the Opposition until a new Tory leader was elected, was also unaware of the change and came to see me. 'Madam Speaker, nobody has consulted me,' he said. 'What does this mean? How many questions will I have?'

I replied: 'John, as far as I am concerned, the Opposition leader had three questions to the Prime Minister twice a week under the old system, so you will have double that under the new one.'

I told nobody else and the penny did not drop with the Government until I called Major six times at Blair's first Question Time. If anybody thought I was going to reduce the Opposition's rights, just because the procedure had changed, they were mistaken.

At our first sitting Gwyneth Dunwoody

proposed with great glee my re-election as Speaker: 'This is truly a beautiful day. The sun is shining. God is in his heaven and I am happy to see a majority of the House of Commons wearing the right colours.' John MacGregor seconded my re-election from the Tory benches and Sir Edward Heath presided. He had first entered the Commons before Blair and Gordon Brown were born. To cap it all, Tony Benn spoke in support of me from the Government backbenches where he had first sat more than forty years before.

Welcoming all 260 new Members, I asked for a little time to put names to faces, but it was not as difficult as I feared. The record number of 120 women MPs helped, because they were easier to remember than the 140 grey-suited men alongside them. Blair said that the arrival of so many women was an excellent start, but that 'some will feel there is still room for improvement'. Sadly, as things turned out, not enough did and the number of women MPs fell to 118 in 2001.

My re-election was well received, but I was especially touched later to read the entry that Sir Alec Guinness made in his diary and subsequently published in his book *Positively Final Appearance*:

There is much rejoicing that Betty Boothroyd is again to be Madam Speaker. Her strong smile, jolly hairdo and shapely legs hearten us all no end, as well, of course, as her fair-mindedness and the firm grip she keeps on the wheel when the ship of state is lashed by squalls. This time, I imagine, with the course firmly set to port, she will probably have a smoother ride.

His optimism was misplaced. John Major's decision to retire to the backbenches as soon as he could added to the feeling that a new phase in British politics was beginning. I understood his decision to stand down after such a crushing defeat. Tony Blair had been given the chance to remould British politics in a dramatic way and he seized it. My task was to make sure that ministers announced, explained and defended their 'New Britain' policies in the nation's chief forum – the House of Commons.

Matters were not helped by the shell-shocked state of the Conservative Party. Alastair Goodlad worked heroically as their Chief Whip to ensure that Tory MPs and spokesmen covered key debates and responded to ministerial statements, but his party grew so self-absorbed that I became concerned at its lack of vigour and initiative in the House. Had the Tories been a more energetic Opposition, they would have made greater use of the procedure that obliges senior ministers to come to the House and explain themselves on serious and urgent matters.

The Tory Party and the media seemed to think that Blair's Question Time on Wednesday was their last bite at the cherry. It need not have been, if the Opposition had made a good case to me for Private Notice Questions (PNQs) to the Government on Thursday mornings, but they were in too much disarray to use the opportunities they had. They seldom bothered and, when they did, failed to meet the criteria. They tended to hold their fire until Thursday's statement on next week's business, which was easily deflected. They lacked energy and ingenuity. They were too stunned by their loss of power to know how to run an effective Opposition. Alastair held the Tories together while they were looking for a new leader and I was supportive of him throughout that difficult time.

I was rather more impressed by the new women MPs and thought their tabloid label of 'Blair's babes' did them a disservice. They were nobody's babes and most of them had a lot more confidence than I had had as a new MP. A few were taken aback by the chauvinism they encountered and got a bad press for complaining, but many soon made their mark and I was delighted. It was not easy for them. Government backbenchers have few opportunities to speak in debates when the parties are heavily unbalanced – perhaps four times a year, at best.

That was one of the reasons why we set up a parallel chamber in Westminster Hall to debate non-controversial issues and local matters of specific interest to backbenchers. There were so many MPs waiting to make their maiden speeches, which are supposed to be non-controversial, that I had to allow them to break with custom and speak on amendments to bills.

The new Cabinet included many colleagues from my party days and one of whom I was especially fond. I got to know Mo Mowlam when I was deputy Speaker and she was an Opposition frontbencher. One year I invited her to stop off in Sri Lanka while I was holidaying there and she was en route to Hong Kong. Typically, she arrived without a swimsuit, but had a gloriously slim figure and finding her a bikini was no problem. We had a great time splashing about in the Indian Ocean and riding elephants, and my friends adored her.

It was after she became shadow Northern Ireland Secretary in 1996 and I was Speaker that I noticed a change in her. She looked grey and ill, and very unhappy, and as she passed the chair I said: 'I'm very concerned about you. Come upstairs and have a cup of tea.' Back in Speaker's House, I told her that she was bound to be responsible for Northern Ireland after the forthcoming election, but she was not looking herself – what was the matter with her? What was going wrong?

Tears welled up. 'I'm sorry you've noticed,' she replied. 'I'm terribly ill. I've got a tumour on the brain. I don't know how serious it is. I don't know at this stage if it's malignant.' I was absolutely shocked. The tumour had been diagnosed in January and she had told only Jon, her husband, and Tony Blair. I was the third person to know and I was very distressed.

Mo lived in Islington and was going to Charing Cross Hospital at Hammersmith for treatment, still not knowing whether the growth was cancerous. She was not allowed to drive, and the expense of taxis, and more importantly the effort of getting to hospital and back home to rest afterwards, was wearing her out. I was desperately anxious to help. I told her: 'The most sensible thing is for you to come here to Speaker's House after you've had your treatment. There's a spare bedroom. You take it as your own and rest here at any time of day or night that you want. You don't have to sit in your Commons office to try to rest, or go back to Islington. You come here.'

Only two other people knew of our arrangement: Nicolas Bevan and Roseanne O'Reilly. I told them that any time Mo came through the office downstairs, she must not be stopped or questioned, but allowed straight up. Roseanne was wonderful. She prepared the bedroom and when Mo woke up after her rest there would be a cup of tea and some Marmite on toast. Mo kept up her regular attendance in the Commons but weeks of radiotherapy caused her to lose her hair and she started wearing a wig.

We were coming up to the 1997 election and the press began to write unflattering pieces about her appearance and her dramatic increase in weight, which rose from twelve stone to fourteen because of the steroids she had been prescribed. Mo told reporters it was because of the junk food she was eating after giving up smoking, and that she had a new hairstyle to stop looking 'a bit of a mess'.

She told me, however, that she thought they were on to the wig and was worried that they might pull a stunt during the campaign in order to embarrass her. What should she do? I advised her to tell the truth, because that would stop them making mischief. She agreed and bravely faced up to it. Thankfully, the tumour was not cancerous and she entered the Cabinet, as planned. I love Mo, thought of her as the daughter I never had and was highly protective of her. But I would have done the same for any Member in her situation.

She was the right person for Northern Ireland at that stage in the search for peace. I stayed with her at Hillsborough Castle, the Secretary of State's official home in the Ulster countryside, where she gave a lovely house party one weekend for old friends and was very relaxed. We walked in the woods, Mo did jigsaw puzzles and we played charades and stayed up until the early hours. The next day we planted 'Madam Speaker' roses in the gardens.

'Well, Betty, where do I go from here?' she asked. I thought her future lay with some large international organisation, like the United Nations, and still think so. Mo has made lots of contacts, who respect her hugely. But although she listened to me and tended to agree, she was not a career planner and nothing further was done. She went instead to the Cabinet Office.

Sinn Fein, the Irish republican party associated with the Provisional IRA, won two seats in the 1997 election and claimed the right to establish a London office in the House of Commons. That posed a real problem for me, because its two

Members, Gerry Adams and Martin McGuinness, refused to swear the oath of allegiance that every MP must make at the start of a new Parliament.

Adams had refused before, when he was first elected in 1983, but made no attempt to claim any special privileges at that time. His party's policy was to demonstrate its popular support by winning seats, but to play no part in the actual parliamentary life of Westminster. That remained the position until 1992, when he lost his seat to Sinn Fein's rival Irish nationalists, the Social Democratic and Labour Party (SDLP), who operated as a constitutional party.

When Adams regained his old seat in 1997 and his chief lieutenant, Martin McGuinness, won Mid-Ulster the situation changed. They continued to refuse to take the oath, but claimed full access to Commons facilities and the right to make the House their party's London base. The *Los Angeles Times*, a neutral observer of the situation, described the political background as follows:

> Both men were elected from Northern Ireland on May 1 as Irish nationalists representing the political arm of the IRA, which has warred against British rule for almost three decades. Both ran on an anti-Parliament, get-Britain-out-of-Ireland ticket. Still Adams and McGuinness announced last week that while they would not take their seats, they hoped to establish a Sinn Fein base at Westminster. A convicted former IRA member was named to head the office.

My concern was not the politics of the situation, which centuries of conflict have yet to resolve, but protecting the rules of the House. Here were two MPs who wanted to use it on their own terms. Passing no judgement on their party's anti-British policies, I explained on 14 May why they could not do so.

'I wish to make a statement about the availability of services in the House to those who do not take their seats after being returned here as Members. This House has traditionally accommodated great extremes of opinion. I am sure therefore that the House will not wish to put any unnecessary obstacle in the way of Members wishing to fulfil their democratic mandate by attending, speaking and voting in this House.

'Equally, I feel certain that those who choose not to take their seats should not have access to the many benefits and facilities that are now available in the House without also taking up their responsibilities as Members.'

The legal requirement on Members to swear allegiance before they could take up those responsibilities was clear. The Parliamentary Oaths Act of 1866 barred from voting or sitting in any debate Members who did not take the oath or affirm their loyalty to the Crown. They could incur a fine of £500 and their seats be declared vacant if they did, thus causing a by-election.

A previous Speaker had ruled in 1924 that Members who refused to take the oath should also be unpaid. To clarify the situation, I ruled that such Members were not entitled to any of the services provided by the six departments of the House and ordered a list to be published to remove any possible doubt. Specifically, my ruling denied such Members the right to office accommodation, the provision of passes, access to restricted areas and the booking of rooms. I ordered these rules to come into force at midnight on 20 May, at the end of the debate on the Queen's Speech. In future, I ruled, Members would be required to take the oath, or write seeking excusal, by the date of the Queen's Speech itself.

Sinn Fein challenged my statement, as I had expected they would. Adams called it 'discriminatory' and 'arrogant', and he and McGuinness came to Westminster the day before the deadline to voice their objections. They were met at the public entrance by Superintendent Robert Woods, assistant Head of Security, and escorted to a meeting with Peter Jennings, the Serjeant at Arms.

A Sinn Fein journalist in their party wrote about the visit in the party's newspaper, *Republican News*. He noted the rich mosaic on the ceiling of the central lobby, representing the four parts of the British Isles: Scotland, Wales, England and Ireland (the last represented by the crests of Leinster in the south and Ulster in the north). 'They're a bit behind the times in this place,' he commented.

He may not have known that, when southern Ireland was part of the United Kingdom and sent MPs to Westminster in the nineteenth century, they swore the oath, even though they disliked doing so, in order to champion their cause on the floor of the House – and very effective they were, too. It was Sinn Fein that was behind the times.

Mary Robinson, the first woman President of Ireland, had visited me in Speaker's House during her visit to London in June 1996 and I had been delighted to see her. I wish I could have given an official dinner in her honour, but there was no time. She had an acute sense of what was needed to improve Anglo-Irish relations, and banging on about the past was not on her agenda – or mine.

All the same, the Sinn Fein reporter clearly relished the experience of walking into 'the heart of the British state' with Adams and McGuinness, past the statues of Oliver Cromwell and William Gladstone, who had played such critical roles in Irish history. After meeting the Serjeant at Arms and the Clerk of the House, who told them that my ruling was binding, they were taken on a brief tour by a sympathetic Labour MP and ate in the Commons canteen. Outside, Adams told supporters waving Irish tricolours that Sinn Fein's vote of 126,000 in the general election had made it the third-biggest party in 'the six counties' of Northern Ireland and that their mandate should be fully respected by the British Government. He went on:

'The decision by the Speaker illustrates the undemocratic nature of British policy towards Ireland. Once again the British state changed the rules, which for a hundred years have specifically allowed MPs who wouldn't take the oath to have access to facilities. What is the British establishment afraid of? Why does it subvert its own laws rather than face the reality that those it opposes have rights? One thing is for certain, we will be back.'

He was wrong in several respects. I had not changed the rules. I had reacted to a political party which refused to take its seats in the House of Commons wanting to use it as an address of convenience. Adams and McGuinness relied on the ruling by Erskine May that a Member who does not take the oath is entitled to 'all the other privileges' of being a Member, apart from sitting in the chamber and voting in divisions. But Erskine May meant such Members being allowed to represent their constituents in taking up issues with ministers and having the right to free Commons stationery and postage to do so. They wanted to use the House in a manner that was totally at odds with its prime function as a forum for parliamentary debate. They thought they had found a loophole by asking for office accommodation without taking the oath. I closed it.

In August McGuinness turned to the courts. He applied for a judicial review of my ruling in the High Court of Justice in Northern Ireland, which kept the controversy going and raised the stakes. If he could persuade a High Court judge to find that my ruling was unconstitutional, unfair, improper and discriminatory, as he claimed, then my authority would be challenged and Parliament would be caught in a constitutional tangle.

As the controversy rumbled on, however, it was Sinn Fein that found itself in a tangle and changed its line of attack. The real target, McGuinness explained, was not Madam Speaker but the oath.

'I intend challenging the legality of the oath and demanding its abolition. It clearly discriminates against Irish nationalists and republicans who dispute British jurisdiction over this part of Ireland. It also denies to us our right to freedom of expression. Irish republican MPs are not second class. Those we represent are not second class. The British government and the British parliamentary system must accept the fundamental principle of equality.'

His problem in taking me to court was that the Bill of Rights protected my rulings – and anything else that Parliament said or did – from judicial interference. Mr Justice Kerr confirmed on 3 October that he had no jurisdiction, because the Commons had 'unfettered control of its own internal arrangements', and that I had acted on behalf of the House as its 'delegate and agent'.

McGuinness was in the United States with Adams at the time, having been refused legal aid. Unabashed, his lawyers stated that they would consider going either to the Court of Appeal, the final court in British law, or the European Court of Human Rights under the terms of the Convention for the Protection of Human Rights and Fundamental Freedoms, which Britain had ratified. Either way, they were not giving up. While I prepared for the next round, Adams and

McGuinness made a final attempt to change my mind.

Events in Northern Ireland had now turned in their favour. Adams was negotiating openly with the Government about a political settlement to the causes of the violence that had claimed 3,000 lives, and was invited to talks in Downing Street. He argued that my denying him the run of the House of Commons was absurd, since he was allowed into 10 Downing Street to see the Prime Minister.

Mo Mowlam told me that Adams and McGuinness wanted to see me and they came to Speaker's House on 4 December. I met them in my study, with no staff, press or photographers present. We shook hands and I listened carefully to what they had to say. I told them: 'As Speaker, I am bound by the law. Swearing the oath or affirming is a legal requirement that cannot be set aside by administrative action. Primary legislation would be needed to change the Parliamentary Oaths Act or the form of the oath. It is your refusal to swear or affirm that prevents you taking your seats – not any action by me,' I explained to them.

'My decision does not discriminate against Sinn Fein; it applies equally to any Members not taking their seats for any reason. Those who do not take up their democratic responsibilities cannot have access to the facilities at Westminster that are made available to assist Members who do.

'You are in effect asking for Associate Membership of this House. Such a thing does not exist. There can be no halfway House.'

Adams did most of the talking, while McGuinness paid close attention. They were charming throughout. As they rose to leave, Adams turned to me smiling and said, 'Madam Speaker, the press are waiting outside. What are we going to say to them?'

I replied, 'You tell them exactly what I have told you. The fat old girl in there is immovable.'

'We cannot tell them that,' he laughed.

'Knowing you, you'll think of something,' I said. I felt as impregnable as the Rock of Gibraltar. I would not budge unless the rules were changed, a point Adams understood. He described our exchanges as 'very frank' and 'quite cordial and friendly'. More significantly, he explained Sinn Fein's real ambitions to the *Irish Times*.

The question of the oath was, he admitted, 'a bit of a distraction' and whether it remained – or was changed to remove the required allegiance to the monarch – was irrelevant. Sinn Fein's basic objection to sitting in the British Parliament was 'the claim of that Parliament to jurisdiction in Ireland'. In other words, his real grievance was not my ruling against Sinn Fein opening an office at Westminster, but Northern Ireland being represented in Parliament at all.

Sinn Fein's original line about the oath standing in the way of it enjoying equal rights with other parties was thus momentarily abandoned. This was not because of anything I said; it was prompted by a sardonic suggestion by Clive Soley, chairman of the Parliamentary Labour Party, that Sinn Fein's problem would be solved if the Oaths Act were changed to allow MPs to swear allegiance to Parliament instead of the Queen. That would call Sinn Fein's bluff, said Soley – and he was right.

Adams replied that while such a change might be good for British democracy, it would not alter Sinn Fein's position, logically flawed though that was. Reverting to the original complaint about the oath, McGuinness then challenged my ruling in the European Court: another first for me as Speaker. His lawyers evidently thought he stood no chance in the Court of Appeal, but that he was more likely to succeed in an international court, which would not be swayed by the Bill of Rights.

Supporting the European appeal, Adams now claimed that my ruling was 'part of the old knee-jerk agenda' about 'marginalising and demonising people, about denying people their rights'. The truth was more prosaic, as I explained in a statement. I was bound by a law that could not be bypassed by administrative action. It was as simple as that.

The European Court finally endorsed my stand, and the law on which it was based, in a lengthy judgment published on 8 June 1999. Its findings did not attract the attention they deserved, because of the way in which they came out on the court's website, where the full judgment remained unnoticed for several days. Had the court upheld McGuinness, the result would have been trumpeted around the world as an exposé of my bias and of British injustice.

The fact that the court dismissed McGuinness's claims completely aroused little interest. My ruling was shown to have 'a clear legal basis' in Britain's domestic law, and in its parliamentary practice and procedure, and I had full legal authority to regulate the services of the House.

The court's seven judges further declared that the protection of effective democracy 'must equally extend to the protection of the constitutional principles which underpin a democracy'. It followed that, as the United Kingdom was a monarchy, the oath was part of its constitutional system. So Parliament was entitled to require its Members to take the oath.

The court's judgment did contain one unexpected element. It disclosed that McGuinness had argued that his religion – as well as his political views – prevented him from swearing allegiance. He claimed that his faith as a Roman Catholic disallowed it, because he could not swear allegiance to a monarch who was prevented by law from being a Catholic or from marrying one.

This was a new one. He was referring to the 1701 Act of Settlement, which requires British sovereigns to be Protestants and descendants of the House of Hanover. It had never previously prevented Catholic MPs or members of other faiths from taking the oath, but McGuinness claimed that it made the oath 'repugnant to his religious beliefs'.

The European Court was unimpressed. It ruled that he had voluntarily renounced his right to sit in the Commons and that his claim to have been denied his democratic rights was 'manifestly ill-founded'. His religious claim was also dismissed, on the grounds that he was not required to swear allegiance to any particular religion.

Nor were McGuinness's constituents denied their rights. They had voted for him knowing that he was required to take the oath if he was elected, and Sinn Fein supporters had the same right to vote in and stand for Westminster elections as anybody else. And his exclusion from the House did not prevent McGuinness from raising matters of concern with ministers, their departments and other MPs. Furthermore, my ruling was not discriminatory because it applied to all MPs 'without distinction'. The fact that it bore more heavily on Sinn Fein than on others was due to their policy regarding the oath. For these reasons, the court concluded that McGuinness did not have 'an arguable grievance' under the European Convention for the Protection of Human Rights.

That, I thought, was surely that. Nobody could accuse the European Court of being prejudiced against Irish republicans. It had ruled against Britain when the families of IRA members who had been shot dead by British soldiers in Gibraltar claimed they had been unlawfully killed. Now it had ruled in my favour against Sinn Fein. But I had not reckoned on the importance that the Government attached to gaining Sinn Fein's goodwill in the prolonged peace negotiations.

Towards the end of 1999 I became aware that

ministers were considering whether a concession to Sinn Fein's request for Commons facilities would help move along the peace process – and especially the IRA's decommissioning of weapons. As Speaker, I was neutral in the matter. Personally, I thought it would be wiser to have something on the table from Sinn Fein/IRA before making a concession that would probably just be pocketed. These views were conveyed to ministers.

On 19 December the *Sunday Times* carried a report in its Irish edition, headlined 'Adams wins row over oath to Queen'. It claimed that I was finalising the details to give him and McGuinness parliamentary offices:

> Boothroyd's concession is part of the delicate choreography of confidence-building measures designed by George Mitchell, the former US senator [chairing the peace negotiations] and the British and Irish Governments to ensure that the peace process stays on course and IRA decommissioning starts by February ... Boothroyd will justify her change of heart on the basis of the new devolved administration at Stormont where McGuinness, who was twice convicted of IRA membership in the 1970s, is Minister for Education. No oath of allegiance is required in the Stormont assembly.

No. 10 denied any involvement in the story and Peter Mandelson, now Northern Ireland Secretary, telephoned my office to declare his ignorance of its origins. But it certainly did not come from me.

An early opportunity arose to make my position clear when Crispin Blunt, a Conservative backbencher, raised the *Sunday Times* article on a point of order and asked for my comments. I recalled the background and told him: 'It is true to say that one or two ministers have been to see me recently. The House would not expect me to divulge any conversations. Others may divulge conversations of that nature; I do not. Should Ministers wish the two Sinn Fein Members to have access to some of the facilities, it would be for the Government to bring a motion to that effect for debate and decision by the House. I am the servant of the House and if it approved such a motion, I would of course ensure that it was put into effect.'

Sinn Fein's *Republican News* noted after the recess that Blair and Mandelson were believed to support their claim to parliamentary services. It added that Martin McGovern, their London representative, 'believed a motion overturning the ban will be brought before the House by the Labour Government within the next two or three weeks'.

I waited, but nothing happened and my ruling was still in force when I retired. Adams returned to the issue in May 2001, saying that he had talked to the British Government 'at the very highest level' and intended to pursue the matter again. He argued that Sinn Fein had a permanent office in London as part of its 'international outreach' and its efforts to influence British public opinion. 'Our people are there very regularly. The problem at the moment is that we have to pay for them.'

After he became Speaker, Michael Martin confirmed my ruling, following another report that Sinn Fein was to be admitted. However, the election of four Sinn Fein Members in the June 2001 general election put fresh pressure on the Government and they got their way. They thus enjoy the perks of being MPs – the parliamentary offices and expenses – without taking part in the work and life of the Commons. I noted that the Prime Minister did not put his name to the Government motion that allowed this breach with our traditions. I believe he should have done. Whatever the politics of the issue, the damage caused to the integrity of Parliament has potentially dangerous and long-term consequences.

CHAPTER SIXTEEN

Landslide

No Government can be long secure without a formidable Opposition.

Benjamin Disraeli

W HEN HE MOVED into No. 10 Tony Blair dropped another old custom I was sad to see go. As usual I was invited to the Prime Minister's reception on the eve of the Queen's Speech at the start of each session, but its traditional purpose was abandoned. There was no advance reading of the speech by the Cabinet Secretary; instead Blair gave a drinks party. Gin and tonic replaced warm wine, and Cherie Blair frowned on smoking. I welcomed the former but was discomfited by the latter. Anji Hunter, Blair's special assistant, must have noticed. 'Do you like to smoke?' she asked. My confirmation of that well-known fact earned me an exemption.

I shared my concern about the lack of experience of both Government and Opposition with an eminent civil servant. He thought they would adjust to their new roles within two or three years and that everything would come right. But it never did during my time.

Blair was determined to make No. 10 more powerful than it had ever been in peacetime. One of his aides told Peter Hennessy, the constitutional historian, that it would be like changing from feudal times to the age of Napoleon.

We were in an unusual situation. Tony Blair was the first Prime Minister to take office without any ministerial experience since Ramsay MacDonald formed the first Labour Government in 1924. The rest of his senior ministers, with the exception of John Morris, the Attorney-General, were in the same position.

The Conservatives found themselves at an even greater disadvantage. They knew their way around the corridors of power, but these were now closed to them. Few of their surviving leaders had any experience of what it was like to be in opposition and the party was still burdened by its divisions over Europe. To make matters worse, the Tories faced a hostile press, watched over by Downing Street's media advisers.

Liberal Democrat MPs tried to exploit the Tory Party's problems in a manner of which I thoroughly disapproved. This happened shortly after William Hague's election as Conservative leader in June 1997. Defying convention, a number of LibDem MPs occupied the front bench of the official Opposition one morning before I entered the chamber. As soon as I heard about it I sent the

Serjeant at Arms and Nicolas Bevan to tell them that their action was unacceptable and they were to remove themselves.

They were reminded that their place as a minority party was below the gangway that runs further along the Opposition benches. Only the official Opposition, that is the minority party with the largest number of MPs – the Conservatives – had the right to sit above the gangway and speak from the dispatch box.

When I appeared Paul Tyler, the LibDem Member for North Cornwall, tried to defend their action, but I was having none of it. 'I have never known grown-up people to behave in such a crass and childish manner,' I declared. 'I think that it is time that Members of this House grew up. If they do not, I shall want to see the leaders of the Conservative and Liberal Democrat parties very soon.' I then told the LibDem wanderers to remove themselves while I was still on my feet. As they shuffled off, I said I was 'ashamed of this morning's proceedings'.

William Hague's election completed the transfer of leadership in both major parties to a new generation. The youngest Tory leader for nearly 200 years, he was unafraid of Labour's huge majority and I admired his incisive questioning of Blair. I attended his wedding to Ffion in the Chapel of St Mary Undercroft in the Commons crypt. In a gallant gesture, he sent David Lidington, his Parliamentary Private Secretary, to escort me and I sat in the front row as they exchanged their vows in English and Welsh.

By the time we rose for the summer recess, Blair and his closest advisers were masters of all they surveyed. Word reached me that Cabinet meetings were mostly cursory affairs. The way Blair ran his Cabinet was not my concern; maintaining the Commons' rights to scrutinise legislation and question ministers was.

I had to remind No. 10 that my approval was needed before the names of new deputy Speakers were put to the House. The cause of this frisson was their intention to offer a deputy's job to a former frontbencher, as a consolation for his not becoming a minister. He, however, had not been a member of the Speaker's Panel of Chairmen, the customary route for promotion to a deputy's position, and I was not prepared to waive my rights. My new deputies were Sir Alan Haselhurst, Michael Martin and Michael Lord. My message to the Government was unequivocal: 'My department is not a dustbin for people you want to get rid of.'

A spate of Whitehall leaks and briefings, about important policy changes that MPs should have been told of first, was harder to control. I took the unusual – possibly unprecedented – decision to delay Gordon Brown's first Budget statement by fifteen minutes in May to allow Peter Lilley, the shadow Chancellor, to question the origin of what appeared to be a Budget leak that morning. The *Financial Times* had reported that the Chancellor would announce the abolition of pension-fund tax credits that afternoon – an important change in fiscal law.

Ann Taylor ridiculed Lilley's charge, but the

Chancellor did announce it. Brown was not pleased at being kept waiting to deliver his Budget statement, watched by millions on television, but I thought Lilley had a case and the right to put it. I had no idea where the *FT* got its story, but I knew that Whitehall's media managers were adept at releasing sensitive information to favoured reporters to prepare public opinion ahead of a formal announcement, pre-empt the parliamentary debate and outflank the Opposition.

I deplored this kind of leak twice that month. On 10 July I said: 'Like other Honourable Members, I often listen to [Government] statements on the radio in the morning in the hope that a further statement in greater detail will be made in the House in the afternoon. Often that does not occur. I deprecate statements or information on policy changes that are made either on the radio or at press conferences. The House should be the first to know when changes of Government policy occur.'

Disclosures of the Government's intention to break the principle of free education and introduce tuition fees for university students brought fresh complaints from Members and I supported them. On 21 July I observed: 'The practice of briefing in advance of a ministerial statement by Whitehall sources has been current for quite a long time. My impression is that over the past twenty years, it has progressively developed to the point where the rights of the House are in danger of being overlooked. The House is rightly jealous of its role in holding ministers to account. If it is to fulfil its function properly, it must be the first to learn of important developments in Government policy. I deprecate most strongly action that tends to undermine this important principle.'

Ministers were not alone in needing to be reminded of their obligations. I took up a complaint from David Winnick, Labour MP for Walsall North, that the BBC was planning to downgrade its parliamentary broadcasting, in breach of its statutory undertaking that 'the BBC shall broadcast an impartial account day by day of the proceedings of Parliament'.

Our fears centred on mooted changes to its flagship radio programmes *Yesterday in Parliament* and *The Week in Westminster*. They were not dispelled when the BBC acknowledged my concerns, but declined to comment until they had reviewed the situation. I wrote to John Birt, the Corporation's Director-General, and Sir Christopher Bland, its Chairman, in July 1997 and placed copies of my correspondence in the Commons library to keep Members informed. It was the beginning of a long battle.

Sir Christopher's lack of enthusiasm for parliamentary broadcasting was soon apparent. 'Radio 4 does need to reconcile the BBC's important obligation to report Parliament comprehensively with its need to remain sympathetic to listeners' needs,' he wrote on 24 July 1997. He claimed that the Radio 4 audience dropped by 350,000 when *Yesterday in Parliament* began and that many listeners switched to other stations.

That was a spurious argument. Radio audiences fell during the early morning for obvious reasons, whether or not Parliament was sitting. Another move, tucked away in the small print of the BBC's proposed changes, also alarmed me. They intended to transfer their more reflective and prestigious programme, *The Week in Westminster*, from its established slot at 11 a.m. on Saturdays to unknown territory: 8.30 p.m. on Thursdays. I was informed that its 500,000 regular listeners would be more than halved by the change.

These were 'important and complex issues', Bland argued. He agreed that all radio networks lost some listeners between 8.30 a.m. and 9 a.m. but claimed that Radio 4 lost rather more. Then, turning his own argument on its head, he said it was true that Thursday night's audience for *The Week in Westminster* was likely to be 'significantly lower' than Saturday morning's, but 'we expect to engage a loyal, and we hope, growing audience'.

Bland and I met on 17 March 1998, when I expressed my reservations in the clearest terms. It was a complete non-meeting of minds. *Yesterday in Parliament* was shunted off to Long Wave, which many listeners have difficulty receiving, and I was treated to a homily about the need for 'judicious scheduling' to maximise listener choice. Bland said that the changes were needed to safeguard Radio 4's future and its commitment to 'effective parliamentary coverage'.

I was appalled. Pushing two flagship programmes to the margins was not my definition of effectiveness.

On 6 April I wrote quoting Bland's own admission that their audiences were likely to plummet, and added:

> It is difficult to reconcile this reality with the rhetoric of your commitment ... My concern is that the BBC is overlooking its duty as a public-service broadcaster to educate as well as to entertain, is marginalising parliamentary broadcasting and is in effect seeking to withdraw from its commitment to the democratic process.

A year later my fears were acknowledged. Audiences for *Yesterday in Parliament* and *The Week in Westminster* were down by 73 per cent and 65 per cent respectively and the effect on Radio 4's popularity between 8.30 and 9 a.m. was non-existent. Even so, Bland still argued that consumer choice mattered most. He wrote to me on 23 March 1999: 'We should not *make* people listen' to parliamentary programmes.

I replied:

> The effect on the reach of parliamentary broadcasting has been disastrous – far worse than even the BBC predicted.
>
> There has been no countervailing increase in the audience for Radio 4 programmes that have replaced parliamentary broadcasting, which was after all the rationale for the changes you introduced. The conclusion is equally obvious. The experiment has failed and the changes

introduced last year should be immediately rescinded.

'I have noted your views and understand your position,' Bland replied on 26 April. 'I have made it clear that we are open to change.' The governors had finally realised the strength of feeling in the House about its favourite programmes. On 22 July Bland wrote to me again, hauling down the flag:

> It is clear, after a year's experience and from audience figures, that the changes in the Radio 4 schedule which were introduced in April 1998 did not give appropriate prominence to parliamentary broadcasting.

The Week in Westminster was returned to Saturday mornings on FM and Long Wave; *Today in Parliament* returned to FM as well as Long Wave five nights a week; the *Today* programme was given a parliamentary slot; and *Yesterday in Parliament* was given more time on Long Wave. The governors decreed: 'Parliamentary broadcasting is a key responsibility of the BBC and its execution should be kept under continuous review.'

I signed off in a final letter to Bland on 26 July:

> It is sad that so much unnecessary damage has been done by ignoring what should have been obvious from the start. Nevertheless I welcome your recognition of what has happened and your acceptance that the damage must be repaired.

Triumph and reconciliation. President Mandela enters Westminster Hall, 1996.

Tony Blair and Sir Edward Heath at the unveiling of my portrait
in 1 Parliament Street, January 2000

Musical evening at Speaker's House with the Prescotts, Marian Montgomery
and Laurie Holloway

Addressing the Duma

A meeting with Gennady Seleznev, Speaker of the Russian Parliament

The Pandit Pant lecture at the
Central Hall of Parliament House
in New Delhi September 1994.
'There were no imperialists
in my family.'

Celebrating the 50th
anniversary of Sri Lankan
independence with the Sri
Lankan High Commissioner

At the Taj Mahal, 1994

Installation as Chancellor
of the Open University,
March 1995

Two Yorkshire tykes in
Oxford. David Hockney
and I with Honorary
degrees

Florida reunion
with the
Golden Girls

At a charity function –
and never scored a goal

Helen de Freitas's birthday
party in my garden at
Thriplow

My favourite snapshot of Mo taken on our Sri Lankan holiday

Up, up and away. Paragliding on holiday in Paphos.

A Sunday morning on London's liquid history

'The Gang of Three'. Taking my seat in the House of Lords with
Baroness Castle and Lord Healey.

It was not quite game, set and match. I would have liked the return of *Yesterday in Parliament* to FM as well, but the governors had gone a long way towards meeting my objections and those of the House.

The BBC later took over the Parliament Channel on cable television, which broadcasts the Commons live, provides continuous coverage of party conferences and general-election campaigns and carries recorded Lords debates and select-committee hearings. As it recognised in its 1999 statement, the BBC has a duty to foster interest in the political process and the obligations of citizenship – a vital part of its public service that Bland's misguided marketing ignored.

In the summer recess of 1997, I had not planned to go to India, but I was invited in such a persuasive way that I could not refuse. My arrangements were altered when L. M. Singhvi, India's long-serving High Commissioner in London, brought P. A. Sangma, the Speaker of India's Parliament, the Lok Sabha (House of the People), to see me some months previously.

They wanted me to represent the Commons at a ceremony to mark the fiftieth anniversary of India's independence from Britain in the central hall of the Lok Sabha, where Pandit Nehru had declared his country's 'tryst with destiny' in August 1947. I was due in Australia shortly afterwards and was sorry that I could not accept. The High Commissioner, however, persisted. 'Look, this is a very important occasion to us. To have you with us as the representative of the

Mother of Parliaments is the finest tribute my country can pay to yours.'

I was immensely touched and agreed to change my plans and go to New Delhi with Nicolas Bevan and Bill McKay, then Assistant Clerk of the House. Unbeknown to me, my presence was not universally welcomed. A vocal minority took exception to my sitting on the dais in central hall with the President of India, the Prime Minister and Speaker Sangma.

One Indian MP wrote to him suggesting that it would be better to honour the freedom fighters who had died or languished in the jails of British India, or to give my seat to a member of the former Indian National Army that had fought with the Japanese in the war. I was accused of representing 'the seat of the colonial regime' that had subjugated India for two hundred years. Sangma, a tough character, would not be budged.

He welcomed me as an honoured guest at a sitting of the Lok Sabha and refused my suggestion that I sat in the audience at the midnight ceremony. 'No! You will be on that platform,' he said. 'You do not represent the imperial power. You represent the country of Attlee, and you come from his party and the Mother of Parliaments.' He was no more than five feet tall, but a man of steel. I did as he said.

I met the President that afternoon and, as midnight approached, I made my way towards the dais in the central hall, greeted on all sides. Some people said as I passed, 'Attlee, we remember Attlee.' I did too, as I sat alongside India's leaders to celebrate the independence that Clement Attlee's government had given them when I was young. My mind flitted back to Fenner Brockway's Movement for Colonial Freedom and I remembered Indira Gandhi's words to a Commonwealth gathering that I attended: 'Welcome to India, land of contrasts. My father spent a lifetime trying to discover it.'

Later I went on to Australia, which was where I heard the news of Princess Diana's death. Nicolas Bevan and I had been touring the country on an official visit and were resting on Orpheus Island on the Great Barrier Reef with our hosts from the Australian Parliament. We were at lunch when the owner of the hotel told us, 'Princess Diana has had an accident and has passed on.' We thought he meant she had carried on after the accident and said how glad we were.

He repeated, this time with greater emphasis, that she had 'passed on' and I asked him to explain himself. When we realised that he had been trying to break the news gently to us, Nicolas telephoned the British High Commissioner in Canberra to be told that the Princess of Wales had died from her injuries. We were at the end of our visit and returned home.

A few days later, John Guinery and I went to Kew Gardens. Returning to central London on the Tube, we saw many passengers, mostly women, carrying flowers to place outside Kensington Palace and Buckingham Palace in tribute to the Princess. The size and emotion of the crowds that watched her funeral service at Westminster Abbey, which I attended, confirmed that the scale of public grief at her loss was greater than I had first realised.

*

I had by now already thought about the timing of my retirement and almost gave the game away in an interview for *Saga* magazine's August issue. 'Will she soldier on until the next election?' it asked.

'There are no rules about it,' I answered. 'But I probably think it would be easier for the Government of the day if I went in mid-term.'

'The mid-term of this Parliament?' asked my interviewer.

'Not necessarily,' I replied with what he described as 'a broad but enigmatic smile'. On that note, the soft-focus, three-page article ended. Fortunately nobody spotted the clear hint that I was likely to quit before the next general election. Had they done so, I would have become a lame duck hobbled by constant speculation concerning my successor. Fleet Street slumbers in August and I was grateful for it.

I had enough problems as it was. The recess had been enlivened by an extraordinary burst of speculation about the Government's policy on entry into the European economic and monetary union. Gordon Brown had given an interview to *The Times* which it had interpreted as a flat rejection of Britain joining the euro in the lifetime of the current Parliament. Advance news of this had taken Blair totally by surprise and he asked Charlie Whelan, Brown's press secretary, for an explanation.

I insisted that the Chancellor make an immediate statement to the House enlightening us all on our return. Brown would have preferred three days' grace, but I made it clear that I would allow an Opposition Private Notice Question obliging him to come to the House without delay. He took my point.

My fears about the difficulties created by a totally unbalanced House were warranted. A rampant Government wanted as little parliamentary interference as possible, while the Tories found it hard to manage themselves, let alone become a competent Opposition. The essence of a parliamentary system is a vigorous Opposition, and in the interests of democracy I found myself in the unusual role of trying to help them pick themselves up from the floor. Blair was right when he said there was little chance of my ever needing to use my casting vote again, but that did not mean I was powerless – far from it. The Government controlled the normal business of the House, as it should. But I controlled the conduct of business, under the powers entrusted to me by Standing Orders, and nothing could affect that.

Ministers were less of a problem than the swollen ranks of apparatchiks around them, whose off-the-record comments sometimes had a greater effect than anything their masters said. I had no quarrel with Alastair Campbell, the Prime Minister's press secretary. He was a tough operator and I had trusted him when he was a political journalist. He came across from No. 10 to tell me that he was anxious not to offend and understood my position. The problem lay with the freelance operations of the new class of spin-doctors who occupied every Government department. Power had gone to their heads and they believed their ministers needed the oxygen of publicity to survive. Somebody said it would be no bad thing if they were laid end-to-end on the bed of the English Channel. I agreed.

Before the year was out, I took the unusual step of using an interview with the *Birmingham Post* to warn ministers and their advisers that I was keeping a close watch on what they said outside the House. Those who put Parliament low on their list of priorities had fair warning. I was not satisfied with winning the odd skirmish – 'I will win the war,' I said. But I never did.

A few backbenchers made life even more difficult on our return from the summer recess. Anonymous complaints were published that I was too tough with Labour's new women Members. My beastliness was alleged to be the talk of the Commons tearoom. It was said that I had been put 'on probation' by the Government whips, which had a familiar ring. It was a repeat performance of the tittle-tattle I had endured under the Tories. Nobody said anything to me directly, of course.

The only specific charge was that I had dealt harshly with the new Labour MP for Crawley, Laura Moffatt. Apparently 'it was horrible to watch', one report said. So horrible that my severity was to be discussed by Labour's women's committee. If it was, nothing came of it.

The Hansard report showed what actually happened. Laura had fallen into the error of prefacing a question with a time-consuming preamble and I corrected her as helpfully as I knew how. I believed strongly that Question Times were golden opportunities for sharp questions and pithy replies – the more, the better. The faster the delivery, the less time ministers have to consult their files, listen to colleagues prompting them or think of an evasive answer. The prize for the best supplementary question ever put went to Tam Dalyell, who punctured a minister's composure with one word: 'Why?'

As Laura began to tell us what she thought of the Tories, I apologised for interrupting, saying she must put a question. When it came it was a very good one. Was Frank Dobson, the Health Secretary, aware, she asked, that 'we desperately need some improvement in Health Service staff?'

Criticism by one or two of her more sensitive sisters about my handling of the matter prompted Laura to write to me on 5 October putting the record straight:

> You may have seen in recent press reports that I was upset following a direction by yourself to ask a question without the long introduction. I feel that this was completely justified and in no way was I being victimised, as alleged by some newspapers. I do hope that we can put this matter behind us and I look forward to the forthcoming session of Parliament.

Diane Abbott, the forthright Labour MP for Hackney North and Stoke Newington, also wrote on 16 November rejecting the sniping against me.

> Some new Labour women MPs have been criticising you recently. They claim that you pick

on them. I think that they are quite wrong. Not only are you an extremely fair Speaker, but you go out of your way to help new Members (of whatever gender).

As you know I am a diehard feminist. But I think it is an odd sort of feminism which involves women MPs attacking one of the most popular Speakers that we have ever had – who also happens to be a woman! I think that these new women MPs complaining about you reflects badly on all women in the House and I hope that we will hear no more of it.

It is true that I made no concessions to women Members because of their gender. Some of them were helped to become MPs by the Labour Party's policy of positive discrimination, but that was no reason for me to apply it. As far as I was concerned, every Member competed on equal terms and women performed none the worse for that.

A number of Labour's women quickly impressed me. Lynda Clark, Yvette Cooper, Gisela Stuart and Sally Keeble went on to become ministers, although Gisela unaccountably lost her post in the 2001 reshuffle. Louise Ellman, Helen Jones, Margaret Moran, Phyllis Starkey, Helen Southworth and Diana Organ also showed great potential.

Among those already established in the House, Patricia Hewitt and Estelle Morris were natural Cabinet material, as was Theresa May on the Tory front bench. Blair sometimes asked me who impressed me and I gave him my impartial views.

After all, I saw more of his MPs than he did.

One cartoonist depicted me saying to a distressed woman MP, 'If you can't stand the heat, get back to the kitchen.' I was dismayed when I saw it, although I liked its sense of mischief. The original now hangs in my home at Thriplow. What I actually told one interviewer was that if women MPs could not stand the heat 'they should stay out of the kitchen'. For that is what Parliament is – or ought to be: a workplace where time is precious and people know what they are about.

The Speaker's Office ran on that principle and was the first department of the House to gain the coveted Investors in People Award for the excellence of its performance. Behind the scenes the workload was colossal. Nicolas Bevan and I planned my schedule with almost military precision, fitting in meetings, conferences, VIPs who wanted to call, and the entire range of Commons business. I spent an hour every Sunday night reviewing the week ahead and making telephone calls. My days in Speaker's House began with the *Today* programme, a brisk walk in St James's Park and a preliminary inspection of the order paper.

No Speaker will admit to deciding in advance which MPs will be called. Suffice it to say that the claims of those who want to speak because of a special interest are sifted well in advance. My first meeting with Nicolas at 9.30 a.m. was crucial. He had marked his order paper with a colour code, to show the party of each MP who was down for questions. I marked mine similarly and we considered the way things were likely to go. I anticipated the likely shape of Question Time, the most topical subjects and how best to call a representative cross-section of opinion.

Select-committee members and members of party groups have a strong case to be called on topics on which they are knowledgeable. 'Regulars' who attend the chamber daily should also be called, and timid Members also need to be encouraged. I tried to see all those who were not called to say, 'Don't despair.' Fitting the minority parties in was more of a problem. The Liberal Democrats had the right to put questions, but the smaller parties were more difficult to accommodate. Debates required careful preparation. I needed to know which ministers and Opposition frontbenchers would open and wind up and to decide whether to allow an amendment.

I met my three deputies and the Officers of the House at noon, after which the day's main events were broadly choreographed. I then considered the claims of MPs who wished to speak. The convention is that Members must catch the Speaker's eye before they are called, but that does not prevent them lobbying in advance in the hope that the Speaker will look in their direction. I took into account the number of times a Member had been called that session and any personal expertise. I knew where the flak might fly most, and from which quarter. More often than not, something happened for which we were unprepared. Some Members took more risks than others.

During the Conservative Government, Dale

Campbell-Savours, Labour MP for Workington and an assiduous parliamentarian, fell foul of the rules twice for attacking his targets in unacceptable terms. He accused the Tory MP Alan Duncan of a property 'rip-off' and Lord Archer, the Tory peer and author, of 'criminality'. He knew he was flouting the rules, but he refused to withdraw and left the chamber without complaint when I reproved him.

After the Conservatives went into Opposition there was less disorder in the chamber. Labour backbenchers had little incentive to kick the underdog Tories and the Tory backbenches took a long time to readjust to their diminished role. One uncharitable Tory ex-minister told me that he no longer paid much attention to his colleagues because half of them were 'nonentities' and the other half 'mad'.

From the outset my view was that William Hague performed better at the despatch box than his detractors allowed. He had the unenviable job of dragging his party back from the wilderness and he was not helped by opinion polls that constantly showed the Tories miles behind.

Despite my efforts, the Government machine continued to leak information that ought to have reached Parliament first. 'What is happening is that this House, and the status of this House is being devalued and I deprecate it most strongly,' I said on 3 December 1997. I then turned to Ann Taylor, the Leader of the House, and hoped there would be no recurrence. But I had little confidence in that happening and prepared for a long war of attrition.

Liam Fox, the Opposition constitutional affairs spokesman, made the sombre observation to me that 'It seems the Government simply wishes the House of Commons wasn't here.' I refused to accept that, but was furious when another Government initiative was leaked within days of my warning. Ironically, it concerned plans (later watered down) to introduce more open government. David Clark, Chancellor of the Duchy of Lancaster, apologised to the House for the leak but the damage was done.

'Time to get rough, Betty,' wrote Sir Bernard Ingham, Thatcher's former press secretary. 'If you don't, Parliament will soon count for nowt.' I could never countenance that. While I was around, the Commons would not be written off or pushed around by the Government, the BBC's management, Sinn Fein or anybody else.

CHAPTER SEVENTEEN

Standards and Privileges

___

*Changes which have occurred over the years in the role
and working environment of politicians and other public
servants have led to a confusion over what is and is not
acceptable behaviour.*

Lord Nolan

As I approached my sixth year in Speaker's House I was familiar with most of the questions that visitors asked, but the query from Madame Tussaud's was original: 'Are Madam Speaker's teeth her own?' They needed to know because they wanted to add my moulded image to their famous exhibition.

As they explained in a letter in January 1998, 'We cannot take a teeth cast if they are not.' Assured that they were indeed my own, a team of four arrived at Speaker's House for the preparatory work: a sculptor, a photographer and two moulders. They wanted a cast of my hands as well, plus a ready supply of water. I obliged with both. Eighteen months later I inspected the result.

While my appearance was being replicated, that of

the Commons chamber was disturbed, along with my sleep. An oak moulding fell from the ceiling and landed close to the Prime Minister's place on the front bench, where it would have seriously injured anybody in the way. Called from my bed, I inspected the damage in the early hours of 29 January while the Director of Parliamentary Works summoned specialist contractors to survey the ceiling and ensure the safety of Members.

Assured that there was no immediate danger of other panels landing on us, the House met as usual and a scaffolding crew moved in next day for the weekend. When one other panel was found to be potentially unsafe, 2,800 six-inch brass screws were inserted into all of them. That, it was said, would guarantee MPs' safety for another fifty years.

Looking further ahead, in February I laid the foundation stone of Portcullis House, the new parliamentary building facing Big Ben, which has a life-expectancy of 200 years. It was designed by Sir Michael Hopkins and stands as a showpiece of contemporary British architecture on one of the finest sites in London – a worthy neighbour of Charles Barry's Palace of Westminster. For the first time all 659 MPs have their own offices on the parliamentary estate. The building was a good investment and a splendid contribution to our national heritage.

My personal fabric needed remedial treatment at around that time. The size and design of the Speaker's chair flatters the occupant's authority but does nothing for the posture. I tended to slide around in it and developed a back problem. My solution was to prop a copy of Erskine May's bulky tome behind me and slip my shoes off when business was quiet, to exercise my feet.

The Government's popularity was undiminished as it pushed ahead with its programme, but Labour Members still cheered Tony Blair when he arrived for Question Time, as if their seats depended on it. On 11 February 1998 Mo Mowlam was answering a question about political progress in Northern Ireland when Blair walked in and the Labour benches roared their welcome. I had already reprimanded the Tories for cheering Hague's entrance. This time I turned to the more thickly packed Government side: 'Order. I won the battle on the Opposition benches. I will win the war on the Government benches.'

That day I was unhappy with the House generally for its performance. The misuse of Question Time had become much worse than it had been during the previous Parliament and fewer questions were being answered. It was time for a short tutorial.

'The primary purpose of questioning ministers is to hold the executive to account. Questions should relate to matters of public policy or administration for which ministers are responsible. I have to tell backbenchers that the purpose of a question is to obtain information or to press for action. It should not be a short speech.

'As for ministers, answers should be confined to points contained in the question, with a short explanation only when necessary to make the answer intelligible ... Members would do well to educate themselves . . . What is required above all are short questions and brisk answers . . . I shall not hesitate to intervene if I think a question or an answer is too long, but it would be much better if the House were to discipline and regulate itself. I hope it will do so.'

Some Members misheard me and thought I wanted them to be crisp instead of brisk. As a result, I became known as Miss Crisp in the Members' tearoom. Evidently my enunciation needed improving.

My campaign to raise the standards of conduct and debate in the House was by this time well into its stride. Some veterans, like Tam Dalyell, would have liked me to be even firmer, especially at Prime Minister's Question Time, but I had to strike a balance between coercion and persuasion. Above all, I had to carry the House with me. I had already gone further than any previous Speaker in calling for accusations of improper behaviour to be investigated.

My call for urgent action in 1996 had prompted an inquiry into the conduct of twenty-five Members that was analogous in its scope to a statutory tribunal of inquiry. Most members were exonerated, but five were found to have fallen below the standards of the House. The inquiry was wholly unlike anything the House had envisaged when it appointed Sir Gordon Downey its first Commissioner for Standards, but I had no other choice if the crisis of public confidence was to be contained.

Inquiries into the case of Neil Hamilton, the former minister, who in 1997 lost his seat to Martin

Bell, the BBC war correspondent, continued after the election. Had Hamilton still been a Member when Downey found 'compelling' evidence that he had received cash payments from Al Fayed and had broken other parts of the Members' code, he would have been suspended for a long time. I admired Bell's courage in standing as an Independent against him. The House needs courageous Members with minds of their own, and I invited him for an encouraging chat soon after his arrival.

Party machines look unkindly on MPs who do not stand in line. Labour's apparatchiks, influenced by American techniques and jargon, describe them as being 'off-message', but that did not matter to me. I wanted as wide a debate as possible, however unpalatable to the majority some of the views expressed were.

Downey's finding that Geoffrey Robinson, the Paymaster General, had failed to disclose all his financial interests in the Register of Members' Interests opened a new phase in the controversy over standards of conduct. The row over a £1 million donation to the Labour Party by Bernie Ecclestone, the motor-racing entrepreneur, meant it was the new Government's turn to face sleaze allegations – and both the press and the Opposition made the most of it. Robinson later apologised to the House, but further inquiries into his complex business activities were pursued with even greater vigour by Downey's successor, Elizabeth Filkin.

Unlike Downey, she had never been a Whitehall insider, which worked in her favour during the selection process. Sir Gordon was an old Treasury hand and knew how the Commons worked from his contacts with the Public Accounts Committee. The House of Commons Commission, which I chaired, thought it was time for a fresh approach and Elizabeth Filkin's varied career in academia, social work, childcare, on company boards and in the public sector was just what the Commission wanted. She struck me as being a tough operator and her work as an independent adjudicator of appeals against the Inland Revenue, Customs & Excise and the Contributions Agency added to her attraction.

I endorsed the Commission's decision to give Filkin a three-year contract, on the basis of a four-day week, at £76,576 a year, and the House appointed her without a vote in November 1998. We believed that she would be painstaking and fair (which she was) and would avoid personal controversy (which she did not). Robert Sheldon, the long-serving Labour MP for Ashton-under-Lyne and chairman of the Standards and Privileges Committee, mistakenly expected the volume of complaints about Members to fall as they adapted to the new rules of conduct.

Downey, he said, had 'laid down a road for others to follow'. But Downey was almost unknown outside the Whitehall–Westminster 'village' because he sought no personal publicity and gave few interviews. That did nothing to hinder his effectiveness; quite the reverse. He examined more than forty complaints against Members and the Standards Committee accepted his findings unanimously in every case, an extraordinary record.

From the start Filkin had a high profile and journalists had never enjoyed such easy access to a senior Commons official. Her independence and specific responsibility for policing the Register of Interests made her a prime news source. I did not mind her being no respecter of persons in the way she conducted her investigations or the lengths she went to in order to uncover the truth. My worry was that MPs were put in the dock by the press on the basis of unsubstantiated accusations made against them.

Some MPs encouraged this attitude by casting doubt on the reputation of Members in other parties. Both sides indulged in this point-scoring by writing to Filkin, sometimes with no hard evidence other than a tendentious press report. Downey had ruled that complaints needed more than newspaper allegations to prompt an investigation.

John Major, however, was investigated on the basis of a report that he had earned large sums on the speech circuit, which were undeclared in the register. Yet his concern to observe the rules was manifest: he had consulted the Registrar of Members' Interests and taken his advice to the letter in declaring his interests. The *Daily Express* nevertheless was to report as a fact that Major was 'set to be rebuked by the parliamentary anti-sleaze watchdog'. In fact he was exonerated and found to have been 'at all times punctilious' in providing the required information.

Filkin made it clear that she believed that MPs who earned large sums outside the House should disclose their earnings in detail and that there were 'many members of the public who think it should be compulsory'. But the rules she was paid to operate do not provide for that and she was speaking out of turn. She did so again when the Standards Committee rejected her finding that Mandelson had broken the rules by not registering his £373,000 loan from Geoffrey Robinson. 'It's entirely up to them,' she said. 'The protection of my office is the fact that they publish in full my views and the press and public can decide whether they share my view or the committee's.' The implication was that she was right and the committee to which she submitted her report was wrong. It was not well received in the House.

Filkin admitted that some complaints made to her might have been politically motivated, but said she was not interested in people's motives and 'If there are facts, I investigate.' That was her job, but her disinterest in the political point-scoring behind complaints encouraged each side of the House to have a go at discrediting the other. It was to her credit that she persisted against considerable resistance, especially in the cases of Geoffrey Robinson, after his resignation, and of Keith Vaz, Minister for Europe, who left the Government after the 2001 election.

I supported her intentions but was deeply concerned by the scatter-gun publicity generated by her activities and urged her to be more cautious in her public comments. Her investigations into Robinson, Vaz and Mandelson showed her considerable forensic skills and shed light where light was needed. She also proved herself a doughty fighter against attempts to obstruct her inquiries, which I applauded. Other cases warranted little more than a reminder or a tap on the wrist, but any offence, whether serious or slight, made news and this created unnecessary tension in her relations with the House.

Sheldon and Downey worked as a partnership, which was how it ought to be. Filkin was an excellent investigator, but lacked political acumen and seemed to have little feeling for the Commons, as she showed when she told a meeting at the Royal Society of Arts: 'There's no doubt some MPs are absent-minded. A few are foolish. And a few, from what I've now seen, deliberately flout the rules because they don't like them and it doesn't suit them.' She added that other MPs – again 'a few' – were 'nasty to the people who come to them for help, are rude to them, and are dismissive in situations where that's very hurtful and harmful to the individual concerned'. This was 'apparent' to her from the complaints she received and raised the issue of MPs' accountability for the work they were paid to do.

'Apparent' is not good enough, however, and Filkin's comments on the quality of MPs' constituency work caused outrage in the House. Every MP meets people in his or her constituency surgery whose problems are better dealt with by other agencies whom they refuse to consult.

Jeff Rooker, who had a splendid record of service in the Commons before going to the Lords, was especially aggrieved by Filkin's comments. He said she should stick to her job, and I tended to agree. Advising Members on the rules was an important part of her responsibilities, but her reputation as a clinical interrogator reduced her effectiveness in that role.

Some of the complaints she looked into also had shallow foundations, notably two concerning the non-declaration of business interests in debates. Iain Duncan Smith, Norman Tebbit's successor as MP for Chingford, who was later elected Leader of the Conservative Party in September 2001, came under Filkin's scrutiny on this score. So did, of all people, Bob Sheldon.

The rule was that Members ought to declare a business interest if it might reasonably be thought by others to influence them in anything they said or did in the Commons. Duncan Smith was accused of not declaring an interest in an engineering company during a debate on defence procurement, but the company had no defence contracts and his interest in it was declared in the Register anyway. So the complaint was rejected.

Sheldon was less fortunate in not declaring his business interest in a debate in which it had no direct relevance. Although the Standards and Privileges Committee decided this was a marginal case and warranted no further action, it warned other MPs to take note of Filkin's attitude. But why? This looked more like nit-picking than sleaze-busting.

I wrote to her about the Commission's concerns about her accessibility to journalists, which was a serious step for me to take. It arose from Filkin's request to the Commission to review her heavy workload and increase her budget to handle it. Our attitude was that we were anxious to help, but that she could reduce the burden herself if she did not talk to the press so much.

However, we were too far apart in our perception of her role for our differences to be easily resolved and I was not surprised when the new Commons Commission decided not to renew her contract automatically when it expired in 2002. To the media she was headline news; to many MPs she had become a witch-hunter. That was clearly a hopeless situation. I felt that the House would be better served by somebody who knew it well, worked quietly in the background and followed Downey's example. That way, Members would have more confidence in the process and misbehaviour would be identified just as effectively.

In his final report in July 1998 Downey referred to an important guideline that seemed to count less with Filkin. It was that 'the onus is placed *very heavily* [my italics] on the complainants to provide the evidence to support allegations of rule breaches'. He also asserted – rightly in my opinion – that the Commissioner must have discretion to dismiss frivolous or malicious complaints and that the House was 'in danger of reinventing the wheel' in the way it handled allegations of malpractice.

We had learned our lessons from the pre-Nolan years. The reforms that followed have worked far better than our critics predicted, but I believe we jeopardise that by destroying the continuity of membership on the Standards and Privileges Committee and producing uneven judgements. The committee should be drawn exclusively from the ranks of senior MPs, as it used to be. Labour's Dale Campbell-Savours and Alan Williams met these criteria during my final years in the chair, as did Eric Forth and Peter Bottomley on the Tory side; others did not. The review of the complaints procedure planned by Sir Nigel Wicks, the new chairman of the Commission on Standards in Public Life, is timely.

In July Tony and Cherie Blair invited me to Chequers for dinner. I had not been to the Prime Minister's official country residence before and was entranced by it. Fellow guests included Mary Wilson, who knew the house intimately from the days of her husband's premiership; Neil and Glenys Kinnock; John Monks, General Secretary of the TUC, and his wife; and Stephen Fry, the actor and writer.

It was a wonderfully relaxed evening. We had a jolly dinner, full of chatter and laughter, after which Cherie took us on a guided tour of the treasures acquired for Chequers. I admired most the ruby ring of Elizabeth I, which opens up to reveal enamel miniatures of her and her mother, Anne Boleyn. With a magnifying glass, one can see their hair decorations picked out in rose diamonds and mother-of-pearl – breathtakingly beautiful.

Elizabeth I has always been a heroine of mine. A powerful, full-length painting of her in the House of Commons shows her surrounded by courtiers urging her to marry, for the sake of the country. She holds a ring in her hand and declares, 'With this ring, I wedded the Realm.' I wondered if it was the same one that now resides, untouchable, in a sealed glass box at Chequers.

Amid its spectacular collection of paintings, furniture and decorative art, the house resounded with the voices of the Blair children. The boys, Euan and Nicholas, played in their bedrooms while their sister, Kathryn, practised the piano. Of all the great houses I have visited throughout the world, nothing remains in the memory like Chequers.

Blair reshuffled his Cabinet eight days later, promoting Mandelson to Trade and Industry Secretary and sacking Harriet Harman. Their subsequent careers showed what a giddy business politics is. Harriet rejoined the Government after the 2001 election, by which time Mandelson had resigned, been reappointed and resigned a second time. Peter displayed great talent in turning Labour's fortunes around, but showed no common sense in managing his own affairs.

An important figure in the life of the Commons also moved on in July. Canon Donald Gray retired as Speaker's Chaplain and was succeeded by Robert Wright, a parish priest in Portsea and an honorary canon of Portsmouth Cathedral. The chaplaincy is held by the Rector of St Margaret's, across the street from the Commons and next to Westminster Abbey, where the rector is also a canon. Donald's virtues included an extraordinary ability to compose Graces that began each line with letters spelling out the name of the guest's country. Places with Z in them posed a problem, but Donald was equal to this, as the Speaker of New Zealand's House of Representatives discovered in April 1998:

> *Never failing and*
> *Eternal source of all goodness*
> *We fully,*
> *Zealously and*
> *Earnestly*
> *Acknowledge your generosity,*
> *Lord of the Universe;*
> *And pray we may*
> *Never cease so to live as to*
> *Deserve your continuing blessing.*

Donald and Joyce, his wife, made many friends among MPs and Commons staff who were in need of friendly counsel and prayer. Before he left, we discussed changes to the daily Prayers for Parliament. They had done yeoman service since the late seventeenth century, but some parts of them were overdue for retirement.

Instead of praying for the Queen's 'health and wealth', we now ask that she be granted long to live. And a separate prayer for members of the royal family has been replaced by a prayer for the Queen, her Government and all those in positions of public responsibility, that they may 'never lead the nation wrongly through love of power, desire to please, or unworthy ideals'. After John Smith's death, I also authorised a new prayer to be said for Members who died in the service of the House.

That September I recalled the Commons from its recess for the third time during my Speakership and only the eighteenth time since the Speaker was given the power to do so, if the Prime Minister requests it. The list of recalls over the ensuing fifty years charts the crises that have endangered the world's peace and that of our own country. MPs were recalled to debate the Korean War in 1950, the Suez crisis in 1956, the Berlin crisis in 1961 and the invasions of Czechoslovakia in 1968, of the Falklands in 1982 and of Kuwait in 1990.

My recall of the House in 1992 allowed the Government to report on UN action in the Balkans and Iraq, as well as on the domestic economic crisis, and in 1995 we reviewed the deteriorating Balkan situation. Events in Northern Ireland caused most recalls – in 1971, 1974 and in 1998 after the Omagh bombing and its heavy loss of life. Sadly, the province's 'troubles' span the decades like no other.

In October 1998 I went to Russia again, at the invitation of the State Duma, visiting St Petersburg and Moscow. Russian concern about Britain's support for tough Nato action against Serbia after its expulsion of Kosovo's Albanian population failed to dampen the warmth of my reception.

Gennady Seleznev, the Duma's chairman, told me formally that the Russia–Nato treaty would be at risk if Nato used force against Serbia. He added, 'The Cold War may be in the air again.' But he understood my neutral position in British politics and I took no offence at him putting his warning on the record. His role in the Duma was quite different from mine in the Commons. Seleznev was a leading spokesman of what remained of the Communist Party and told me that Yeltsin 'should not wield the enormous power he has'. He believed Russia needed 'a strong government and a strong Parliament' and the President's ability to dismiss the Cabinet without accountability was unacceptable.

In my Duma speech I advocated a workable concordat between the executive and Parliament. 'An essential role of Parliament is to keep the government on its toes, challenging, scrutinising, demanding explanations, but not setting out to destroy the government. Parliament in a sense complements the government rather than competes with it.'

While I waited for Vladimir Zhirinovsky to finish before I could speak, Seleznev explained that he usually had a lot to say and was difficult to control. I knew Zhirinovsky's reputation as an ultra-nationalist and that he had run for the presidency against Yeltsin in 1996. I was interested to meet him.

At lunch afterwards, attended by the Duma's caucus leaders, Zhirinovsky arrived carrying bottles of vodka with labels bearing his picture, which he proceeded to hand out. Some of my hosts were embarrassed by his flamboyance and asked, 'What would you do with somebody like this?' Uproar followed when I explained that I had the authority to tell a Member who became repetitious and tedious to sit down. Seleznev was immediately besieged with demands that the Duma follow the same rule.

At a British Embassy party, where I was in the

receiving line greeting guests, Zhirinovsky returned at length to the intolerable degree of communist influence in Russia. Speaking in hesitant English, he slowed things down so much that I said, 'Look, we're having a jolly time here, so why don't you go home and look for Reds under the bed!' That did the trick and he moved on, amid great hilarity, as news of my banter spread. I subsequently met Zhirinovsky at a North Atlantic Assembly meeting in Scotland, but his party lost its popular appeal in Russia and he became a figure of fun.

Understandably, perhaps, the Russians showed less interest in my views about Parliament's role in a modern democracy than other former communist states. My assurance that Russia 'is and always will be a great nation' made the news but little else.

A charming man escorted me throughout my visit: Aleksandr Paradis, chairman of the Russian-British Parliamentary Group, who learned English through a British Council scholarship. During the interval in a performance at the Bolshoi, he said he had told his uncle, who lived in Moscow, how moved I had been by the Leningrad Memorial to the victims of the 900 days and nights of the German siege. His uncle had replied, 'I know how Coventry suffered and I would like that lady to have the medal that I won in the Battle of Moscow.' I was completely taken aback, but very moved. Aleksandr explained that its inscription meant 'For Those Who Fought for Our Soviet Land'. The medal has an honoured place in my home and I shall always treasure it.

*

After the first elections to the new Scottish Parliament and the Welsh Assembly the Commons ran into problems with its own constitutional settlement. Anomalies were bound to arise from transferring responsibility for substantial issues like health, education, social services, transport and domestic law from Westminster to Edinburgh. The Welsh Assembly in Cardiff had lesser powers of policy-making but, even there, many local matters that Welsh MPs had put to Welsh ministers at Westminster were no longer our concern.

Tam Dalyell's famous West Lothian question remained unanswered: why should Scots and Welsh MPs have the right to intervene in purely English affairs, whereas English MPs have no right to intervene in similar issues decided in Edinburgh and Cardiff? Short of setting up a devolved English Parliament, which was not being proposed, there is no real answer to that.

Devolution complicated my task, making it harder to select MPs in debates to ensure the right balance between the regions and increasing the pressure on my discretionary powers. Friction was inevitable.

After complaints about the scope of Welsh questions, I issued new guidelines on 12 July 1999 stipulating that Commons questions must relate to matters for which ministers were responsible. That meant limiting the range of questions to Scottish and Welsh ministers at Westminster and refusing questions that related to devolved policy and detailed expenditure.

Tam Dalyell asked if the Scottish Parliament

would observe the same self-denying ordinance in respect of UK matters beyond its competence. All I could say was that the new Commons guidelines would be sent to Edinburgh, but I was happy to leave that conundrum to Sir David Steel, presiding officer of the new Scottish Parliament. That displeased some Scots MPs, who accused me of silencing their right to speak on Scottish matters. 'We were devolving power-making, not the right to have an opinion,' said one. The right to hold opinions, however, was not at stake. My guidelines concerned questions to ministers about their specific responsibilities. We could not carry on after devolution as if nothing had happened.

I invited Prince William to see something of Parliament at work before the pre-election temperature rose. He came one morning, without advance publicity, with his housemaster from Eton College and two friends. I took them on a ninety-minute tour from Speaker's House to the Commons library, the Members' lobby, the division lobbies and the chamber itself. I made a special point of explaining to him how much the Commonwealth had contributed to the restoration of the Commons after the chamber's destruction by German bombers on 10 May 1941. Australia gave the Speaker's chair, Canada the table and New Zealand the dispatch boxes. Smaller countries did their bit too, contributing reading lamps and stationery racks in the division lobbies.

We then looked in on a session of the Home

Affairs Select Committee, which carried on (as it is obliged to do) without acknowledging the presence of 'strangers' – even royal ones. As a courtesy, I had forewarned the committee's chairman, Chris Mullin, Labour MP for Sunderland South, who nodded us in.

It was an educational visit, which had been agreed with Prince William's school and Buckingham Palace, and we ended in Westminster Hall, where the prince will doubtless receive loyal addresses from both Houses one day.

Monarchs have not entered the chamber since Charles I marched in with an armed escort in a vain effort to arrest five Members in 1642. Two consorts – Prince Albert, Queen Victoria's husband, and Prince Philip – have watched debates from the gallery but subsequently stayed away after objections were raised. I wanted Prince William to see something of the Commons as part of his constitutional training and was glad he did.

I encouraged personal contact between the royal family and MPs and both sides seemed to appreciate this. I had a particularly high regard for Princess Anne, the Princess Royal, for her hard work and forthright views and enjoyed good relations with other members of the royal family. They like people to be themselves, which came easily to me. The Duke of York, whom I invited to dinner with MPs in Speaker's House, introduced himself at a state banquet at Windsor Castle with the greeting: 'Hello, I'm York.' 'Hello, I'm Westminster,' I replied. We got on famously after that.

CHAPTER EIGHTEEN

Babes and Mandarins

*A completely honest answer always gives you the
advantage of surprise in the House of Commons.*

from *Yes, Prime Minister*,
by Jonathan Lynn and Antony Jay

I HAD SOME cause for satisfaction as I began my
last full year in the chair. Ministers were now
more wary of having to apologise for departmental
misdemeanours at the dispatch box as I continued
my battle in defence of Parliament's rights.
Whitehall's élite corps of Permanent Secretaries
also promised to try harder to meet their
obligations to MPs by answering their questions
properly, replying promptly to letters and
depositing policy papers in the Commons library
before their contents became stale news.

Only the Treasury showed any hubris at being
told that I wanted a great improvement in performance all round, but that did not surprise me. The
Treasury's self-regard surpasses that of other ministries, despite the fact that some of its

parliamentary answers left a lot to be desired. I quoted two examples in a letter to Sir Richard Wilson, Secretary to the Cabinet, on 3 July 2000. Andrew Robathan, Tory MP for Blaby, had wanted to know how much the abolition of the married couples' allowance would cost an average couple of working age. On the same theme, Cheryl Gillan, Tory MP for Chesham and Amersham, asked how many families who had qualified for the married couples' allowance would not be allowed the tax credit that was replacing it.

Dawn Primarolo, the Paymaster General, avoided the first question by talking about the general benefits of Government policies to house-holds and families with children and Andrew Smith, Chief Secretary to the Treasury, used the same ploy to avoid the second question and jeered at Gillan when she protested. If the Treasury thought it was being clever in taking that line, I did not.

Sir Richard, an outstanding public servant, relayed my concerns to his colleagues. By their own admission, only 60 per cent of letters from MPs were answered within a reasonable time and the performance of one-third of the larger ministries and agencies was even worse, at 50 per cent. If MPs were treated so poorly, what hope did members of the public have of getting a satisfactory service?

Overall, my efforts had mixed results, but the Government machine learned that I was a bad loser. In my last full year as Speaker, Kate Hoey, the Sports Minister, made a formal apology for her department's release of a new national sports strategy before Parliament was informed of it. I also asked the Standards and Privileges Committee to investigate the leak to the Foreign Office of a select committee report on arms to Africa. That incident led to prolonged controversy and reflected badly on the Government's attempts to pre-empt criticism, however considered it was.

I was delighted when the Liaison Committee of senior MPs, representing all the select committees in the House, challenged the system that made it easier for Labour and Tory Governments alike to avoid the rigours of parliamentary scrutiny. Like me, the committee believed that it was time to redress the balance between the executive and the Commons. Pundits were writing that the House of Commons was being swept aside by the importation of American political techniques and a quasi-presidential style. I refused to accept that and No. 10 knew my views. I agreed with the reformist MPs.

The Liaison Committee was an unlikely forum for revolt against the power of the whips. Using its broad but little-known powers, it issued two ground-breaking reports in my final months in the chair, calling for radical changes in the way that the members of select committees were chosen.

Ever since Margaret Thatcher's Government set up the watchdog committees in 1979, their composition was decided by the party whips and nodded through the House. These committees had nothing like the clout of Congressional committees on Capitol Hill, but the innovation took root and some committees grasped the opportunities to examine Government policies. With greater independence and resources, they could perform even better. The Liaison Committee's proposals sent shudders through both the Government and Whitehall. Its declaration that 'It is wrong in principle that party managers should exercise effective control of select committee membership' was regarded as revolutionary.

In its 1997 election manifesto Labour vowed to change the culture of Whitehall and rebuild 'the bond of trust between government and the people', but in May 2000 the Government rejected virtually every suggestion that the Liaison Committee put forward to improve the process of parliamentary investigation. It claimed that the existing system for deciding which MPs should sit on select committees had 'stood the test of time'. That was nonsense, of course, as the committees proved. I could not say so openly, because it was a matter for the House and not for me personally, but I resolved to speak my mind when I was free to do so – and did.

The Government's publication of three Annual Reports during my final years in the chair was no substitute for engaging Parliament more openly. The reports were rightly criticised for their selective content and the absence of one in 2001 marked the end of the experiment. The Liaison Committee invited Tony Blair to appear before it and answer questions about the reports and the Government's broad strategy. Blair refused, claiming that he had no specific departmental responsibilities, that previous Prime Ministers had not appeared before select committees and that he did not intend to break the tradition.

Fundamental issues like this were temporarily overshadowed by a bizarre campaign for change on a different front. It concerned my decision that women Members should not suckle their babies in committee meetings of the House. In the brouhaha that followed, my critics accused me of being narrow-minded, old-fashioned and ignorant of the needs of motherhood. Gwyneth Dunwoody, whose three children and ten grandchildren were all breastfed, knocked that calumny for six by agreeing with me that babies were best fed in comfortable, relaxed surroundings – not in the televised hurly-burly of Commons sittings. There were other considerations, too.

The fuss began when new MPs with babies were told by the Serjeant at Arms that they were not allowed to take them into the chamber, the division lobbies, the Members' tearoom and quiet parts of the library. That left a grey area, not covered by his injunction, of committee sittings. I cleared that up on 6 April 2000 by deciding that the general rule should also apply there. This meant that only MPs and specified officers of the House were allowed in the non-public areas of the chamber and committee rooms, where the taking of refreshment was also not permitted – in other words, no babies and no breastfeeding.

Julia Drown, Labour MP for Swindon South, asked Sir Alan Haselhurst, the deputy Speaker, for a meeting to take the matter further. She wanted to bring with her Margaret Hodge, Minister for Childcare, and Tessa Jowell, Minister for Education and Employment. She said she also wanted to invite Yvette Cooper, a junior public-health minister. We heard no more about Yvette, who had more sense, but the involvement of two ministers of the Crown in a purely internal House of Commons matter was bad enough.

Tony Blair, Margaret Beckett (Leader of the House) and Ann Taylor (the Government Chief Whip) were said to be appalled. I myself was astonished. Hodge and Jowell's intervention prompted the BBC to report that ministers, and by implication the Government, were seeking a change in the breastfeeding rule, which was not the case. Jowell wrote to me on 17 April to say that she was surprised and concerned by the report and was fully aware that it was a matter for the Commons and me. She added that Hodge, MP for Barking, wanted me to see an all-party group to discuss Commons facilities for parents with babies but that this was 'a separate matter'.

Jowell's public comments, however, were not about better facilities, but about the iniquity of the ban on breastfeeding in committees. 'Absolutely breathtaking,' she said. 'We really have got to move into the twenty-first century and put some of this archaic view of the world behind us.' Other Labour backbenchers spoke in a similar vein. Sally

Keeble, MP for Northampton North, thought the ban epitomised 'the complete nonsense of an institution that won't move on', and Barbara Follett, MP for Stevenage, talked of 'antediluvian' attitudes.

The row seeped into the wider controversy over the need for more 'family-friendly' working hours. Anne Campbell, Labour MP for Cambridge, sponsored a call by more than 100 Labour Members for debates to be timetabled, filibustering banned and daily sessions started at 11.30 a.m. instead of 2.30 p.m. Six women Members with young children were said to be thinking of quitting the House because it was too much like a men's club for their liking. In the event, only one did.

I made my position clear at a meeting in Speaker's House on 9 May. Drown, Hodge and Jowell were all there and I invited Caroline Spelman, Conservative MP for Meriden, and Jackie Ballard, Liberal Democrat MP for Taunton, to join us to make the gathering more representative. Ballard was delayed, so we went ahead without her.

Julia Drown asked to attend committee meetings with her young baby, who needed breastfeeding. I replied that I was sure the whips would give her time out to feed her baby in one of the rooms set aside for women Members, but she said she had fought so hard to get elected that she did not want to miss anything. Jowell, trying to be helpful, asked if I would reconsider the ban if the baby was really sick. My answer was that babies who needed special care should not be taken to the Commons, but should be looked after at home.

Hodge noted that John Lewis, the department store, had a room where customers could feed and change their babies and that we should have similar amenities. I told her there were three Lady Members' lounges, which I had inspected and found to be clean, comfortable and peaceful, and that nappy-changing facilities could be added. There was also a large family room and Members could, of course, use their own offices. If Members wanted better facilities, the remedy lay in their own hands and I hoped that the domestic committees of the House would see what could be done to help them.

However, I would not be dissuaded from my refusal to allow breastfeeding in committees. It was not conducive to the efficient conduct of public business. Nor did I think that Commons sittings, either in the chamber or committees, provided the calm environment babies needed when they were being fed, whether by the breast or bottle. I was becoming the great nanny of the state and did not care for it. What was more, if the Government tabled a motion to overrule me, the Prime Minister's name must be at the top of it. I then asked if the Members present were going to issue a press release about our meeting. When they said they were, I stood up and replied that I would issue my own – only the second time I did so (the first being after my meeting with Sinn Fein). The issue petered out after that, and at the time of writing, the ban remains in force.

Like Gwyneth, whom I had fought alongside during the anti-Militant days, I found the attitude of a few of the new Labour women hard to understand. Tess Kingham, MP for Gloucester, became so disillusioned with the Commons that she retired after only four years, explaining, 'I just can't stomach the culture of Westminster.' By that she meant 'the petty, poisonous machinations of Parliament's whipping system', and what she called the 'silly games that have very little to do with scrutinising legislation', such as Opposition attempts to wear out the Government by tactical means, including late-night sittings. The idea of the Opposition frustrating the Government by whatever means possible evidently appalled her. Sir Patrick Cormack, deputy shadow Leader of the House, said that Kingham failed to understand what being a Member of Parliament was all about, and I understood his exasperation.

In the last six years of my Speakership I took inspiration from the students of the Open University (OU), which made me its Chancellor in 1994. I held honorary positions in many organisations, but the OU was special. I succeeded Lord Briggs (better known as Asa Briggs), who retired on the university's twenty-fifth anniversary. I was able to accept the post because the office carried no salary, involved no political commitment and did not interfere with my duties to the House. Unlike Lord Briggs and the titular heads of other English universities, I had not gone on to higher education. A London student suggested my name to an OU tutor, who passed it on to the committee looking for suitable candidates. I was told that I fitted the bill because I had an outgoing personality, had made it to the top of my career by my own efforts and was demonstrably non-partisan. My neutrality mattered because the OU was founded by Harold Wilson's Labour Government and its ruling body wanted to dispel any lingering misconceptions about its independence.

Our common Labour roots, however, were undeniable. Joe Haines, Harold Wilson's press secretary and confidant for many years, witnessed the enormous difficulties Wilson faced in founding the OU, against the resistance of Oxbridge colleagues, who belittled 'Harold's pet scheme' and believed that proper degrees could only be won amid dreaming spires and peaceful cloisters. That did not deter Wilson, whose academic reputation outshone those of his snobbish contemporaries. He clung to his vision, despite the economic crisis that dogged his Government in the 1960s, and his faith was rewarded. The OU soon disproved the sneer that it represented a dumbing-down of academic standards, and its achievements and innovations became universally admired. Iain Macleod, who as a liberal Conservative ought to have known better, got it spectacularly wrong when he called Wilson's idea 'blithering nonsense'. But he was not alone.

I accepted the Chancellorship on the basis that I would not be involved in the internal affairs of the university but would devote my energies to presiding over as many degree ceremonies as I could and to using my influence behind the scenes, if asked to do so. The determination of OU students to win their degree is legendary. That makes the award ceremonies more emotionally charged than any other event I know. Many graduates are elderly, and younger members of their families applaud their achievements as they stand before me. It is a magic moment. In other universities young people accept their degrees while their proud parents and grandparents look on. In ours that occurs less often, although we are open to people of all ages, abilities and backgrounds.

The undergraduates include students in their thirties with full-time jobs, women who combine study with bringing up a family, those who are unemployed, retired single people, widowed or disabled people, grandparents whose children were the first generation in their family to go to university. The OU also has prisoners who study alone in their cells, and foreign students who follow one of the many 'distance-learning' courses and keep in contact with their tutors on the Internet. What matters is the will to learn and the courage to attempt a demanding syllabus that may take many years to complete at the student's own pace.

Being the OU's Chancellor is the appointment I have cherished most, apart from the Speakership itself. My sympathy with its aims and my pride in its success combine with the deep satisfaction that I am carrying on the work of Jennie Lee, Labour's first Minister for the Arts, who nurtured the OU during its infant years. The OU's Yorkshire connection also gave me a personal link. Wilson came from Huddersfield and Asa Briggs from Keighley. We shared the same practical attitude to life.

Since becoming Chancellor, I have sometimes wondered whether my intense ambition to be a politician might have drawn me to enlist as a mature student had the OU existed at the time. But when would the right time have been? I was always too busy for anything but politics, although 'being too busy' is an excuse that OU students never use, however hard the going.

The letters they and their relatives send me after every graduation show how much it means to be able to fulfil their potential and enjoy richer lives. One, from 'Caroline, a proud daughter' in Devon, told me how her eighty-five-year-old mother had given up a place at Cambridge in her youth to look after her mother. 'Now she has a degree and has just pipped her granddaughter to the graduation post.' Alongside her that day was Norman Stagg, a former national officer of the old Postal Workers' Union, who won his degree a week before his seventy-ninth birthday. He left school at fourteen and was an OU student for seven years.

Some observers felt that my campaign to reassert the rights of Parliament stood as little chance of success as the OU in its early days. 'Parliament has lost power and authority to the executive, to Europe, to the courts, to the media,' Robin Oakley, the BBC's political editor, wrote in the *House*

Magazine, as Blair's Government reached the halfway mark:

> The executive is almost totally dominant. It cares little for Parliament because it doesn't have to. The votes are assured and it can get its message across to the people directly in interviews on radio and television and in the 'exclusive' articles by the Prime Minister which now appear almost daily.

Peter Kellner wrote in the *Evening Standard* that I was the only person who made the Government pause and think, but he too doubted my chances of succeeding, because 'solving this problem is beyond the power of even the most determined Speaker'. I refused to accept that. The Commons can do anything it likes if it has the will, however large the Government's majority. Prime Ministers who appear unassailable can soon be toppled, as Neville Chamberlain and Margaret Thatcher found to their cost.

Maintaining a high public profile was an important part of my fight to defend Parliament's rights. The stronger my reputation in the country and beyond, the more hesitant adversaries would be in taking me on. Government governs, but I would not be bullied or ignored, whichever party was in power.

I was inundated with invitations. Commodore Timothy Laurence, the delightful husband of the

Princess Royal, escorted me in the royal procession into the state banquet for the Queen of Denmark at Windsor Castle. I also appeared on the BBC's *Songs of Praise* from Westminster Abbey and took the salute at the march-past of Jewish ex-servicemen at the Cenotaph. I was especially delighted to become patron of the campaign to erect a memorial to the women of the Second World War and President of the National Benevolent Fund for the Aged. My diary had never been so crowded.

I welcomed the American Bar Association to Westminster Hall, alongside the Lord Chancellor; received a group of young Tongans on their way to the Isle of Barra; met the High Commissioners of New Zealand and Namibia, the Hungarian Speaker, the new Russian Ambassador and Madam Mubarak, the wife of Egypt's President Hosni Mubarak; and said goodbye to Chief Emeka Anyoaku, the Commonwealth Secretary-General. I suspect my overseas visitors were curious to see what I was really like, when I was not on their television screens calling for order. I tried to put them at their ease. In May I returned to my old stamping ground in Strasbourg for a conference of European Speakers and opened an extension to St Hugh's College, Oxford, in a ceremony attended by Barbara Castle and Roy Jenkins.

Meeting VIPs at Speaker's House sometimes involved sensitive political considerations. Anglo-Spanish difficulties over Gibraltar put the visit of the Prince of Asturias, heir to the Spanish throne, into this category and my long association with China brought me an invitation to meet President Jiang Zemin privately at Buckingham Palace during his state visit in 1999. I raised the issue of human rights with him, as I did with every Chinese leader I met. I did not accept his position, but that did not stop him inviting me that night to join him in singing 'Our Hearts Were Young and Gay' to an appreciative audience at his banquet for the Queen in the Chinese Embassy.

I was less popular in other quarters. The *Guardian* wrote that many ministers would be 'glad to see the back' of me and longed for a more emollient successor. I had told the House that they would be the first to know when I chose to retire, but by the summer of 1999 I could do nothing to stop the runners and riders being assessed. The impression was that I would go either at the new millennium in January 2000 or at the following general election. Neither of those dates was on my shortlist, but I kept my own counsel.

I greeted the twenty-first century with a party in my private apartment in Speaker's House from where we had a magnificent view of the throng below and the fireworks over the Thames. I had been invited to the Millennium Dome celebrations, but declined. Nothing would have tempted me away from Westminster that night.

Sir Edward Heath's fiftieth anniversary as a Member of Parliament gave me the opportunity to honour him with a dinner three months later. I invited him to choose the guests. Old battles with

Labour, the Liberals and even the Lady who followed him were put aside for an extraordinary celebration and the guests included Lady Thatcher, Jim Callaghan, Denis Healey, Tony Benn, Charles Kennedy and David Steel – as unlikely a political reunion as can be imagined. Sir Edward also remembered other former Prime Ministers of both parties by inviting Mary Wilson (Lady Wilson of Rievaulx), Clarissa Eden (the Countess of Avon), and Mary Soames (Lady Soames), all personal friends.

So we sat down with six Downing Street generations – three former Prime Ministers, the widows of Harold Wilson and Sir Anthony Eden and the daughter of Sir Winston Churchill. Tony Blair joined us for pre-dinner drinks, but was unable to stay. Michael Cockerell was making a television documentary of my life at the time and recorded Blair chatting amiably to Sir Edward across the generational divide. 'You were Chief Whip in the Fifties?

'Yes.'

'Not during Suez?'

'Yes.'

'You were Chief Whip during Suez?'

'Yes, I handled the whole of Suez.'

Lady Thatcher's greeting was more personal. 'You look very fetching in red.'

'Thank you. Blue also suits me, actually.'

'If you have white hair, it does. You're lucky.'

My thoughts now turned increasingly to the future. My plans were fairly well advanced. I intended to retire that year but to keep it secret until the last moment. Meanwhile, I wanted to do something to strengthen the position of Parliament at the centre of our democracy. I was appalled by the May Day rioters, who defaced the Cenotaph and Churchill's statue in Parliament Square and tore up the turf. Some of those arrested turned out to be professional, well-educated people who were hell-bent on anarchy. This was the violent edge of political indifference and it worried me stiff.

I strongly supported moves by David Blunkett to improve the teaching of citizenship and democracy in schools and became patron of the Advisory Group on Citizenship, under the chairmanship of Professor Bernard Crick. Sir Donald Limon, former Clerk of the House and a group member, kept me informed of its deliberations. He was ideally equipped to offer an insider's view of the real mechanics of Parliament.

Other members of the group included Kenneth Baker, the former Education Secretary, Judge Stephen Tumim, former Inspector of Prisons, and Michael Brunson, Political Editor of ITN. Michael took an active interest in the Citizenship Foundation's mock-parliaments competition in schools and suggested that I wrote a foreword to their report, which called unanimously for citizenship to be taught as part of the national curriculum.

I was delighted to do so. I disagreed with Chris Woodhead, then the Chief Inspector of Schools, who argued that the teaching of literacy and

numeracy was a sufficient basis for adult life. When
I left school I was more knowledgeable about civic
life than many children are today, not only because
of my family's political activities but because our
teachers taught us about the community in which
we lived. We learned about public services and
were taken to the police station, the fire station
and council meetings to see how they functioned.

In my foreword I wrote that the diminished
importance attached to the teaching of citizenship
in schools had been 'a blot on the landscape of
public life for too long, with unfortunate consequences for the future of our democratic process'.
The dreadfully low turnout in the 2001 general
election confirmed that, and the recent surge in
violent demonstrations at international meetings
across the world makes me even more fearful. We
tolerate the so-called 'democratic deficit' at our
peril.

I returned from a week's break in Cyprus, my
favourite bolthole, on 4 June. I wanted to be on top
form in the run-up to the announcement of my
retirement, but I had gone to Cyprus with a cold,
which turned into bronchitis when I returned.
After a walk in St James's Park, feeling cold and
unwell, I was prescribed anti-congestive tablets by
Ronald Zeegen, my medical adviser and a good
friend.

The next day I had to be reminded to call Charles
Kennedy, the Liberal Democrat leader, for his
second question to Tony Blair at Prime Minister's
Question Time, and my streaming cold and high

temperature forced me to leave the annual meeting
of the Hansard Society in Westminster Hall. A
viral infection was diagnosed.

I had thought of retiring at Easter, but settled on
announcing it in July to enable me to fulfil long-
promised visits during the summer recess to Latvia,
Estonia and Ukraine; chair the conference of the
Commonwealth Parliamentary Association, which
was opened by the Queen; and give MPs plenty of
time to consider my successor. I would remain
Speaker until the day that the House returned in
October. That would enable Parliament to be
recalled, if the need arose.

I told Buckingham Palace of my impending
retirement a week before I announced it. There was
no procedural need to let the Queen know, but I
thought it right to do so, in view of the Speaker's
constitutional link with the Crown and the
kindness with which the Palace had always treated
me, not least when they loaned me the royal paintings. I was reminded of that during the Queen's
reception for backbench MPs on 10 July. Walking
into the Queen's Gallery, I saw Benjamin Haydon's
painting *The Mock Election*, which I had on the
walls at Speaker's House for five years.

Before leaving the Palace, I handed in a letter
telling Sir Robin Janvrin, the Queen's Private
Secretary, that I would announce my retirement on
12 July. At Westminster, apart from Nicolas Bevan
and Bill McKay (who had succeeded Donald
Limon) I told only Margaret Beckett, Tony Blair,
William Hague and Charles Kennedy, in that

order, what I intended. Margaret was quite tearful and touched to be told first, as Leader of the House. She said that she would not even tell her husband Leo who would be upset, because we had known each other for more than forty years after meeting in Lincoln, where he was a Labour activist and Geoffrey de Freitas was MP.

Tony Blair had expected me to stay until the general election, but my mind was made up. The Procedure Committee had recommended in 1972 that the Speaker should retire in mid-term and I agreed with that. There was a clear advantage in my successor having a run-in before the general election, and Members could choose from among those whose qualities they already knew.

My deputies and other officials attending my noon conference on 12 July were also unaware that the day's events contained a surprise. I intended to keep my promise that the Commons would be the first to know. My new flat in Pimlico was being prepared. A seat in the House of Lords awaited. Invitations lay on my desk to pay official visits to Bangladesh, Canada, Pakistan, Uganda, Zimbabwe, Bulgaria, Denmark, the European Parliament, France, Georgia, Hungary, Lithuania, Romania, Slovenia, Spain, Sweden, Egypt, Jordan, Korea, Syria, Tunisia, Vietnam, Bolivia and Venezuela. But my globe-trotting days as Madam Speaker were almost over and it was too late to accept further engagements. My time was nearly up.

CHAPTER NINETEEN

Be Happy for Me

*If I had a second innings, I'd do the same thing all
over again.*

Ian Mikardo

BEFORE ANNOUNCING MY retirement, I made my
annual pilgrimage to the Wimbledon champion-
ships as a guest of the All England Lawn Tennis Club.
John Guinery and I sat in the royal box with Sir Denis
and Lady Thatcher, Virginia Wade and others to see
Venus Williams beat Lindsay Davenport in a thrilling
match. I read later that Zina Garrison, the black
American player who had inspired Venus and her
sister Serena when they were youngsters, had planned
to send Venus a note reminding her to bend her knees
when play became tense. Thinking that might
unsettle her, Zina wrote instead: 'The time is now.'

I felt the same way about leaving the Speakership.
During my eight years in the chair I had worked with
two Prime Ministers and a series of party leaders and
it was time to quit my own Centre Court. Clutching
my four-paragraph statement on 12 July 2000, I

waited for the right moment to deliver it. The chamber was full for Prime Minister's Questions, the press and public galleries were packed and the only thing on most people's minds was whether Tony Blair could come back fighting after a spate of summer mishaps.

His performance at the previous week's Question Time was judged to have been below par and the Tories had their tails up. Two of William Hague's backbenchers had become so agitated during his 5 July clash with Blair that I had warned them they were in danger of being sent out. In a move to regain the initiative, Blair had called a Downing Street press conference before Question Time on 12 July. He denied that he was suffering an *annus horribilis* and played down recent difficulties. That did not deflect Hague who, to the delight of his own side and Labour's fury, probed the Government's sensitivities about joining the euro. 'The House must come to order. I cannot hear,' I cried. That calmed things down a bit but it was hardly an ideal atmosphere in which to tell them I would soon be off.

There was no reason why the House should have been less than its usual robust self. July is invariably high-spirited as Members prepare for their summer holidays. Apart from the main party leaders and Margaret Beckett, nobody had any foreknowledge of what I was going to say. Nicolas Bevan had put out a one-line notice on the Commons screens that I would make a statement at 3.30 p.m., but that was merely to prevent Members drifting off immediately after Question Time.

The BBC's *Westminster Live* programme stayed on air, but against all the odds my secret held. Only one newspaper came close. The *Evening Standard* reported the previous day that I had begun work on my memoirs and asked Nicolas about them. He told them I was doing autobiographical research 'so that when she retires she will have something to be getting on with'. Fortunately, they did not press the matter and deduced that I would stay on as Speaker for another year.

The broadcaster Michael Parkinson described me on the morning of 12 July as 'tough, plain-speaking, four-square, no-nonsense, up and at 'em, in despair at the antics of her flock, yet tolerant and forgiving'. I could live with that and later repaid his compliment by appearing on his television show. Otherwise, the news front had been quiet as far as my future was concerned, which was just as I planned it.

When I told Members that afternoon that I intended to relinquish the Speakership immediately before the House returned from the summer recess some of them voiced their astonishment. 'Oh,' they cried, when I added that I would also resign as Member for West Bromwich at the same time. I looked up from my statement. 'Be happy for me!' I appealed.

Suddenly they were all smiles and began applauding. Members and spectators in the public galleries clapped as warmly as they had done when I was elected. Minutes before, the two sides had been growling at each other during Question Time. Now they were suffused by mutual goodwill for the woman who had often barked at them but now asked for understanding. Their dismay at my announcement vanished as quickly as a ray of sunshine takes to cross the floor of the House. My appeal to their higher sentiments had succeeded and we were all glad of it.

Just as quickly we were back to business. Margaret Beckett announced that I would make a substantive valedictory speech two weeks later, after which the Government would propose a motion of thanks. The only business when they returned from the recess on 23 October would be the election of a new Speaker. Sir Edward Heath would preside – the only Father of the House to do so in three Parliaments.

A contest was certain. By giving three months' notice I set in motion the longest election campaign in the history of the Speakership. Seven centuries of fixing the succession had ended for ever with my election in 1992. I wanted to ensure that this time every Member knew what was going on and had plenty of opportunity to express an opinion – or, if they were ambitious enough, to put their name forward.

Unknown to me, Sir Edward was approached on the day of my statement by some Members who said to him: 'Can't you persuade the Speaker to stay on, and then she can preside over a debate in which the method of election will be changed?' After making enquiries into my probable response, he told them I could not. I took the view that the House must choose my successor without my participation.

Some Labour officials were rather more concerned

with the imaginary dangers of losing the West Bromwich by-election caused by my resignation. They fretted about the state of the local party organisation and the possibility of a low turnout. Who they imagined would rob Labour of certain victory was beyond me – and so the result proved.

The Prime Minister was typically gracious. He had called me 'a national treasure and institution' when he unveiled my portrait in the Commons offices at 1 Parliament Street a few months earlier. 'We acknowledge your impartiality and objectivity,' he said then. That was all that mattered to me.

We met again on 18 July at a ceremony in the gardens of Clarence House, the London home of the Queen Mother. Joined by Margaret Beckett, William Hague and Charles Kennedy, we were there to deliver a message of congratulations from the Commons on her approaching one-hundredth birthday. She insisted on standing while Derry Irvine and I read the greetings from the Lords and the Commons.

Mine expressed the people's gratitude for her lifelong example of 'trust in the Lord, and courage and service in war and in peace'. Speaking without notes, she replied: 'I am deeply touched to receive these messages of congratulations on my one-hundredth birthday and I thank you for the kind things you have said. I feel very grateful that in the last decades I have had the opportunity to serve my country and its great people. And I pray that happiness, peace and prosperity will continue over this dear land.'

At long last she sat down and called for celebratory drinks. I had to return to the chair, so I made do with sparkling water. The Queen Mother wished me well on my retirement and I returned to the House for the rest of the day's engagements. I also wanted to study the farewell speeches of my predecessors before expressing my feelings about Parliament in my own way.

I was still a new Member when Selwyn Lloyd retired in 1976. He signed off with a lament that I could only echo twenty-four years later. He chided the House for its 'long-windedness, sedentary inter-ruptions, points of order which are not points of order, inability to scrutinise Bills and Statutory Instruments as they should be scrutinised and many other matters' that made the Commons an imperfect institution. But he recognised too that the Commons was 'admirably fashioned to express the will of a high-spirited and free people'.

I agree whole-heartedly with that, but much has changed in a quarter of a century and some of it is for the worse. The executive power has grown stronger and Parliament has lost ground. Governments have become more intent on winning their battles in the media than on facing controversy on the floor of the House. For years I had cajoled MPs, ministers, bureaucrats and the media for not observing the highest standards. My valedictory speech 26 July was my last opportunity from the chair to urge the Commons to assert itself before it suffered further reverses.

I began by comparing the respect that people

showed for Parliament on my overseas visits with its lower standing at home and called for a renewal of basic principles. 'I know from my postbag how much disillusionment about the political process there is among the general public. The level of cynicism about Parliament, and the accompanying alienation of many of the young from the democratic process, is troubling. It is an issue on which every Member of the House should wish to reflect. It is our responsibility, each and every one of us, to do what we can to develop and build public trust and confidence.'

I had done my best to ensure that Parliament held the executive to account and I underlined its importance. 'That is the role for which history has cast the Commons. It is in Parliament in the first instance that ministers must explain and justify their policies. Since becoming Speaker in 1992, I have made my views known about that to both governments. I have taken action to ensure that those who advise ministers should not overlook the primacy of Parliament. It is the chief forum of the nation – today, tomorrow and, I hope, for ever.'

Parliament's other prime function, the scrutiny of legislation, was also ripe for improvement, but there was no simple solution and I advised against trying to find one by conducting the debate on party lines or blaming the Government for everything. Better legislation would only come from better scrutiny, perhaps through the greater use of pre-legislative arrangements.

I had become convinced that the specialist select

committees should be able to call witnesses and take expert evidence on the aims and contents of every Government bill submitted to Parliament before it went to a standing committee for clause-by-clause examination. The select committees would probe the bill on a non-party basis before the standing committees got to work. In that way, its purpose would be thoroughly aired and tested in a more neutral forum before it went through the political mill.

Experience had taught me that the quality of parliamentary scrutiny mattered just as much as the length of time we pored over legislation. I was a staunch believer in putting in the hours necessary to examine the Government's programme, and if that meant working long days, or forfeiting time off during the recesses, then so be it. In my view Parliament and the democratic process takes priority over domestic pleasures – important though these are.

Does this make me a dinosaur? I do not think so. When I became Speaker I said that the Commons had never been just a career for me. It had been my life. After eight and a half years that was truer than ever. I ended my farewell with the passage from Ecclesiastes about there being 'A time to weep, and a time to laugh; a time to mourn, and a time to dance'.

'Well, my dancing days are long past and I promise the House I shall not mourn the fact that an all-important phase of my life has come to a natural end. However, it is time for laughter as well, as we remember all the lighter moments we have enjoyed. I say to you, rejoice in your inheritance, defend your rights and remember always that the privileges the House enjoys were dearly won and must never be squandered. You elected me in the springtime and I shall retire in the autumn, which marks a fitting seasonal conclusion to my period in office.

'Therefore I say to you all, in a phrase that you all know well, but which has never been more true than now: Time's up.'

Disregarding standing orders, the House and public galleries again applauded. Moving the motion of thanks, Tony Blair steered clear of my more pertinent observations and made a graceful speech of the kind he does so well. His comment that my time in the chair had been characterised by my 'transparent love of this place and all that it stands for' touched the right note, as far as I was concerned.

Some Members who got on the wrong side of me may have had reservations about his praising my judgements as 'unerringly sound and fair', but there were smiles all round when he said how effective my stifled yawn had been in bringing boring speeches to a close. 'We would have liked you to continue,' he said. 'It's your decision, not ours, that time's up.'

Then came the memories. William Hague recalled my ordering Ann Widdecombe's microphone to be switched off when the formidable Tory frontbencher was in full flow but out of order – 'not something many of us would ever dare to do'. Charles Kennedy revealed that in our private conversations he called me 'Madam Speaker' and I called him 'luv'. Peter Snape, my old friend and West Bromwich neighbour, joked that we had never had a cross word, largely because he never dared answer me back!

Peter Pike, who had elicited the answer 'Call me Madam' thirteen years earlier, reminded me of the Nelson and Colne by-election, when he and my campaign team slogged on to the end, even though everybody knew that I could not win. 'Suddenly a massive van arrived and four people carried out a potato pie. One of the Nelson party members was a master baker and we had the biggest potato pie that I have ever seen in my life.'

John MacGregor, a former Tory Leader of the House, picked up on my plea for Parliament, as did Tony Benn and others whose ministerial days were behind them. MacGregor said: 'You have recognised the realities of this place. We are not good at scrutinising various aspects of the executive.'

It was Sir Edward Heath's prerogative to reflect on his experience of a half-century in the House. 'You, Madam Speaker, have occupied the chair during two quite distinct periods of British politics. First, you were Speaker for a government on the decline who had been in office for eighteen years. Secondly, you were in office for a new government of a different party, with one of the largest majorities in history. Looking back over it, I cannot recall any incident in which your conduct or comments aroused any real difference in the chamber. That is the most remarkable thing in all the years I have been in the House.'

Writing next day, Roy Hattersley thought I would miss the splendour of being Speaker. 'Not a bit of it,'

I told him. 'I'll miss the job, but I always knew the trappings wouldn't last. I was happy without them before and I'll be happy without them again.' It was true – I had come full circle. After the farewells were said, John Guinery and I returned to the restaurant above The Albert in Victoria Street for a celebratory dinner, just as we had done eight years previously.

Among the letters I received in the following weeks, one from a former constituent summed up what politics means at the grass roots:

> Just to say thank you for all your good work. You helped reinstate the 79 bus in September 92 so I could get to my early shift at Sandwell and Dudley Railway Station. You helped my mother recently with a problem with trees. When I left your area to get married you even sent a good luck letter, which I have got framed. Good luck in the future.

Like most MPs, I wanted to change the world, but the 79 bus meant a great deal to that working man and he was happy to settle for that.

Michael Foot wrote a sweet letter, saying that he was only sorry some of my oldest and dearest friends, like Jo Richardson and Ian Mikardo, were not still around. Shirley Williams also wrote warmly, as did John Redwood from the Tory benches. Jack Weatherill sent me an advance welcome to sit with him on the non-party cross-benches in the Lords. Even the BBC's religious slot, *Thought for the Day*, had something to say: Lavinia Byrne told listeners that she had been riveted to hear the 'clickerty,

clickerty, lickerty, spit' of my heels as I walked in procession through the central lobby to the chamber, and wondered whether dance can help us in our daily lives. 'Yes, absolutely and utterly. In your retirement, Madam Speaker, dance on!' she said.

Press comment, as ever, was a mixture of the rough and the smooth. Some pundits held me responsible for the loss of authority by the Commons, and the *Guardian* lamented that 'given the way modern politics works, she was always going to fail'. Peter Preston, the paper's former editor, described me as a 'folk heroine, a woman coping with vigour and humour in a man's world', but who had failed to 'turn the clock back'. According to him, the Commons had become irrelevant and the rule of the whips was 'absolute'. There was more of the same in the *New Statesman*, where I was accused of timidity and inactivity in protecting Parliament's rights. Had these pundits known of my struggles with Richard Ryder and of other tussles behind the scenes, they might have been less dogmatic.

My record must speak for itself. The Commons has been written off many times before and I make no claim other than to have done my best to fulfil the pledge I made when I sought the Speakership. That was not to turn the clock backwards or forwards; it was 'to offer myself as the voice of the House, sensitive to the concerns of every Member, aware of the supreme duty of the Speaker to safeguard the rights of this House'.

Beyond that, I promised nothing. Nor could I, as I explained to the procedure committee when they

considered the way Speakers are elected after the
seven-hour session that ended with Michael Martin
defeating eleven other candidates to succeed me. I
was asked if candidates should be allowed to
campaign for election, make speeches and answer
questions at hustings. 'I am totally opposed to
manifestos and hustings,' I replied.

Speakers do not enjoy the powers that some MPs
imagine, so what is the point of candidates for the
chair setting out their stalls? 'The power lies with
you, it lies with the House of Commons, it lies with
the Members,' I told the committee. 'The Speaker
can do nothing unless you give that Speaker
authority.' As for Speaker Martin's election taking
what some people thought an unconscionable time, I
took the view that MPs ought to be able to spare one
day every eight years to choose the right person for
the job. Admittedly the process was cumbersome
and tedious, but the House knew what it was doing
and all candidates stood a fair chance.

I also had second thoughts about the proposal that
Speakers should be elected by secret ballot. I
understood the case for it – in fact, for a whole year
I did not look at how Members had voted in my
election because I did not want to be influenced by it,
even subliminally. But I was persuaded against secret
ballots for other reasons. 'This House does not have
secret ballots,' I told the committee. 'It is hostile and
foreign to us – unless it is in the party caucuses . . . we
are all grown-up, we can justify what we do and I
think it is better to be open about it.'

I was less bothered about whether a new Speaker

should have to troop to the Lords to receive the royal
approbation. Jack Weatherill said that he liked the
ceremonial, but Sir Edward (who gave evidence at
the same time as us) was laid-back about it. 'All I
want to do is get a decent House of Lords,' he said.
'Come and join us,' I replied – but he will not do that.
Like Churchill, his mentor, Sir Edward prefers to
remain a commoner, albeit a very distinguished one.

The broader constitutional point is that the
Commons retains the final authority in all matters of
national policy. It limits its powers to avoid clashing
with bodies to which it has ceded part of its
authority, such as the European Union, but its ultimate sovereignty remains intact.

What I could and did do was use every
opportunity I had to bang the drum for Parliament's
rights and hope that others would continue the
struggle. To my great joy, that is happening and will
not easily be reversed. The liaison committee's call
for reforms has been taken up by the newly formed
Parliament First group, supported by an all-party
alliance including Mark Fisher, the former Labour
Arts Minister, Tam Dalyell, Sir George Young,
Gwyneth Dunwoody, Kenneth Clarke, David
Davies, Bob Marshall-Andrews, Richard Shepherd
and Archie Kirkwood. No fewer than 150 MPs
signed Mark Fisher's Commons motion that 'the
role of Parliament has weakened, is weakening and
ought to be strengthened'; calling on the Government to reconsider its rejection of the liaison
committee's call for stronger select committees. They
deserve to succeed.

I took no part in the 2001 general election but was shocked by the crassness of the Government's subsequent attempts to remove Gwyneth Dunwoody and Donald Anderson from the chairmanships of the transport and foreign-affairs committees. I was not surprised by the strength of the protest that this aroused on the backbenches. Downing Street's attempts to defend the dropping of two senior and independently minded Members from their posts did not help matters.

It seemed to me that Parliament was being manipulated and that I had to speak out. 'Select committees are not an arm of government. They are a mechanism of Parliament to scrutinise government,' I told *The Times*. 'The two people concerned have huge reputations in the House and have won great respect for the jobs they have done as chairmen as well as outside the House. It is outrageous that the Government cannot stand the heat of a bit of criticism.'

When the controversy broke, I urged MPs to exert their authority and defy the whips. My hopes and expectations were fulfilled on 16 July 2001 when the Government's list of nominees for the new select committees was forced to a vote and was rejected by 301 votes to 232. It was the Government's first parliamentary reverse since 1997. Hilary Armstrong, the new Chief Whip, had little choice but to say that it would respond to the will of the House. Gwyneth's and Donald's names were restored to their rightful place a few days later and the reform camp won a significant victory. For me, this is what modernisation ought to be about – protecting and enhancing Parliament's rights, not suckling babies during committee sessions or regarding MPs as lobby fodder to be summoned after breakfast and sent home before dinner.

It was no secret that I viewed some aspects of so-called 'modernisation' with a beady eye, but that was because I questioned the effects of what was being proposed, not the principle of change. I reminded the modernisation committee of the three principles that they pledged themselves to support after the 1997 election:

1. The Government of the day must be assured of getting its legislation through in a reasonable time, provided it obtains the approval of the House.

2. The Opposition in particular, and Members in general, must have a full opportunity to discuss and seek to change provisions to which they attach importance.

3. All parts of a bill must be properly considered.

How, I asked the committee, did the 'programming' of bills (which pushes legislation through the House) and the Government's guillotining of debates meet the third criterion? Whatever stratagems the Government of the day uses to gets its bills passed in the fastest possible time, there is a limit to the legislation that the Commons can handle if all three criteria are to be met.

The Government had tabled 2,537 pages of new legislation at the time I made my views known to the committee during the 1999–2000 session. That was considerably more than the 1,901 pages for the whole of the long 1997–8 session and the 1,590 pages in 1998–9. It was obvious what was happening: legislation was being rushed through without time to consider it properly, producing some bills that needed wholesale amendments on the floor of the Commons and in the Lords to make sense of them. I do not call that progress.

Starting our sittings at 9.30 a.m. instead of 2.30 p.m. also had a detrimental effect that the modernisers overlooked. The earlier start ate into the time needed by officers of the House, Opposition parties and Government departments to make enquiries about the business on the daily order paper – let alone the time needed by the Speaker to consider requests for emergency questions and debates. I also regretted the restrictions on the public's access to Parliament by the extension of morning sittings.

The low turnout in the 2001 election confirmed the fears I expressed in my valedictory speech concerning the decline of interest in the democratic process. Parliament must open its doors wide to people who wish to come inside, look around and understand what we do. Nothing pleases me more than visitors seeing for themselves what the Mother of Parliaments is all about. The public's interest in the way our democracy works must be rekindled if we are to overcome the alarming growth of apathy in our elections. We must begin by diagnosing our own failures as parliamentarians and then take steps to remedy them.

The Hansard Society has done valuable work charting the way. While I was its president it appointed an expert commission, which found that Parliament's scrutiny of government was neither systematic nor rigorous. The commission's report, *The Challenge for Parliament*, endorsed the call for stronger select committees, without detracting from the chamber's importance as 'the forum where ministers are held to account for the most important and pressing issues of the day'. Its proposals for a larger number of short debates and more opportunities for questions, ministerial statements and 'public-interest debates' not tied to legislation are all worth pursuing. The chamber should be more responsive to issues of public concern.

I have some suggestions of my own. We should consider an annual calendar for both Houses of Parliament with fixed recesses for Christmas, Easter, the Spring bank holiday and the summer. It need not be set in stone, and Members would have to soldier on if there was a slippage in legislation. However, it would be a declaration of intent and would put both sides on their mettle. Canada operates this system successfully, and it would give Westminster a clear idea of what was expected of it, instead of leaving MPs to speculate endlessly about the Government's timetable, as they do now.

The House might also consider sitting for five full days in three out of four weeks, leaving the fourth week for constituency work, visits to European institutions and other fact-finding activities. If the Government of the day abused the system by making important announcements during the 'week away', then the Speaker could use the chair's powers to accept requests for emergency debates and statements when the Commons returned, putting ministers on the spot and upsetting the Government's timetable.

Fewer MPs would help to raise the authority of the Commons. Do we really need 659 MPs in a devolved Britain, where Scotland, Wales and Northern Ireland have their own assemblies? Other countries with larger populations have fewer national legislators. Modern communications make it easy for MPs to keep in touch with the public and their localities and the Commons has vastly improved its support services in recent years.

When I started work at Westminster constituents rarely telephoned their MPs. Today e-mails, faxes and pagers are commonplace, many Members have interactive Internet sites and Westminster's corridors resonate to the sound of mobile telephones. Deciding the optimum number of MPs is for others to debate. I shall not be drawn into the numbers game. Any reduction would require legislation and a willingness by MPs to cull their own numbers, of course. The electoral map would have to be redrawn, with many boundary changes. But the need is surely obvious. Whether the Commons has the foresight to answer it is another question.

My Speakership ended with a flurry of visitors, including Gennady Seleznev, the Duma chairman, who flew in from Moscow in his own aircraft, accompanied by a doctor and retinue. My last guests for an uproarious musical evening around the grand piano at Speaker's House included Norma Major and Timothy Laurence.

My final official visits were to Ukraine and the Baltic States, and then to New York for a conference of Speakers and presiding officers from across the world. In the Ukraine, Latvia and Estonia I argued – as I had done in Slovakia and Poland – that oppositions have rights as well as governments. But, as on all my tours, I did not push Westminster's claims as a role-model. 'It is the system I know and love. It has developed over centuries and stood the test of time. It has withstood war and economic depression. It suits British circumstances and temperament. But we are not complacent about it. It has had to adapt over the years to changing pressures and circumstances. That is part of the reason for its success and durability. It continues to change. If it did not, it would ossify and fall into decline and disrepute.'

The Queen received me in a farewell audience at Buckingham Palace on 11 October and heard how I had spent the morning lining drawers for my new flat in Pimlico. She had a busy schedule that day: a meeting of the Privy Council followed my audience, at which Rhodri Morgan, First Minister of Wales, was sworn in. I recalled how the royal visit to Tipton in my constituency on 24 July 1994 had been one of only two occasions when I took time off from my duties. It took place on a Friday morning when business was light, and I flew on to The Hague for a conference of European Speakers and a meeting with Queen Beatrice. The other occasion was when I received an honorary degree at Oxford. Otherwise, I had a full attendance record.

I left Speaker's House for the last time without regret in the first week of October. The tears and high emotion following my retirement announcement were long spent. My life-peerage was gazetted on 24 October 2000 and I took my seat in the Lords on 16 January 2001 as a cross-bencher, supported by Barbara Castle and Denis Healey. Barbara suggested I should sit on the Labour benches, but I was not about to break the tradition that ex-Speakers stay above the party fray.

I would have preferred to have been called Baroness Betty Boothroyd, but I was told it was against the rules to have one's first name in a title, so I became Baroness Boothroyd of Sandwell, the Black Country borough that incorporates my constituency. The authorities did offer me a new shape for my coat of arms, stipulating that I could have a shield (previously reserved for men) instead of the lozenge-shaped arms traditionally reserved for women. I declined the invitation. My arms hang on the walls of Speaker's House, along with my portrait; the same lozenge shape hangs alongside the shields on the staircase of the House of Lords. My maiden speech about the achievements of the Open University was the first policy speech I had made in Parliament for fifteen years.

My last farewell call was on Sir Richard Wilson in

the Cabinet Office. After a half-hour's banter, he saw me out to a dark, rainswept Whitehall. 'Where's your car?' he asked. 'I do hate to see people like you just walk away.'

'Don't be dotty, Richard. I'm unofficial now,' I replied. 'But I do have my Freedom Pass' – the Londoners' senior-citizens pass that allows free bus and Underground travel. I walked off, waving it cheerily.

'Watch out,' he cried. 'You're backing into a No. 11 bus.'

Political commentators always speculate about what will happen if the serving Prime Minister is run over by the No. 11 bus, which runs past Downing Street, but I had no such fears. The No. 11 was just what I wanted. It took me home – a free woman.

Index